Killer Kids, Bad Law

Killer Kids, Bad Law

Tales of the Juvenile Court System

PETER REINHARZ

Barricade Books, Inc. New York

Published by Barricade Books Inc.
150 Fifth Avenue
New York, NY 10011

Printed in the United States of America.

Book design and composition by CompuDesign.

Library of Congress Cataloging-in-Publication Data

Reinharz, Peter.
    Killer kids, bad law: tales of the juvenile court system / by
    Peter Reinharz.
        p.   cm.
    Includes bibliographical references.
    ISBN 1-56980-070-7 (hardcover)
    1. New York (State) Family Court (City of New York)
    2. Juvenile courts—New York (N.Y.)
    3. Juvenile justice, Administration of—New York (N.Y.)
    I. Title.
KFN5116.5.R45 1996
345.747'081—dc20   95-51179
[347.470581]   CIP

First Printing

For Hillary, Alex and most of all for Patti. Their constant support is a reminder of the importance of the family in our society.

CONTENTS

FOREWORD

American juvenile justice suffers from an identity crisis. Those who see the growing youth crime statistics as violent *crime* are pushing for more incarceration and "transfer" of young offenders to adult court. Others see the crimes of juveniles as a failure of a social service system to meet the needs of a desperate population or as the failure to seek their rehabilitation.

Unfortunately, the court, in trying to reconcile both arguments, has failed in the quest for public safety as well as in meeting the needs of young offenders. The New York State Family Court—like other juvenile courts across America—must consider community safety concerns along with their traditional array of child welfare laws. In developing a plan for every young offender, the best interests of the child always compete with the need for community protection. While such an equation sounds easy to balance, implementation may be virtually impossible.

Legislators, advocates, chief executives, and members of the bar often fail to recognize that the best interests of the child and the need for community safety are frequently mutually exclusive. The best interests of most young offenders may require offering very specialized services with a regimen strict enough to impart basic socialization skills. These programs may be expensive—and like most protocols designed to correct human behavior they are replete with failures. Failures along the road to personal reform may result in murder, serious injury to innocent people, or just the destruction of property. Thus, assuring community safety while searching for the best interests of the youth may require one simple approach: long periods of incarceration.

I have run the country's largest juvenile prosecution unit for nearly a decade. Over the years, I have seen the rise and fall of "crack" cocaine, the change in the character of youth crime from minor offenses to the violence of group assaults and homicides, and the failure of the courts and the legislatures to deal with these changes. Where pickpockets once seemed the norm, now robbers, rapists and drive-by-shooters barely raise an eyebrow. Ripoffs of lunch money have been displaced by gang extortion and robberies of delivery men. Drinking on the corner and marijuana use have become group assaults for the fun of the hunt. Yesterday's victims of pranks are today's victims of violence.

I want you to see the world of juvenile crime from where I sit. This book is a prosecutor's view of a piece of the criminal justice system that has gone awry. It is my summation against the case for preserving an outdated juvenile justice system. It is not designed to be an objective primer about one of America's paramount crises. Other people have very different ideas about these issues—having viewed juvenile crime from a totally different perspective.

The perspective of the prosecutor, however, gives the reader a front-row view of the effects of juvenile violence. The police, victims, and courts are examined up close in the aftermath of the crime. Rather than portraying juvenile violence as a societal failure or the absence of a safety net within the social services community, the prosecutor's view provides a vivid and often raw account of people brought together solely by the predatory acts of an antisocial adolescent.

Although virtually all names have been changed, the stories are based upon actual cases which have taken place under my watch or have been told to me by people who work in the system or who have had contact with the system. A few of the stories offer an amusing view of daily life in the juvenile justice system, but most portray the constant tragedy that hangs over the entire process. The legal articles which follow describe—in technical detail—problems created by the courts and the legislature that have inhibited the development of a rational juvenile crime system. Together, the stories and articles provide the reader with this prosecutor's view of the facts and the law.

I have also included a glossary for those unfamiliar with the terms and abbreviations used in the juvenile justice system. These terms are often marked in *italics* to aid the reader.

I want to thank Edward I. Koch, former mayor of the City of New York, for reading samples of the book and for helping me in my quest for publication. I also want to thank former New York City Corporation Counsel and now Federal Judge Allen G. Schwartz of the Southern District of New York for hiring me as an assistant corporation counsel, getting me started in the Family Court, and for helping me get this work published.

I thank Judge Stephen J. Bogacz of the New York City Family Court for his help in reviewing the material for content and for his careful editing. I also want to thank Judge Judith B. Sheindlin, former supervising judge of the Family Court in Manhattan and a real "mover and shaker." Her relentless pursuit of common sense was a refreshing aside in a system perpetually on the wrong course. Judy's energy and no-nonsense attitude are an inspiration to many lawyers, and I am proud to count her as a friend. Over the years Judge Sheindlin and I shared a kindred spirit which sought to bring reform into New York's Family Court. Most of the time we didn't get what we wanted, but the fight isn't over yet.

—Peter Reinharz

GLOSSARY

People meeting those who work in New York's Criminal and Juvenile Justice Systems probably think they have entered a new language zone. These systems are filled with abbreviations and initials that are tossed about by cops, perpetrators, lawyers, judges and everyone else attached to the criminal justice programs. This glossary will help you, the reader, understand what we are saying. These stories and comments will help you understand what we are—and are not—doing.

ACD: Adjournment in Contemplation of Dismissal. The case is adjourned (postponed) for a period of up to six months. If the *respondent* stays out of trouble during the adjournment period, the case is dismissed. If the youth gets into trouble, is excessively truant or is somehow brought to the attention of law enforcement authorities, the case is added to the calendar and the prosecution continues. An ACD is not a finding of juvenile delinquency.

Adjustment: The diversion of a case away from court processing by the Probation Department. After a juvenile is arrested, he or shc is sent to the Probation Department for a conference to see if the matter can be diverted from court. The Department may hold a case open for 60 days to determine whether the adjustment services are working. When the matter is not adjusted—and very few cases are even considered suitable for adjustment—the matter is referred to the *presentment agency* for prosecution.

Appellate Division: Intermediate appellate court. You appeal here from the Family Court. After the Appellate Division, a *perp's* last shot is the *Court of Appeals.*

ATD: Alternative to Detention School. This is a school run by the NYC Department of Probation. It is used pre-*disposition* only. Kids awaiting *fact-finding* or *disposition* may be ordered to attend this school instead of being locked in a detention facility. Prosecutors love to send kids to ATD because the staff is honest about those kids who violate the terms and conditions of the school. Upon violation, the *perp* is likely to *go in.* Where the kid does well, he gets a better shot at remaining in the community.

ATI: Alternatives to Incarceration. This is a general term that refers to any program that keeps a *perp* out of jail. Legislators, mayors, and governors all support the development of ATI programs because they are cheaper than prison. That cost analysis fails to consider the cost in extra lives lost, property taken/destroyed, and medical costs to victims by keeping violent people on the streets. No matter what a politician tells you, there is no substitute other than jail for a violent criminal.

billable hours: Manner in which attorneys charge for their services.

Community Care: *DFY's* supervision in the community following residential placement. Youths reside in their own home and are assigned counselors to supervise their activities and school attendance.

Conditional Discharge: The least restrictive type of *disposition* allowed under the Family Court Act. For a maximum period of one year, the court may impose terms and conditions upon the respondent as a final disposition of the case. The conditional discharge is a finding of juvenile delinquency, as opposed to an *ACD*, which results in the dismissal of the case at the close of the period of supervision.

Corporation Counsel: The attorneys for the City of New York and the prosecutors of *juvenile delinquents* in the NYC Family Courts. When a *juvenile offender* is charged in the adult system, the *District Attorney* handles the case.

corporeal identification: The identification of a *perpetrator* via a *lineup* or *showup.* The suggestibility of such an identification is tested in a "Wade" hearing. If the court finds that the identification arranged by the police is suggestive —that is, tends to indicate the *perp*—the identification is suppressed and may not be used as evidence at trial.

Court of Appeals: The highest court in New York State. Cases are heard here after a decision is rendered in the Appellate Division. There are seven judges on the court, which prides itself in being the leading liberal court in the United States.

crack: A smokable form of cocaine popular in the cities because it is cheap and potent. It is sold in small vials and looks like tiny white rocks. It is the most addictive form of cocaine because the smoker inhales the pure narcotic into the lungs, and it is then absorbed within seconds into the bloodstream. People have told of their addiction after one or two experiments with the drug.

Criminal Procedure Law (CPL): New York's code

governing criminal proceedings.

DA: District Attorney. The prosecutors in the Criminal Justice System, also responsible for the prosecution of *juvenile offenders.*

Designated Felony Act: A classification of juvenile delinquency cases that reflect the most severe offenses in the Penal Law, and may also include recidivist juveniles. These are cases tried in the Family Courts—and are distinguished from those offenses where a youth is tried in the adult criminal system. Penalties for designated felony findings may be much more harsh, but the need for these penalties must be proven at a dispositional hearing.

detention: Holding a juvenile pending a hearing or transportation to a placement facility.

DFY: New York State Division for Youth. The state corrections department for juveniles. After disposition, they take the kids who are put into placement by the Family Court. Facilities range from group homes to secure prisons. These places are the training grounds for Attica. DFY is presently being reorganized by Governor Pataki. All references in this text to DFY relate to the pre-1995 organization.

dirtbag: A criminal, in police parlance.

disposition: The sentencing phase of juvenile delinquency proceedings in New York.

dispositional hearing: The hearing at which the Court renders the order of disposition, usually involving probation supervision or placement.

DJJ: New York City Department of Juvenile Justice. Although the New York City charter (the city's constitutives) enables

DJJ to set up ATI (Alternatives to Incarceration) and pre vention programs, its main purpose is to detain youths awaiting court action, and those kids awaiting transportation to DFY. DJJ runs *Spofford*—the most famous juvenile detention facility in the world.

DOC (NYC): Department of Corrections. This is where adult criminals are held. It is a perp's last stop before state prison.

Family Court: The court that has exclusive original jurisdiction to hear *juvenile delinquency* cases.

Family Court Appearance Ticket (FCAT): A paper issued to an arrested juvenile and his/her parent upon release of the youth by the police. It directs the youth to appear in the Probation Department's Intake Service branch for *adjustment* consideration or pre-court processing.

Family Ties: An alternative to the placement program run by New York City's Department of Juvenile Justice.

FCA: Family Court Act. The statutes that define the powers and procedures of the Family Court. Included in the Family Court Act is the Juvenile Delinquency Procedure Law, which defines all the procedures for the prosecution of juveniles in Family Court.

get paid: To rob someone.

going in: Getting locked up.

Grand Jury: A group of citizens who may vote to indict a person for a felony or other crime. The Grand Jury sits for a term of approximately thirty days and hears evidence presented by the prosecutors. When they vote—by majority—for an indictment, they are said to vote a "true bill." Grand Jury proceedings are confidential.

Housing Police: The police department responsible for patrolling the housing projects in New York City. It was merged into the NYPD by Mayor Giuliani.

I & R: Probation's Investigation and Report. When a finding of guilt has been made following the *fact-finding* hearing, the Department of Probation is mandated to conduct an inquiry into the youth and his family. The contents of the I & R are regulated by state regulations and by the Family Court Act. These contents include, but are not limited to, a family history, a school history, legal contacts with the police and court as well as a recommendation for disposition.

initial appearance: Euphemism for an arraignment.

jammie: A handgun.

Juvenile Delinquent (JD):   A youth under 16 years of age charged with a crime in the Family Court. A finding of guilt is not a criminal finding, but the proceedings are very much in the nature of criminal cases. The JD trial is not in front of a jury—the judge makes the findings of fact.

Juvenile Offender (JO):   Kids in New York under 16 years of age, but tried in the adult system. While the process is similar to adult procedures, the sentences for these "JO's" are less than for an adult committing the same crime. In New York, there is no "waiver" into the adult system. Kids who commit the most violent offenses (mostly 14- and 15-year-olds—only intentional murder for 13-year-olds) are automatically put into the adult system. There has been much talk about the failure of the "JO law." Leading that charge has been the defense bar as well as many child-advocacy groups. They may have a point. Most of the juvenile offenders in the adult system receive less prison/placement time than their counterparts in the

Juvenile Justice System. Kids in the adult system, while facing a true criminal conviction, are often granted a community-based sentence as compared to the near certainty of placement for the most violent offenders in Family Court. While this is not the basis for the defense bar's objection, they may be right that the system has failed to accomplish what was intended.

Legal Aid Society: Defense Counsel. Also called Law Guardians. This is a private organization under contract with the state to represent juveniles who cannot afford counsel. The Family Court group is called the Juvenile Rights Division. They are akin to a public defender in jurisdictions outside New York City.

lineup: An identification procedure used by police and prosecutors. *Perps* pick a number to hold, and sit next to similar-looking persons. A witness then views the array (usually through a one-way mirror), and attempts to identify the perp. The suggestiveness of such a procedure is challenged by a defense lawyer in a *Wade* hearing. If the court finds that the lineup was unconstitutionally suggestive—that it tends to indicate the perp—then the identification via the lineup is suppressed (disallowed at trial). If the court finds that the lineup was fair, then the lineup identification may be admitted at trial.

material witness order: An order by the court directing a witness to appear and testify. If the witness refuses to testify or to appear, the court may jail the witness and admit him or her to bail.

MHS: The Mental Health Service which evaluates offenders at *disposition*. The term "MHS" also refers to the agency's written report on the young offender.

mutt: Derogatory term for a *perp*.

NSD: Non–Secure Detention. These are usually group homes run by or for the Department of Juvenile Justice (DJJ). They are supposed to hold the less violent offenders, but often a violent kid is placed into NSD.

NYPD: New York City Police Department. There are various police agencies in the City of New York. NYPD is by far the largest. Other major police departments are the New York City Transit Police (subway and bus crimes) and the Housing Police (patrolling the public housing projects). Also the Port Authority Police (commuter bus terminal at 42nd Street and the PATH commuter trains), along with the Amtrak and Long Island Railroad Police. NYPD's top brass supposedly oversees all these agencies, but control is very limited. There are other police departments in the City of New York, but they have limited scope for the purposes herein. The House and Transit Departments are now part of NYPD.

OCA (Office of Court Administration): The New York State Agency that oversees the operations and budget of the courts and judiciary. The agency is charged with lobbying on behalf of the courts in the legislature and with the executive branch. The Chief Judge of the Court of Appeals has recently been the Chief Executive Officer of the OCA.

One Police Plaza (1PP): NYPD Headquarters. A large brick building at the Manhattan foot of the Brooklyn Bridge. The place is a maze, and no one has fond thoughts about doing business there. It has been said it is the largest collection of bureaucrats in the history of the civilized world. It has also been suggested by some police officers that something in the building—fumes, stale air or even the paint—has the profound effect of lowering IQ levels.

Patrol Guide: The "bible" of the Police Department. It contains the rules and regulations for all the cops.

Penal Law: The statutory crimes of the State of New York. Robbery, murder, burglary, rape, arson, etc. are all defined in the Penal Law. Different degrees of each offense define the levels of culpability for adult offenders.

Perp: Perpetrator.

Per Se **error:** This is a legal error that is not questionable. Even explained and with good reason, it is still error. It will require the reversal of a conviction/finding if the error is not "harmless error." In some types of cases, like the complete failure to provide *Rosario* material, the Court may not conduct a harmless error analysis.

Petition: The accusatory instrument in the Family Court. A petition must contain the charges against the youth, and there must be sworn non-hearsay allegations attached to the petition to support each charge therein.

PINS: A Person in Need of Supervision. Like juvenile delinquency, this is a "status offense." It concerns unruly behavior, truancy and children beyond parental control. Courts cannot hold PINS children in secure detention, so most PINS proceedings have little or no ability to control the child. Children who run away are returned on warrants only to run again. Parents usually file the petitions in the hope that the courts can do what they have been unable to do—control the child. Children are assigned lawyers who advocate zealously on behalf of their client against the interests of the parent (who is not entitled to representation). In most cases, the process is a waste of time and money, and usually reinforces the child's defiance.

Placement: The juvenile delinquency code's euphemism for incarceration. It refers only to long-term care after a case is finished. It is distinguished from detention, which is the short-term care of kids awaiting further court action or transportation to placement.

Presentment Agency: The Family Court Act's euphemism for prosecutor.

Preventive Detention: The right to hold a youth in custody based upon his or her propensity to commit a crime. Under the Family Court Act, youths may be held via preventive detention when the court believes that . . . "[H]e may before the return date commit an act which if committed by an adult would constitute a crime."[1] The constitutionality of preventive detention was upheld by the Supreme Court in *Schall v. Martin.*[2]

Probation: Supervision ordered by the Court. The Department of Probation is charged with supervising offenders remain within the community. The Department also handles the Intake Services for the Family Court. Youths arrested go to the Probation Officer, who will determine whether an "adjustment" is necessary. Youths committing less serious offenses may be appropriate for adjustment— they may be referred to a variety of diversion programs. Less than 6 percent of all cases get adjusted. Most offenders are beyond the need for diversion services by the time they come to Family Court. The Department of Probation also prepares an Investigation and Report (I & R) on every case in which the youth has been found guilty. This report is similar to an adult's Pre-Sentence Investigation (PSI)—only the Family Court Probation Officer is supposed to consider the offense as well as getting a detailed view of the offender's family, school and social history.

purge (relating to contempt of court): To do an act

required by a court that will result in vacating the contempt order.

Remand: An order by the court to detain a youth.

Removal: The process of transferring a Juvenile Offender case from the criminal justice system to the juvenile justice system.

Respondent: Juvenile charged in the Family Court. In an attempt to "decriminalize" these proceedings, and to prevent "stigma" from attaching to these young felons, the Legislature in New York has created statutory euphemisms for the general terms of the Criminal Justice System. Make no mistake, however, these offenders are real criminals. Ask their victims.

restrictive placement: A series of placements available for *designated felony acts.* It commences with placement in a locked facility and moves through limited secure and then community-based placements.

skells: Derived from the Italian term for villain (*scellerato*), it is a common police term for a perpetrator.

strapped: Armed with a gun.

supra (Latin): Above or upon. Used for citations when referring to a case, treatise or statute previously cited.

vic: A victim.

---

1. Family Court Act of the State of New York §320.5.

2. 104 S.Ct.2403, 467 U.S. 253, 81 L.Ed.2d 207 (1984).

Part I

The Kids

1.

"Make no mistake about it. This kid is going to be a stone-cold killer."

Anne Morgan felt the stiff, raw December wind blowing off the Hudson River as she hurried toward her building on West 91st Street in Manhattan. She wanted to get home and put away the groceries. It had been a long day at work, and the constant cold breeze in her face made Anne want to run into her building. It was the first full day of winter—although the biting cold made it feel more like February. She noticed the darkly dressed teen loitering in front of her building as she fumbled with her purse and packages to find a key. She couldn't make out his face in the early evening dimness, but the reflected light from her lobby told her it was a tall, heavy-set boy wearing a black knit hat. As she opened the door to the building and entered the vestibule, she sensed a presence rush up from behind. Before the door could close she felt an attacker's hand cover her mouth and twist her head. Anne struggled to break free as the attacker reached from behind and slammed his left hand into her abdomen. With the wind knocked out of her, Anne was thrown into the corner of the vestibule—and out of sight of any passersby on West 91st Street.

The attacker pushed Anne into the vertical cornice that traveled up the wall to cover the heating pipe. Anne felt the sting in the left side of her head as the *perp* grabbed her hair and pushed her head back and against the protruding cornice. He battered her body with his left fist and with his right hand tugged at her purse, which had become twisted around her arms during the attack. With all the strength she had, Anne Morgan screamed into the face of her attacker. Startled at her defiance, and concerned now about detection, the youth scrambled out the door and into the dark street. Anne Morgan, dazed and bleeding, slumped to the floor.

Cindy Garner walked east on West 88th Street toward the supermarket on Broadway. She was thinking about several items that needed to be added to her shopping list when she felt an arm grab her around the neck and drive her small frame down to the concrete sidewalk. "Give me all your money," screamed the youth in the black parka hovering two feet above her. Cindy reached for her purse and paid the ransom, but the attacker was not through. He yanked her up by her hair and coat and jammed his fist into her side. "I have a knife. If you scream or run I'll kill you." He then calmly told her to walk with him to Broadway, where he would go with her to a cash machine and she would withdraw all her money. He put his arm around the young woman's waist and told her to pretend they were the "perfect couple." He gave her a squeeze and pulled her closer as they walked to the bank. When they entered the ATM lobby, the sounds of sirens were approaching. The perp gave his victim a final gratuitous punch and ran out the door.

For Johnny Rojas[1] this was the exhilaration of the hunt. It wasn't about the money, although the money was nice. The attacks on the women felt good. He enjoyed the sensation of domination, and he liked exercising that feeling through violence. He told the court psychologist that he felt no sense of remorse for either of these crimes. He laughed loudly when asked if the face-to-face confrontations caused him to consider the victim's pain. Between his giggles, he answered simply, "I feel nothing at all." Rojas explained that he did it for fun, because he wanted to see how it felt.

Johnny Rojas, however, knew very well how it felt to play the hunter. Less than six weeks before the robberies on Manhattan's Upper West Side, he had been released from *DFY* for drug possession and larceny. He also told investigators and the court psychologist that he had done other robberies, including the knife-point car-jacking of a cab. Three days prior to this arrest he abducted another woman at knife-point on the Upper West Side and took her to a cash machine, where he robbed her. For these robberies, Johnny laughed, he had never been caught. None were done for the money. Rather, it was the fun of playing predator and watching the fear of the prey. Sometimes, when he did not get any money, there was just the satisfaction of beating the victim.

When Anne Morgan testified at a hearing about the attack in her lobby she fought in vain to control her tears. In between sobs she described the feeling of being trapped by her attacker inside the lobby of her home, and she told the court about the constant blows to her head that eventually caused her to faint. She went on to describe the rage of her attacker as he mercilessly jammed her head into the wall. As the blows kept coming, she believed she was going to die in her own vestibule. When she stared into the eyes of her attacker, she saw the soul of Johnny Rojas, at that moment, Anne Morgan said she knew her attacker was ready and willing to kill her. It was the depth of the anger in those cold eyes that caused her to scream.

The senior psychologist wanted to talk about this case off the record. Throughout her career she had interviewed hundreds of violent offenders, but none had ever displayed a total lack of empathy—even if feigned—combined with a love of predation and a willingness to engage in violence for sport.

She told me, "You have to do something about this kid. I'm trapped by the inability of the Family Court to deal with this guy. They want me to consider community safety, but that is impossible here. Safety is not even an issue. I can only recommend limited secure placement as the max; but Rojas needs to be caged, forever. *"Make no mistake about it. This kid is going to be a stone-cold killer."* The psychologist winced when she related Cindy Garnor's ordeal, as described by her attacker. It seemed unfathomable that this act had taken place only a few moments after Rojas had crushed the head of Anne Morgan into the wall of her vestibule. Johnny Rojas' thirst for the hunt had not dissipated when he beat Anne Morgan senseless. The few minutes it took him to travel the three blocks to Cindy Garner's street were all that he needed to psyche himself up for another mugging. Had the police sirens not alerted him in the ATM lobby, and had he not been caught as he ran out, would there have been another victim that evening? Was the hunter going to kill? The psychologist believed that Anne Morgan and Cindy Garner were lucky to escape alive. She was not sure that Rojas' next victims would be so lucky—nor was she sure that all his previous victims had actually survived their encounters with him.

Johnny Rojas is another of the thousands of failures who have come through the juvenile justice system and have grown—and continue to grow—more violent with age. He is, however, among the most grotesque of the failures, even in light of the myriad of social services that have been delivered without success. Social services will not change the adolescent who thrives on the hunt. Programs and counseling will not defuse the exhilaration of an attack or the sense of power gained when looking into the eyes of a woman in fear. "Rap sessions" run by former delinquents and gang members in a

DFY (Division for Youth) facility will not teach a *"stone-cold killer"* to stop behaving like a predator. These programs will, however, teach Johnny Rojas and all the others like him that they can externalize their responsibility and that they can blame their crimes on society, their school or their environment.

Despite his truancy and special education background, Johnny was educated enough to relate the usual excuses for his behavior. The psychologist noted that Johnny was able to explain away every robbery, assault and theft. He was quick to condemn his environment and his poverty for his crimes. He told the psychologist that if he were able to move to the Dominican Republic, then all the violence would stop. Perhaps this was why he was so willing to admit to his criminal acts; he really believed that he was not accountable for his violent actions.

What are the signs of a *"stone-cold killer"?* Should DFY have seen the signs as readily as the court's psychologist? About one year prior to crushing Anne Morgan's skull and abducting Cindy Garner, Johnny Rojas sat in a detention room in Manhattan's Family Court with a court-appointed psychiatrist. Rojas was being evaluated for possible placement in his drug and larceny cases.

The doctor noted that Rojas had been enrolled by his mother in a Head Start program at age three. He was originally put into a standard elementary school class at age five, but soon thereafter he was placed in a special education environment. Clearly the early intervention of Head Start and special education, so often cited as a panacea for the growing criminality in our cities, was useless in light of his limited academic capabilities (he had an IQ of 74), as well as limiting his propensity for violent crime. In fact, it is clear that every one of the hundreds of thousands of dollars wasted on Johnny

Rojas' early education would have been better used in building the permanent prison space which will eventually hold
him for life.

By the time Johnny Rojas was in third grade he had
already been suspended from school for fighting. His aggressive personality continued to escalate through elementary
school and into junior high, where he was arrested for possession of an electronic stun gun. He told the psychiatrist that in
addition to carrying the stun gun, he regularly carried a knife.
He used the knife in several fights and nearly died at age 13
when another youth stabbed him in the chest. He declined to
tell the psychiatrist how many people he had stabbed prior to
or following his own wounding.

Johnny was beyond the control of his mother at about
age nine. He stayed out "at least until 3 A.M." regularly, and
refused to do anything to help his mother around the house.
His mother filed a *PINS (Person in Need of Supervision)* petition
against him when he was 13 after he began to steal her money
and jewelry. She also asserted that he was openly smoking
marijuana and using cocaine in the house. Johnny denied her
allegations, saying that this was only the "word on the street."

Shortly after the PINS petition was filed, Johnny was
arrested for beating a boy almost to death. Johnny claimed justification because the other youth was "messing with me" and
deserved to be killed. The victim in that case, according to
Johnny, was afraid to press charges, so the matter was dropped.

The psychiatrist's evaluation, prior to this initial placement with DFY, concluded that Johnny Rojas had poor
insight and limited impulse control. His judgment, she said,
was impaired, and if he remained in the community his violent
activity would probably escalate. Although Johnny told her
that counseling was "bullshit" that he didn't need, the psychi-

atrist recommended that he be placed in a facility that would provide him with some group counseling, in the hope that he would find either a role model or a peer who could talk some sense into him. The prognosis, she would say later, was extremely poor.

Apparently, the NYS Division for Youth saw Johnny Rojas differently from the rest of the criminal justice system. He was released from placement after serving only nine months of his term. Although this nine-month period included the time that he was moved to a more secure facility for his continual fighting and overall aggressive behavior, this conduct was not enough to keep him in DFY custody. In effect, DFY determined that Johnny Rojas was too violent for placement in a limited-secure facility but deemed it appropriate to place him back into the community. Perhaps overcrowding within DFY forced Johnny out of placement, but the reasons for his release were not made known by the agency at the dispositional hearing following the attack on Anne Morgan. Johnny may have been doing better in the more secure environment—which may have prompted the boy's discharge to the community. Instead, any improvement in behavior should have indicated to DFY that a firm structure was the best way to control the young offender. Less than two months after his release, however, he assaulted Anne Morgan and abducted Cindy Garner—all for what he described as his own fun.

Had DFY based its decision to release Johnny Rojas on the facts within the court records, rather than on population politics or outmoded social theories, Anne Morgan and Cindy Garner would have been spared a lifetime of pain. Long after Rojas is incarcerated for a life term, or more likely dead as a result of the violence integral to his existence, these two women and his unknown victims will be looking over their shoulders, living in fear and expecting the worst.

Johnny Rojas should have been an easy call for DFY. All the signs indicating continued violence were in the court-ordered evaluations. Any questions about the boy or his likelihood for crime, even for an off-the-record comment, were only a phone call away. Instead of taking a responsible position, DFY released Johnny Rojas, as they do with virtually every offender placed by the Family Court. They called no one, not the prosecutor, the judge, the victim, or the court-appointed evaluators. The court's file was not requested by DFY at the time of Johnny's release, and despite the warnings in the psychiatric report that the youth was dangerous, there was no notification to the police department. DFY merely released him without word or warning upon an unsuspecting public. His return to custody was a foregone conclusion. Unfortunately, by the time he came back to DFY, there were other victims—some of whom are scarred for life. While these issues may not be important to DFY, courts and prosecutors have to wonder why community safety is so easily compromised by a system that has safety as its primary obligation. How many more like Johnny Rojas are there in DFY? This question is only important to the public. For DFY it is irrelevant since they will let them all out without regard for the number of victims they create.

Rojas will undoubtedly be released again prematurely. He will be bigger, stronger, faster and angrier when he is returned to the city. But he will be the same violent offender. Such information, it is clear, is irrelevant to DFY. This correctional agency views community safety and incarceration as mutually exclusive items. But the release of Johnny Rojas will be important to the residents of Manhattan's Upper West Side. They will have to remain on their guard because DFY refuses to take that responsibility. Citizens had best remember the words of the court psychologist when DFY chooses to ignore them: *"Make no mistake about it. This kid is going to be a stone-cold killer."*

2.

As Americans are bombarded with political speeches from candidates who want to get "tough," "smart," or even deadly about crime, it seems clear that concrete plans to prevent recidivism among violent criminals have been lost in the rhetoric of the campaigns. Those who seek incarceration of violent offenders also seem obligated to suggest that the high cost of prison must be reduced by using alternatives for first offenders, youthful offenders and nonviolent criminals. While this double-speak is an essential part of the political process for compromise with those legislators who choose to represent the rights of criminals at the expense of our society, it guarantees continuation of the policies that historically produced the violence, and now the total failure of the criminal justice system.

Instead of looking at the data regarding *who* is committing crimes, reformers and advocates within and without the American criminal justice system have focused upon new programs and "alternatives" as the future for law enforcement. As every new prison cell is constructed, the race to develop alternatives accelerates. Drug treatment, boot camps and community supervision make up many of these alternative programs—although the low rate of incarceration among all convicted criminals means that the *real alternative* in criminal justice has become prison. Popular theories suggest that finding the "root causes" of crime will somehow allow us to prevent crime in the future. Unfortunately, too many activists confuse the causes of crime with the actual effects of violent behavior. Poverty, homelessness and drug abuse are as easily understood as the by-product of criminal behavior as they are the "root causes." Too much policy, especially that relating to sentencing alternatives for felony offenders, is driven by unquestioned articles of faith that presuppose that violent crime is caused by some independent factor that may be ameliorated with public money and good will. As fiscal prudence becomes a necessity in government, it is time to ensure that only the most effective criminal justice programs are the ones that remain funded. Unquestionably, the best program for crime control is incarceration—without the alternatives.

Nowhere is the quest for alternative sentencing as strong as it is in the juvenile and youthful offender criminal justice systems. And nowhere is failure more apparent than in these programs. *Rehabilitation* is the goal sought in New York and in so many other states, although the likelihood of rehabilitation is virtually never explored at dispositional hearings or sentencings. Instead, judges and prosecutors are bound by laws that require the offenders to be placed in the least restrictive environments that supposedly do not pose a threat to community safety. Perpetrators are placed into programs with the *hope* that there will be behavioral modification. Neither the probability of reform nor the extent of rehabilitation following release from a program is ever examined. This is so because courts and prosecutors know that any success is likely accidental—and probably unrelated to the program or the court process.

In New York City, as in most urban criminal justice systems, first-time offenders are rarely incarcerated. Community supervision is almost always the preferred disposition, so that the youth remains free within the same community that he previously victimized. Traditional juvenile justice theories support this view as a means to protect an errant youth whose criminal actions are blamed more upon the folly and inexperience of adolescence than upon his lack of internal controls. Even those who *are* incarcerated by juvenile courts are often held only for short periods of time, until they are released back to the same parents who could not control these kids less than one year before.

Among the programs in New York City seeking to combat the incarceration of young offenders, none has provided more impact with less substance than the grant from the Annie E. Casey Foundation. The foundation describes itself as the largest philanthropy in the United States whose mission is to improve the lives of disadvantaged children and families. In the early 1990s, the group decided that improving the lives of disadvantaged kids also included the need to address a "national crisis" in the overuse of secure detention for juveniles. The foundation sought grant applications from all across the country for five sites where money could be used to develop alternative programs to the use of secure detention for juveniles. The printed overview describing this initiative noted that between 1982 and 1989 there was a 31 percent increase in the rate of admission to secure facilities in the United States. Youths arrested in the late 1980s were likely to be held longer than those arrested in earlier years, and all this detention was supposedly in the wake of a national *decrease*—at least as measured by the Casey Foundation—in violent juvenile crime.

The administration of Mayor David Dinkins jumped into the Casey initiative. New York City sent juvenile justice system managers to conferences and meetings all over the country to study the secure detention policies and reforms in other jurisdictions. Of course, any suggestion that the juvenile crime problems of Fort Lauderdale could be compared to those in New York was ludicrous, except to the Annie Casey promoters. The fact that robberies in New York City's Family Court were doubling in number between 1986 and 1993, and that felony assaults and loaded gun possession were rising even more quickly seemed lost on those seeking to limit secure detention. New York City reported a rise in detention throughout the 1980s, but this was consistent with the rapid escalation in violent juvenile crime during that same period. Yet the Annie Casey Foundation had found a philosophical and fiscal partner in the Dinkins Administration. In a city starved for money, the Foundation was offering a grant of more than $2,000,000 to an administration that was already willing to accept their premise as natural law.

Hundreds of man-hours from Commissioners, Deputy Commissioners and other high ranking officials were sought in order to propose a New York City program that would meet the Annie Casey objectives and get the grant money. So driven was the pursuit of this cash, that the groups, subgroups and steering committees spent more time on analyzing detention than was done on the administration of major criminal justice projects such as sentencing reform and gun interdiction. Probably the greatest test of patience was the grueling summer conference in July of 1993 in Pawling, New York. About 50 to 75 high-ranking city officials and other administrators, including a Deputy Mayor, met for a three-day conference during a record heat wave. District Attorneys, defense lawyers, judges, advocates, program administrators and detention providers sat through planning conferences, debates and even a violent movie about life in the streets. Questions were posed about how to ensure the success of the grant initiative (one answer suggested that the Mayor had to be re-elected— he was not), and about solving the alleged disparities in "minority over-representation" (where one anonymous answer included the need to arrest more white people).

One of the results of the Casey initiative was the development of a "Risk Assessment Instrument" to determine whether the probation department was correct in recommending secure detention for offenders when they appeared at arraignment. Proponents of the plan suggested that objective criteria needed to be defined to ensure that detention was recommended in a nondiscriminatory way. Thus, under the plan, offenders would be judged against a set of factors that would be applied to everyone who was arrested. The apparent fairness of this proposal is overshadowed by the fact that the ability to recognize the need for detention is a common sense call. The relevant statutes already define criteria that allow detention when the youth is likely to commit another crime or if that youth is a risk to appear again in court. Judges have been using these criteria since they were ruled constitutional by the U.S. Supreme Court, and among the more than eight thousand detention orders made by New York City's Family Courts each year, less than twenty-five writs of *habeas corpus* are filed by defense counsel alleging improper use of detention. The detention system in the City of New York was not broken, but the Casey people were going to spend money to fix it anyway.

Among the originally proposed criteria within the

Probation's Risk Assessment instrument to determine the propriety of a detention recommendation were the criminal and warrant histories of the offender. The fact that the youth had a warrant in his past would not suggest detention. In fact, a youth with a prior robbery history, with a warrant within that history and where all background, family and school information were unknown was still required to receive a recommendation for release. The Casey initiative, with its mandate to reduce detention, was going to do just that, even if it placed the community at risk of further violence.

It is undisputed that young offenders are the most likely criminals to repeat their crimes. Despite the beliefs among juvenile justice workers that minors are often victims of their own adolescence or of society's ills, studies show that violent young offenders are more likely than any other group to return to prison within a few years of their release. A recent study in New York State tracked thousands of offenders who were released from state prison in 1987. Over 70 percent of the felons released at ages 16–18 were returned to state prison within five years. Those who were 19–20 at the time of release had a return rate of 66 percent, those 21–24 came back at the rate of 58 percent, and those 25–29 returned at a rate of under 55 percent. As offenders increased in age, rate of return to custody continued to go down, until those over age 50 had a 22 percent return. Similar studies for other years demonstrated the same theme; the older an offender is at the time of release, the less likely he is to repeat his criminal activity.

National figures also demonstrate that younger offenders are a greater risk for recidivism. According to the latest released figures in the FBI's Uniform Crime Reports (UCR), violent crimes such as robbery and assault begin taking place at about age 13 and continue to rise until about age 20. After several years of leveling off, the numbers of those arrested for these violent crimes start to drop at about age 25. A more rapid drop occurs after age 30, and the decline in violence continues as the criminal population enters middle age.

The New York study and the national figures demonstrate that criminal justice policies toward violent crime have been universally misdirected. Present laws look to excuse the violence of first offenders as youthful indiscretions by granting "Youthful Offender" status. This limits or eliminates jail time and also converts the conviction to a noncriminal finding. Even when incarceration is ordered, it is usually for a shorter period of time and in separate youth facilities. Offenders are given schooling, counseling, therapy and behavior modification programs in the quest for rehabilitation. States pay little attention to the data that suggest, however, that young violent criminals are the most likely to return to prison, often at the expense of another innocent victim.

Nothing short of an overhaul of criminal justice philosophies will begin to correct a system that appears doomed to failure. Instead of releasing offenders via presumptions that mandate *release* after short periods of incarceration, a presumption of *incarceration* ought to be applied to every violent young offender. That youth would have the burden at sentencing and beyond to demonstrate that he or she is an appropriate risk for community-based supervision. Since violence tends to escalate as youths enter their later teens and early twenties, the presumption of incarceration would have to ensure that most of these offenders would not return to the community until they start to age out of their criminality. Only those who could demonstrate to the courts that their rehabilitation and socialization are sincere would enjoy the benefits of early release under strict supervision.

This view is a complete rejection of the traditional juvenile justice system of leniency and forgiveness. Putting society's hopes in alternative programs and community-based supervision, where most young offenders are placed these days, has proven to be a failure. As violent crime rates across America have fallen over the last three years, recidivism among violent young offenders rejects this trend. If we really want to see changes in the UCR and in the recidivism rates of state corrections studies, we have to rethink policies about violent crime by youth based upon the numbers. We need to accept the simple premise that the older an offender is at the time of his release, the less likely he is to return to the criminal justice system. Giving the young offender a second chance as a matter of right probably means giving that offender another opportunity for violent crime.

The Annie Casey grant is designed to ensure that every offender has the maximum opportunity to victimize New York. The foundation has been urging the City of New York to move forward on its plans to eliminate its only detention facility for juveniles, *Spofford Juvenile Center.* For the last several years, New York City has been building two new facilities to replace Spofford, one in Brooklyn and the other in the Bronx. Spofford, which holds up to 320 youths, is deemed unsatisfactory because of its remote location and its poor design as a detention center. Instead, two modern 100-bed facilities, recently upgraded to 125 beds, are set to replace New York's only secure juvenile facility.

The problem with the replacement for Spofford is apparent from the numbers. Throughout the late 1980s and into the 1990s juvenile crime, especially crimes of violence, has been on the rise. Spofford has been at or near capacity for much of this period, and the small size of the two new detention centers will not meet the city's present detention needs. Yet the Annie Casey Foundation has been anxious to receive assurances from the current mayoral administration that the downsizing of detention will occur. Perhaps the Casey foundation knows that without the large holding capacity of Spofford, the objective of the grant—to reduce the use of secure detention—will be assured. So far, the Giuliani Administration which inherited the Casey grant, with all its baggage, has wisely avoided making that promise.

Poor urban planning is ensured when the designer chooses to remain a captive of his own philosophy rather than willing to recognize hard facts. So it has been with the Annie Casey grant and the zeal to replace Spofford. For a $2 million payoff, the City of New York has sacrificed man-hours, common sense about the need for more jail space, as well as the safety of its public. As juvenile violence continues to grow year after year in New York, the Casey foundation and its supporters persist in arguing that releasing more of these youths from detention will not affect, or perhaps will diminish, the wanton violence of teen crime. The rising numbers of juvenile felonies each year in the Uniform Crime Reports and the recidivism rate among young offenders (as reported by the NYS Corrections report) tell a very different story. By keeping the youngest and fiercest felons out of jail, the previous mayor accepted the Casey money and embraced the Casey ideology. When this philosophy inevitably results in the release of an offender who would otherwise not have been out in the community, and this youth robs, rapes or kills a New York citizen, the rest of us, along with the politicians who talk "tough," "smart" and even deadly about crime, can take comfort in knowing that we were fairly compensated with a cool $2 million or so.

3.

Miguel Feliz's[2] knuckles were white as he clutched the loose-leaf binder. He had come to court to watch the proceedings concerning the girl whose photos were scattered throughout the pages of the notebook. He was showing the prosecutors and police officers pictures of Maribel, the petite fifteen-year-old, with her friends from Fashion Industries High School and from the neighborhood. The notebook was appropriately black, the color of mourning. Miguel Feliz had come to court to watch the murder trial of his daughter's killer.

Maribel Feliz was a vivacious teenager with an interest in style. She attended the city's high school for people seeking a career in the fashion industry. She was a good student and was popular with her classmates. She was described as a warm and loving child who had a special relationship with her father. The day before she was murdered, her father stopped by the local schoolyard where he saw his daughter playing handball. Unlike most teens who are embarrassed at the sight of a parent, Maribel stopped the game and ran to her dad to give him a kiss. She was a happy child with a bright future for herself and for her city. Twenty-four hours after Miguel Feliz kissed his only daughter in a Manhattan schoolyard, he identified her body to police officers in the city's morgue.

September 20, 1991 was just another day for Latesha. She was awakened by her aunt, who told the overweight fifteen-year-old to get ready for school. Latesha didn't like school, so she had only been there once since the start of the last term. She wanted to tell her aunt that she did not feel well, but if she feigned illness she would not be allowed to go to the party that evening. So Latesha got dressed, all the while telling herself that she did not feel well, just to placate her aunt. As usual, she would pretend to go to school, but would meet up with her friends and "hang out." Even though her mother had put her in a special school, Latesha was not interested in going to class. Besides, her mother was living with her new boyfriend, so Latesha felt no obligation to her mother. She had been dropped off at her aunt's house for a weekend visit and had been living there for weeks. It was just the way things were.

Outside the building in the Brooklyn projects, Latesha met up with Tamara and Tracy. They invited her to Tanisha's house to hang out for a while. They said that after Tanisha got dressed they were going to meet up with some boys and head into Manhattan.

Inside Tanisha's apartment the girls planned their agenda for the day. They decided that they would "chill" with the guys for a while and then start robbing people of their earrings. All four girls loved the big gold earrings that dangle and flash from the earlobe as an invitation to theft. They were not stealing the earrings for profit. They just wanted to take the ones they liked. To complete these robberies, the girls decided that they would need "protection," so Tamara and Tracy took knives from Tanisha's kitchen.

On their way to the subway the four would-be robbers met up with the boys that Tracy and Tamara had mentioned earlier that morning. Like the girls, the boys were not attending school that day. They were heading to Manhattan's Upper West Side to wait outside Printing High School for people to rob. For most kids a school provides education. For some kids, a school is an unlimited source of victims.

The boys were members of a group called the Decepticons. Latesha described the Decepticons as a group that "goes around robbing people and beating up people for laughs and fun." Included in the Decepticons were her cousin Lance and some other of New York City's worst recreational predators. The Decepticons were Latesha's people. She enjoyed their company and, most of all, their violence. Although Latesha denied it later, the other girls told police they wanted to do robberies to gain acceptance within the Decepticon clique.

After hanging around the school for a while, the group got restless. As they started to stroll around the Columbus Circle area, one of the boys saw a kid with a Walkman and told Latesha that he really liked that cassette player. Within a minute Tamara and Latesha had completed the robbery and offered the tape player as a present. Soon Latesha saw a set of "hoop" earrings that she just had to have. Unfortunately, they were on the ears of another girl, but such a formality was of no concern to Latesha. She ran up behind the girl, yanked one earring off her earlobe, and punched the girl in the face for sport. Within seconds, the other girls had joined the fray and were beating the victim to pass time. As Latesha would later testify at her trial, that day the four girls were "all for one," and during the attacks were all *on* one. Unfortunately, this unity cost Latesha the earrings. The fighting caused the earrings to get crushed, so Latesha had to wait for another victim with dangling hoops.

Latesha did not have to wait long. Tracy spotted a girl

with gold bangle earrings and ran across the street to do the robbery. The victim darted into a nearby building, but to no avail. Within minutes, Tracy emerged victorious with stolen earrings in her pockets. The girls and boys had a laugh and continued toward the subway station at 59th Street and Columbus Avenue. It was approaching midafternoon and Latesha could go back to her aunt's house and pretend to have attended school.

In the Columbus Circle subway station, the boys decided it was their time to do robberies. They started beating up other students and taking money and train passes. These predatory acts seemed consistent with having a good time, and both girls and boys were intent upon enjoying themselves to the fullest. The girls entered a downtown "A" train as the boys jumped onto the "C" local. The girls rejoined their male friends on the "C" train at 42nd Street as they continued to scope the passengers for potential victims.

Like a pack of starved rats, the group fixed on Maribel Feliz as she and her friend entered the car at 23rd Street. The two girls had just left class at Fashion Industries High School and were on their way to the schoolyard to play handball. Maribel wondered if her father would stop by the playground again that day.

The big gold earrings looked even bigger against Maribel's tiny frame. As the train rattled and shook on its way downtown, the earrings swayed and glittered with the rhythm of the subway. Latesha and her friends could not help but cast an envious gaze upon Maribel's earrings. When the subway train pulled out of the 14th Street station, Lance told the girls to take the earrings. He handed Tamara his knife, neatly wrapped in a sheath, to guarantee compliance with the demand. Tamara approached her victim and said, "Run the earrings." Although not realizing this to be a demand, Maribel understood that this girl was threatening to steal the earrings that she had received as a birthday gift from her mother. Tamara continued, "Bitch, I'll kill you. Run the earrings."

Before a reply could be given, the other girls joined in the attack. The fact that each assailant was larger and heavier than the petite victim was inconsequential to the marauding thieves. They grabbed her hair and pulled the small girl forward. As she bent over, they punched her back, head and body while the boys encouraged the beatings with shouts of "Fuck her up." Tamara pulled the knife from the sheath displaying the jagged edge and sharp point. She raised it up over her head and, in a swift downward thrust, drove the weapon deep into the back of Maribel Feliz.

The teenage victim fell forward and dropped to the ground. Her four attackers cheered and ran toward the next car. Maribel stood up and staggered forward a few steps before she collapsed at the pole. While Maribel Feliz lay bleeding on the floor of a subway train, her attackers were heard laughing as they scrambled to the next car. Before the reality of their actions could be appreciated, the four predators sprinted away from their prey with the full exhilaration of the hunt. For a moment there was no accountability; for a few fleeting seconds there was the novelty of their first kill. As teenagers they had reached a milestone. They had grown more sinister in their adolescence and had conquered their own limits. Yet in all the excitement they never even bothered to take the earrings.

The train pulled into the West 4th Street station and the four attackers jumped out of the train in a rush to escape. As they headed down the platform, a bystander in the car where the stabbing occurred called for a police officer. Immediately a Transit Police Officer arrived and radioed for medical help.

That same policeman had seen the four girls running on the platform and managed to round up three of the attackers on the scene.

Unfortunately, as the officer pursued the girls, Maribel Feliz was dying. Her faint heartbeat would soon disappear, for the knife had sliced a deep cut through her lung and aorta. Blood was running out of the young woman's back and mouth. There was more blood on the floor, on the doors and on the seat next to the spot where she had finally fallen. Although she was officially declared dead at the hospital a few minutes later, the last moments of Maribel Feliz's short life—and her final vision—faded away on the cold and filthy floor of subway car #3427 on the "C" train in the West 4th Street subway station.

The Criminal Justice System cannot console a grieving parent whose child has been murdered. No legislator, judge, penalty or execution will ever replace for Miguel Feliz the warmth of Maribel's kiss the afternoon before she died. Four vicious and mindless attackers destroyed the lives of an entire family, and all the retribution, rehabilitation and due process will never fill the void that eternally exists in the hearts of the Feliz family. On the other hand, the impotence, forgiveness and statutory leniency of an outdated juvenile justice system will surely enhance their pain.

Although Latesha's trial controlled the fate of her fading adolescence, her concentration paled next to the grief of a father in mourning. From the opening moments of the trial, until the final words of summation, Latesha sat slumped in her chair between her lawyer and her mother. There was irony and injustice in seeing a mother who had often rejected Latesha sitting by her side in a show of support, while Miguel Feliz returned every day with only his black binder and his memories. The protections were all in place to ensure that Latesha received a fair trial. No statute, regulation or constitutional provision could provide a similar guarantee for the victim or her family.

The evidence was straightforward and virtually uncontradicted. The witnesses to the killing testified that Latesha beat the helpless teen while her friends assisted in the crime. The autopsy report that coldly described the cutting of a body that had once been a loving and devoted daughter came into evidence. All of Maribel's organs were weighed, examined and described in the matter-of-fact language unique to medical examiners. Lost in the report was the person of Maribel Feliz, the person whom Latesha had ruthlessly and needlessly slaughtered. Latesha's confession to the police was moved into evidence, and soon thereafter the court found Latesha guilty of murder.

The real challenge in the case, however, took place at the *dispositional hearing.* Because the murder charge was a *designated felony* offense, Latesha faced a maximum period of incarceration of up to five years. This disposition, if the court so decided, would be served initially in a secure facility, with gradual lessening of restrictions as time progressed. In any event, it was certain that even in the most severe applications of the dispositional plan, Latesha would be free to reclaim her lost life by her 21st birthday. The New York State legislature, through a dispositional scheme that has remained unchanged since 1976, has guaranteed that the lives of honest citizens remain cheap. Maribel Feliz was no exception.

The viciousness of the crime and Latesha's own statements seemed to assure the imposition of the five-year maximum sentence. With little emotion, and in a surprising demonstration of unconcern, Latesha "periodically looked through a magazine that had been lying on the table"[3] when she answered a probation officer's questions about the incident. Latesha showed no remorse for the homicide since she maintained that she was not involved in the actual killing. Directly contradicting the statements of eyewitnesses and of her own co-perpetrators, Latesha insisted that she had merely been a spectator to the murder. Although she admitted to doing robberies with the group all day long, and that the group was "one for all," she somehow sought to convince the court that every other piece of evidence was either inaccurate or untrue.

In keeping with her consistent denial of responsibility, Latesha maintained a cold reaction to the death of Maribel Feliz. The psychiatrist inquired whether Latesha could put herself in Maribel's position on the train. What, asked the doctor, did she think the victim was feeling during the attack? Latesha said she could not know the victim's feelings because she could not see her face. Further, she would never have thought to intervene on the victim's behalf because "it wasn't me."

Latesha's indifference contrasts disturbingly with the warmth of the person she brutally murdered. The bright, vivacious student that was Maribel Feliz had a special relationship with her father. As Miguel Feliz described his daughter to the investigating probation officer, he could not hold back his tears. He told the officer about the schoolyard encounter and how he learned of Maribel's death from the television news. He has little appetite and finds limited comfort in his religion. Yet all the consolation of friends and family does not prevent him from hearing her footsteps on the floor or seeing her vision in the playground.

The court gave Latesha the maximum five-year penalty. Miguel Feliz had small satisfaction from that disposition. As he walked out of the courthouse, he headed into the street ready to follow the trials of the other offenders. He would not miss one proceeding; he owed that to Maribel and to himself.

As he left the court, he held in his hand the notebook that bound his memories. Maribel was now only an image on paper within the binder, yet the pictures were so much of his life. The killers had never seen the photos—they had only seen Maribel once. Yet that short deadly moment translated into eternal heartache for Maribel's family and friends.

One day Latesha's mother will be waiting for her young daughter's release from *DFY*. On her release date there will most likely be smiles, hugs, kisses and tears of joy. On that same day in the future, Miguel Feliz will still have his notebook.

4.

It wasn't Craig Peters' first time selling drugs. It was his last.

Craig was a sixteen-year-old punk from the Bronx. He was an exception to the rules that are proffered by the excuse-makers. Craig came from a two-parent home. Both his folks worked. Both his folks cared. He had two siblings who were not children of the streets. He had been enrolled in a "Head Start" school program when he was three years old. Craig did not fit the usual profile for today's juvenile criminal. If he had, he probably would be alive today.

Mrs. Peters[4] knew that her son was in trouble. She had been to the Family Court before. She had filed a *PINS* case against her son, alleging that he was incorrigible and beyond her control. But she didn't realize that the legislature had changed the PINS proceeding to an administrative process. She would have to seek counseling and all other services before she could go to court. Mrs. Peters knew she did not have that kind of time. She knew her son was in danger, and she knew he was likely to get into further trouble. When he was arrested in December of 1991 for selling *crack* on 14th Street in Manhattan, she knew that Craig was completely out of control. Her son needed to be sent away.

The fundamental concern of every defense attorney, and of most judges in the juvenile justice system, is that the accused receive due process. All defendants must get their constitutional rights—even if it is likely to kill them. Legal Aid lawyers and other guardians of the law are not concerned with the best interests of their young criminal clients; they are there to do exactly what the kids want them to do. The fact that a youth's decisions are likely to get him killed is immaterial to the advocate. The life of the offender takes a back seat to his rights.

The first time that Craig was arrested his mother scolded him as he sat handcuffed in a police precinct. She warned him that crime and violence are forever linked and that even petty antics would get him killed. But Craig's teenage brain instinctively believed in his own immortality. Like most teenagers, he was sure that bad stuff only happened to other people. When he failed to heed his mother's warning, Mrs. Peters brought the PINS case against her son. He told his mother not to worry because all the dead kids were chumps. He knew what he was doing because he could handle himself in the street.

Craig's feelings of invincibility were reinforced by the Juvenile Justice System. His first delinquency case, a robbery in 1990, was dismissed in Bronx Family Court because the prosecutor could not meet the rigorous speedy trial deadlines of the Family Court Act. Unlike the criminal system, which excludes time for defense motions and adjournments (within the permitted 180-day limit for trial), a trial in Family Court must commence within 60 days of the arraignment. When Craig's first case could not meet the speedy trial time requirements of the Family Court Act, the youth walked out of the courthouse. He did not understand the reason for his exculpation, nor was he interested in pursuing the procedural details. He simply knew he beat the rap—with the help of the court.

Mrs. Peters recognized that the deal her son's attorney had struck with the prosecution and with the court on this latest arrest would be another empty gesture from the juvenile justice system. Her son had sold *crack* on the streets, and the courts would do no more than put the boy on probation for a year and a half. No jail, no placement and no enforceable restraints. She knew her son would never keep his promise to the court to maintain a curfew and seek a job. His attitude needed fixing, but the court and the lawyer would not listen. They were as deaf to her pleas as the youth they sought to supervise.

The probation officer doing the *I & R* realized that Craig was headed toward a life of crime and violence. When the officer asked the youth to explain his involvement in the drug sale, he told her that it wasn't a big deal. With a dismissing wave of the hand, he said that the cops never really found the stuff *on* him and that the conviction was bogus. He apologized for the incident, but only because he got caught. The court system, opined the young offender, was a "waste of time." Of course he promised that he would not break the law again. He made that promise on the advice of counsel, although he could not contain his laughter when he offered this assurance to the probation officer.

Craig was happy that his lawyer had gotten him such a good deal. He had to plead to a felony drug charge, but he knew that the court would place him on probation if he took the plea. He knew his lawyer had told both the court and the prosecutor that he was a good kid who kept his curfew, obeyed his mother and went to school. Lying was worth it if it kept you out of Spofford—even when your own mother wanted you off the streets.

Probation was going to be easy for Craig. It would not mess with his lifestyle, and it would not prevent him from making money through the crack dealers on the street. Reporting once a week was a joke, especially if you didn't go to school, and the rest of the time could be used for drug dealing, girls and shopping for jeans or sneakers. He really wanted to thank his lawyer for arranging things so nicely for him.

Three weeks after he was placed on probation, the young man was selling crack in new territory, right around his Bronx home. He had been given the post by a Jamaican guy who was looking to muscle in on the Dominican trade in the area. On a warm June evening, Craig and his buddies walked down the street just before midnight in defiance of all territorial claims staked by the Dominican dealers. Just in case, he had a 25-caliber semi-automatic pistol in his waistband. He felt tough. He felt invincible.

The car came screeching around the corner. The Dominican guys had noticed the swagger in Craig's walk. He seemed to be a cocky kid with a desire to provide some free market economy on their street. They, however, had turf to protect, and the life of Craig Peters was insignificant compared to the potential loss of profit. Craig's hand never touched the gun in his belt. Fourteen bullets from an AK–47 assault rifle and from a 9 mm automatic ripped through the flesh of the sixteen-year-old. In his final split-second, Craig learned the ugly truth about the drug business and about the streets of New York. His mother was right.

Craig's father happened to hear the shots as he watched television in their nearby apartment. He ran outside to see the commotion and saw the cops pull up to the body. Somehow he knew it was his son. He ran to the body as the blood ran from Craig's lifeless form. He carefully placed the boy's limp and bleeding head into his lap.

Craig was already dead the day his lawyer got him the good deal. His youth and his greed—promoted in part by his freedom of choice in the court—had written the script for his murder. Although nobody can be sure about the future, Craig's mother (despite her lack of a law degree) was able to recognize the imminent danger encircling her son. Thirty days prior to the boy's death, the probation officer in the *I & R* paraphrased a mother's thoughts and intuition. . . . "The respondent's mother is the first to acknowledge that he is totally out of control and has requested that he be placed for his own safety." But placement was not to be. Instead, sixteen-year-old Craig Peters was sentenced to probation—and a predictable death.

Each year hundreds of New York City's kids are shot. Gunshot wounds kill more teens than any other cause. Kids involved in the drug trade are the most likely to face a certain violent end. Craig was too young to know any better, but his mother knew full well that the boy's life expectancy ran from Saturday to Saturday. Yet the legal system still perpetuates the idea that juvenile justice requires a kid to control his own destiny. Due process, or a warped interpretation of it, gives the young offender's lawyer more input than a parent. Among the rights never discussed in court, or in conference with the lawyer, is the right to die. Craig exercised that right.

Thousands of Craigs continually pass through New York's juvenile justice system. Most of them will not die by the gun, but the number of shooting victims increases steadily each season. The real killers, or at least partners in the crime, are the people who provide the opportunity. Advocating the right of a child to choose his or her own destiny conflicts with the basic tenets of custodial care. Given such an opportunity, most youths will make the wrong choice every time. Ask a teenage boy to choose between a stylish collection of sneakers and safety, and the choice is all too clear. It may also be deadly.

As a father finally let go of the dead son cradled on his lap, a defense attorney slept peacefully somewhere in New York City. Away from the crime, away from the ghetto and the crack, the lawyers live in a world of private schools and fine restaurants. But Craig's death does nothing to change their advocacy. The following day there is another kid with another mother begging for help. Once again it is rights over life, it is "freedom" over sense.

A fifteen-year-old must be held accountable for his crimes. He cannot, however, be blamed for his belief in immortality. That is a privilege of adolescence. Craig was sure that he would never fall prey to the hand of an assassin. His mother, father and probation officer all knew better. So who really killed Craig Peters?

5.

In the city it is often said that the apple doesn't fall very far from the pushcart. Generations of offenders beget other offenders. So it is for Che Novarro.

Che fits the common offender profile for the 90s. He is confrontational because he sees it as a means to self-respect. He is impulsive since he has always been taught that the system reacts to the loudest screamers. He is a coward because, when it comes time for crime and predation, he relies upon the assistance of others. In short he is dangerous, violent and beyond rehabilitation. His father made him that way.

On a Tuesday morning in early March, Che, Victor and Malik were supposed to be in school. They told the group home counselors that they were going to class, but the boys had other plans. They left the group home with two screwdrivers, although none of the youths had any interest in carpentry. They were out to visit friends and were looking to "get paid."

The three youths took the IRT #3 train out of East New York into Manhattan. They thought about stopping at Brandeis or at Park West High School, but somewhere along the route they decided to ride toward the Bronx. That way they could check out the train for victims and do the robbery while traveling through Harlem. The boys knew that in Harlem they could make their escape into a familiar neighborhood with little chance of detection.

Che saw the Chinese guy first. The *skells* know that Chinese, Korean, Vietnamese and Indian people are as afraid of the police as they are of the villains. Asian victims are less likely to come forward, so Che knew that he had hit the jackpot. Che fixed his gaze on the man with the Walkman as the train traveled north out of the 96th Street station. The man's eyes were closed as he listened to the music from his personal cassette player. Although there was a second Chinese man seated next to Che's intended target, the experienced hunter recognized easy game.

Che walked over to his chosen victim as his two partners in crime kept a watchful eye on the four or five others seated in the subway car. To begin the operation, Che lightly kicked the man's feet as he pretended to trip over his victim's extended legs. The man opened his eyes to find Che standing directly over him. Che lowered his gaze to the Walkman and ordered "Give it up or I'll kill you." He shoved the end of the yellow-handled screwdriver into the man's face as he screamed his demand.

The victim understood no English, but he did not need a translator to interpret the nature of a mugging. As he tried to stand up, Che punched the man in the face and on the side of the head. Without a word, and directly on cue, the other assailants joined in the attack with punches and kicks. To facilitate their attack, Malik and Victor alternately restrained the man so that all three could enjoy pummeling their victim without fear of his returning the blows. As hard as the boys hit, they could not wrestle the player from their bloody but determined victim.

Another passenger on the train had seen enough brutality. He ran into the next car and notified the conductor of the ongoing assault. The train stopped short of the 110th Street station and waited a few moments for the police to arrive. When the train pulled into the 110th Street stop, police boarded the train and arrested the three youths. Although they had scattered in an attempt to avoid arrest, the victim and the eyewitnesses were happy to identify the attackers and their screwdrivers.

After his arrest, the group home administrators did not want Che to return to their facility. The youth had been fighting with staff and residents and was a consistent behavior problem in the group home. The boy routinely confronted counselors by asserting that he was being denied "his rights," and then resorted to violence to bring home his point. Che had been in numerous group homes, so he knew that fighting with a counselor was a contest he could not lose. The counselors had to avoid physical confrontation at all costs. Because of these behavioral problems, Che was remanded to Spofford.

Spofford was an old family tradition in the Novarro household. As the Probation Officer found out when she prepared Che's *I & R,* the respondent was his father's carefully constructed product. Che is guaranteed to develop into a killer, simply because his father, George, has engineered it that way. George Novarro was a bad kid. He was a truant who ran with New York's gangs in the 50s and 60s. He lived in the streets and fought in the streets. He committed robberies, purse snatchings and other offenses that had resulted in a stay at Spofford and later in an upstate "training school."

The inability to rehabilitate the unredeemable is not limited to the courts and counselors of the present generation. The hopeful do-gooders of a generation past had failed to change George Novarro, just as today's zealous hopefuls will fail with his son. Within three weeks of being released from a one-year term in a reformatory, replete with services to speed his rehabilitation, George Novarro was arrested for murder. Yet the social workers, judges and corrections reformers that dominated New York's criminal justice system in the 1960s were determined to prove that *understanding* the young George Novarro—and the reasons he had become so violent—would help bring about his inevitable redemption.

George Novarro, they thought, was a malleable youth; therefore, there had to be hope. Leniency for the young offender got him a 7-to-15-year sentence. The court recognized that upon his release from prison George would still be a young man and hoped that he could then begin a productive and honest life.

George was sent to the state prison in Attica, New York. He told Che's investigating probation officer, however, that prison was not a time for honest reflection. Instead, George said he became more radical in his political views. His opinions and actions got him transferred from prison to prison. Corrections officials did not appreciate an angry radical in their midst, so George Novarro traveled the prison circuit. After ten years of revolutionary thought behind bars, George was paroled just before Christmas in 1973.

Although the prison officials had little use for George Novarro's radical politics, there were many segments of society in the early 1970s that welcomed his nonconformist philosophy. These people saw the former inmate not as a murderer but as a hero, or at least a role model for other would-be offenders. He was a reformed criminal, they averred, and could be a symbol of hope among people in despair. George was given a job as a counselor with the Legal Aid Society.

While at Legal Aid, George Novarro met Rene McCord, another counselor. They started dating, and in typical 1970s anti-establishment fashion, they soon had their out-of-wedlock child. In keeping with their politics, they named their son Che.

Yet political and social rebellion were only the beginning of the turmoil within George Novarro. He was an abusive spouse and father. George told Rene that he had good reasons for beating their young son; it would make him a man when he grew up, rather than just a "punk."

George's philosophy of parenting through violence had its immediate rewards. At age nine, Che tried to stab his mother with a kitchen knife. He was taken screaming out of the house and was placed in a children's psychiatric facility for nine months. When the doctors let him leave the facility, Che's mother took her son to Virginia. Rene McCord had learned that George Novarro's views and actions were dangerous. The murderer with radical antisocietal views, who was employed as a counselor by the Legal Aid Society, had finally been diagnosed for the villain he was. Although Rene McCord could not see the truth about George Novarro as a mate, as a mother she saw it all too clearly. She ran for the life of her son.

Rene McCord had a hard time raising her son in Virginia. At the age of nine, the boy was already a product of his father's nurturing. Counseling and therapy cannot provide the missing elements of normal socialization that should have been instilled by a responsible father. Che became too much of a behavioral problem for his mother and her family in Virginia. After several years, Rene McCord had no choice but to return to New York with her uncontrollable son.

Things did not improve for the family upon their return to New York City. As Che got bigger, he got more violent. Soon he understood, just as his father had taught him, that physical force could intimidate his mother. By asserting his machismo, Che was free of her apron strings. He wanted to be in control, and he would use his size and power to get whatever he wanted.

His mother, however, refused to give up. She did her best to limit George Novarro's invidious influences upon their son, but she saw that the boy was headed for trouble. He was getting into fights at school and had already been arrested. He was beating her at home so often that she was afraid to stay in the house. Rene McCord brought her son to Family Court and had him placed in a group home. There, she was told, he would get the counseling and care he needed. There, she was assured, they would do their best to straighten him out.

Che provided a similar history to the probation officer and to the court-appointed psychiatrist. Although he denied his father's beatings, he did acknowledge a predisposition toward fighting. He told the clinician with pride that he was kicked out of several group homes for fighting. Che asserted that he would argue with staff for his rights and that he was a "ringleader" among the group home residents. The youth saw nothing wrong in his present crime other than that he had to suffer the penalties of getting caught. Remorse was nonexistent—"Chinese people got a lot of SONYs"—so he could rationalize his actions. Not surprisingly, Che was placed with *DFY.*

Che Novarro is too young and George Novarro is too tired to recognize that their lives are a series of parallel events separated only by the "generation gap." Che's youthful ignorance makes him immune from recognizing that his father's present life on welfare and food stamps[5] is a certainty for his own future—if he lives. Both have been detained at Spofford, and both have been sent upstate to youth facilities. Each has advocated violence as a means to an end, and each has seen himself as a leader among peers. Che and his father have been involuntarily moved from facility to facility because they were either activist or "ringleader," and both have broken the heart of Rene McCord. The only difference between father and son is that at this point only George Novarro has been jailed for murder.

Unfortunately, Che's future is all too clear. Che is not yet old enough to be hired as a counselor at Legal Aid, but Judge

Ruth Jane Zuckerman chose to offer leniency at disposition, just as the courts had done for George Novarro a generation before. Judge Zuckerman, keeping the faith of her ideological past as a professor of law and adopting the standards of those who had served as her mentors through her education in the 1960s, gave Che credit (against his placement with *DFY*) for his time in Spofford. Additionally, despite his violent crime and his savage attraction toward brutality, she chose not to impose the optional six-month minimum period for residential care. She did not think that Che was a "special" case requiring a guaranteed time of incarceration.[6] Like the court that had sentenced George so many years ago, and like the Legal Aid Society that had hired and supported a killer, the Family Court, in the person of Judge Ruth Jane Zuckerman, now decided that tolerance was in order for George Novarro's son.

George and Che have both found support from people and organizations that have repeatedly made excuses for or ignored their behavior. A previous generation of leaders rejected all common-sense indicators in favor of criminal justice "reforms." Those who have inherited today's positions of power refuse to acknowledge the history of that failure. Instead they blindly choose to repeat it. In the city, from the perps to the power people, the apple doesn't fall very far from the pushcart.

6.

Baby Boy Ruiz[7] was born a normal, healthy eight-and-one-half pound infant. He is called "Baby Boy" because in his one minute of life, no one took the time to name him. With placenta and cord still attached to his little body, his teenage mother put her fingers around his throat and strangled him. Despite her admissions to police and caseworkers, a court found that she was not a murderer. The judge, the cops and the caseworkers, all of whom had become streetwise in a city that educates via America's meanest streets, could not fathom the cruelty of a mother giving life and taking life within the same minute. Nancy Ruiz had redefined brutality for even the most hardened New Yorkers.

Frank and Kevin thought that it was going to be an easy tour that night. They were sitting in their ambulance at 85th and Columbus for twenty minutes, and there had not been a call. It was mild for December, and they were glad they would not have to put up with sleet or snow. The first call seemed routine, a teenage female bleeding from the vagina and having pain. It was probably the usual miscarriage, an easy run for even a novice Emergency Medical Technician (EMT).

The call was a few blocks away on Amsterdam Avenue. Within two minutes they arrived at the apartment building to find a teenage male waiting at the lobby doors. He ushered the two men upstairs to examine his sister. He said she was not pregnant and that she was complaining of bad cramps.

The young man opened the apartment door and directed Frank to the bathroom, where his sister Nancy was seated on the toilet. He introduced Kevin to the rest of the family, his mother Matady, his Aunt Juanita, and his sister's fiance, Manny. They were all standing in the kitchen of the railroad flat apartment watching Nancy sweat as she sat perched on the toilet less than eight feet away.

While Kevin started asking medical and family history, Frank was in the bathroom trying to assess the fifteen-year-old's condition. She refused to stand and asserted that she was too weak to move. Her vital signs were poor, and it appeared that she had lost a lot of blood. There didn't seem to be visible bloodstains in the bathroom, and Frank couldn't see any blood inside the toilet. He asked Nancy to move, but she wanted to stay seated. She did not want to go to the hospital and thought she just needed time to recuperate.

Kevin and Frank knew that Nancy was in trouble. Her blood pressure was very low, and they were concerned about her hemorrhaging. When her condition failed to improve over the next fifteen or twenty minutes, they pulled her off the toilet and put her into a nearby chair. Frank continued to talk to the patient and her family while Kevin looked down into the toilet.

Nancy told the two EMT's that she was a virgin and that she recently had menstruated. Meanwhile Kevin was moving the toilet tissue that had been carefully folded back and forth within the toilet bowl. So much tissue had been used that the top layers of tissue were still dry. Kevin carefully folded back each layer of tissue looking for a clue to the girl's ailment. He was still convinced that this was just another teenager afraid to admit in the presence of her mother that she was sexually active. As Kevin continued to peel away each layer of tissue, he was surprised to see no blood and began to wonder if the girl had been bleeding at all.

While Frank was trying to find out more about the extent and nature of the bleeding, he heard Kevin's loud groan from the bathroom. Frank jumped to his feet at the sound and ran to the bathroom. Wordlessly, Kevin pointed to the toilet. Frank looked into the bowl and there in the water was the rump of an infant. The baby was twisted into the drain, so that Frank's immediate instinct to grab it was met with resistance from the pipe. He pulled the child from the water, walked to the next room and looked at the blank stares of the family. Not a word was said about the dead, wet newborn he held in his hands. Frank and Kevin saw no sorrow; they saw no shame. The conspirators had been found out, and now they were defiant in their silence.

Matady suddenly screamed that it was not a baby. It was a "monster," she said. She had seen her daughter drop seven globs of blood into the toilet, and they had come together in the shape of a baby. It was voodoo, she asserted, and the result of an evil spell.

Minutes later a physician at St. Luke's-Roosevelt Hospital declared Baby Boy Ruiz dead. His uncle, who had rushed the EMT's into the apartment, refused to look at the body because it was "a monster." Nancy's fiancé called the dead infant a "devil baby" and shrugged off the entire incident with disgust for the dead child. Matady and Juanita told the doctors and nurses that Nancy was never pregnant and that this was the result of evil dust that had been sprinkled at the entrance to their apartment. Again and again the family proclaimed Nancy's chastity while they arrogantly disassociated themselves from the dead infant. When asked by police to identify the child as it lay cold on a table in the hospital morgue, the family refused. Without a final touch or glance from his mother, grandmother, aunt, or uncle, Baby Boy Ruiz was identified by detectives, so that he could be buried in an unmarked grave in Potter's Field. In his short life and in death, the child had had but one experience—rejection.

When detectives arrived at Nancy's hospital room they received the same accounts provided to the doctors. Matady told the officers that she had taken Nancy to the voodoo doctor several hours before the birth and that the doctor assured her the girl was not pregnant. Matady told police that she had not sought a conventional medical opinion regarding Nancy's condition at any time during the prior months. She continued to insist that the child was really a monster, the result of an evil voodoo spell, while feigning the lack of sophistication she assumed the police would expect from a recent immigrant. Detectives knew, however, that Matady had been living in New York for nearly twenty years and that Nancy and her brother had both been born in hospitals following extensive prenatal care. She clearly possessed the experience to seek a qualified medical opinion and could be expected to recognize pregnancy from her own life experiences. Yet the mother asserted that, although Nancy and she slept in the same bed, she never saw any signs of pregnancy. She swore it had to be voodoo.

In the days following the birth and death of Baby Boy Ruiz, Nancy and Matady continued to be questioned by police, caseworkers, hospital staff and even the District Attorney's office. Their commitment to the voodoo explanation began to fade as more details of the fatal evening surfaced. Nancy finally admitted to a sexual relationship with a past boyfriend, although conjecture regarding the "evil spell" never vanished entirely. The teenager then offered investigators a series of fabrications about the conception, birth and death of Baby Boy Ruiz. She said that she and the child's twenty-five-year-old father had started having sex when she was about thirteen years old. They had intercourse on their first date in Riverside Park and thereafter continued to have sex in the park and in his family's apartment. Within a few months, Nancy became pregnant. Shortly thereafter, she broke up with her boyfriend and started dating Manny.

Nancy told detectives that she wanted to tell Manny that the child was his, but the timing was not right. She and Manny had been having sex for about three months prior to the birth of Baby Boy Ruiz, and he would never believe that a full-term baby could be born in that short a time. She also said that she did not want to lie to Manny.

Nancy then told police that the death of the child was an accident. Nancy recalled that on the night of the incident she was in the living room of her apartment when she started feeling heavy labor pains. She called to her mother, and they went into the bathroom where she said she straddled the toilet and dropped the baby into the bowl. She claimed that the baby drowned and that she was too scared to tell anyone the truth. Matady corroborated this version of the evening's events to police and caseworkers.

Nancy and her mother had not figured that the autopsy would reveal another cause of death. When Nancy was told by police that the infant had died of strangulation and that the presence of air and lack of any water in the lungs indicated that the child was dead before it was placed into the toilet, she changed her story again. She asserted that because of fear, she and her mother had fabricated the stories about the voodoo, the monster and the baby slipping into the toilet. They revised their fiction and now said that she gave birth to the child while lying on the bathroom floor. As soon as Baby Boy Ruiz exited the birth canal, Nancy said she asked her mother for a glass of water. Rather than taking water from the bathroom tap, Nancy said Matady went into the kitchen. During the time that Matady was in the kitchen, Nancy asserted she accidentally yanked the umbilical cord, causing instant death. She then shoved the child into the toilet and covered it with toilet paper until the *EMTs* arrived.

Investigators knew from the physical evidence and from Nancy's continually changing accounts that the teenager was lying about the death of the child. Yet experienced homicide detectives could not convince the girl to divulge any incriminating statements. They tried to find witnesses to support their theory that Nancy or Matady killed the infant, but nobody in the Ruiz household was talking. The other people in the apartment that night continued to say that they did not know that Nancy was pregnant (including Manny, who admitted having a sexual relationship with her). Juanita, Manny and Nancy's brother all denied that they heard any noises or screams coming from the bathroom the night that Nancy gave birth. They thought Nancy was overweight and suffering from an upset stomach.

While the police continued with their investigation, Wanda Rogers, a caseworker from New York City's child protective services unit, was also questioning Nancy. Not being bound by the same limitations as the police regarding questioning of suspects, caseworkers are free to use methods of interrogation that might not meet strict criminal justice guidelines. Nancy told Wanda that her mother left her alone in the bathroom and that she turned the child over and it stopped breathing. The caseworker, however, insisted upon full details from the teenager. Wanda told Nancy that she would continue to press the investigation until she provided an account that was consistent with the evidence.

Rogers' questioning continued over several different sessions. Each time Nancy provided a little more information than she had previously. The teenager thought that if she told the worker a little more, then Ms. Rogers' questioning would cease. The worker, however, knew that each interrogation would reveal additional inculpatory information, so she continued to press on with the questioning. Wanda Rogers was a fine investigator and an excellent interrogator.

After several days with both mother and daughter, the caseworker finally learned just how much of the truth Nancy Ruiz was prepared to disclose. Nancy tried to convince her questioner that the baby was born in the toilet, but Wanda insisted that such a position was impossible in light of Nancy's petite frame and the height of the bowl. Besides, said the caseworker, there is no way that an eight-pound infant can just slip out of a vagina into a toilet. There had to be pain, and there had to be pushing.

Nancy then admitted to lying on the bathroom floor and having her mother help with the birth. Nancy continued and, for the first time, admitted killing the newborn:

> My mother was at the bathroom door when the baby started to come out. She told me to get on the floor. I was leaning against the bathtub with my legs open. My mother kept telling me to push. My mother helped the baby out. Then she gave the baby to me to hold. I started to wipe off the blood with the toilet paper. My mother left the bathroom for a minute when I was holding my baby. He was soft and had a lot of blood on his body. His eyes were closed. He was crying. I was putting the bloody toilet paper in the toilet. I flushed the toilet *then I put the baby in the toilet.* I don't know—I got scared. When my mother saw what I did, she started crying and screaming at me. [emphasis added]

Wanda then asked why Nancy or the mother failed to remove the child from the toilet. Nancy's answer was immediate, "I don't know." Nancy and Matady next informed the caseworker that they put the child into the toilet with a plastic bag to avoid getting fingerprints on the dead body. They flushed the toilet over and over again in an attempt to dispose of the body, but the infant was too large for the drain. This explained why the baby's body (and the surrounding water) was totally clean when it was retrieved from the toilet.

Nancy and Matady expressed relief to the caseworker that they had finally admitted to killing the baby. Although the evidence was clear that the child was strangled, Nancy's confession to drowning the infant would be the only time that she expressed culpability for the killing. Matady explained to the caseworker that her cover-ups and fabrications were done as a result of love for her daughter. She said, "You have to understand that Nancy is my child. She's part of me. Whatever happens to her affects me. I'd do anything for my child."

One more thing, added Matady. "Will my daughter and I have to go to jail?"

The following day Nancy and her mother put their repentance aside and went to see the police and the district attorney. Again they asserted that Matady was out of the bathroom when the child was born and that the baby had slipped while Nancy was holding him. A day following the confession, the dead infant's mother and grandmother were again labeling the infant's death an accident.

Nancy and Matady did not expect that the police and the prosecutors would find the statements they made to the caseworker. They relied upon their experience with the social services system and upon their expectation of the government's incompetence. In fact, for the next several months, Matady and Nancy were proven right. The police department never spoke with the caseworker, and the assistant district attorney assigned to the case never subpoenaed the records of the child protective services department. Each system pursued a lengthy independent investigation without ever bringing the matter to court. While justice was delayed, Nancy became pregnant again.

As time passed the assistant district attorney saw little chance of successfully prosecuting Nancy as a *Juvenile Offender.* The ADA, nearly one year after the Baby Boy Ruiz' death, had still not seen the confession taken by Wanda Rogers. The physical evidence, along with the family's inconsistent fabrications, would never convince a jury beyond a reasonable doubt that Nancy Ruiz was a murderer. Thus the matter was transferred to the Family Court for prosecution, where charges of conspiracy, tampering and manslaughter could be pursued via a juvenile delinquency prosecution.

In contrast with the Criminal Court, the Family Court moved matters quickly, and within one month of transfer Nancy was charged with the killing of her son. The Family Court prosecutor had the presence of mind to look at the police file and at the caseworker's file. When the eight to ten different versions of the events were considered along with Nancy's confession that she killed the child by placing him in the toilet bowl, a *petition* was filed charging Nancy with the killing of Baby Boy Ruiz. Nancy was arraigned and released pending a *fact-finding hearing.*

The trial commenced with the testimony of the two EMTs, who described the call to the Ruiz apartment, as well as their shock when they saw the dead infant jammed into the toilet. They were followed by several police witnesses who supplied the court with various accounts offered by Nancy concerning the birth and death of her newborn son. Wanda Rogers, the caseworker, spent several days on the stand telling the court about Nancy's different versions of the events and how she finally admitted to killing the child. All the testimony was filled with descriptions of voodoo and Santeria (religious occult practices among some Caribbean groups), along with the callous reaction of a family that had just witnessed the death of their youngest member.

The people who work in the Family Court are not squeamish. The judges, lawyers, clerks, court officers and everyone else see the worst aspects of urban America on a daily basis. There are few surprises for the veterans of the Family Court, but this case got the attention of even the most cynical people in the system. When two medical examiners, including the chief medical examiner, testified that a perfectly normal eight-and-one-half pound baby was strangled within a minute or two of birth, a wave of discomfort ran through people who rarely blinked in the face of tragedy. When each medical examiner ventured an opinion on the amount of force necessary to close a newborn's windpipe, along with their estimates about the period of oxygen deprivation necessary to cause death, it was clear that Baby Boy Ruiz's demise was no accident. Photographs of the dead child were placed in evidence, with markings on the infant's neck to indicate the points where his killer had placed her fingers and squeezed. The facts were grotesque, and no one wanted to believe that this level of brutality was possible from a young mother or that it was sanctioned by her family.

Among those who did not want to believe the brutality of the crime was the judge. Though often sympathetic to the prosecution, this time she continually searched for a reason or excuse to avoid facing the cruelty perpetrated by Nancy Ruiz.

She kept asking the police witnesses and the caseworkers about the role of Nancy's mother in the homicide. Perhaps the failure of the confession to conform to the evidence of strangulation gave the judge reason to find doubt despite Nancy's admission of guilt.

The defense presented no witnesses. Not one family member was called to explain their silence while the two EMT's tried to diagnose Nancy's medical condition that night in the apartment. Nor did anyone offer an explanation for their silence when a dead full-term infant was pulled from the apartment's only toilet. A clearly conspiratorial, and probably murderous, family relied upon their privilege against self-incrimination to stay off the witness stand. Matady, who had told Wanda Rogers that she would do "anything for [her] child," never even came to court during the trial.

The judge was certain that someone in the apartment had murdered Baby Boy Ruiz. She was sure the infant had been strangled and that no accident could have caused the death. The court, however, remained unsure as to whether the killer was Nancy or Matady. The judge ignored Nancy's confession to Wanda because she thought the teenager might be covering for her mother. Matady faced a far longer prison term for the homicide than her daughter, so the judge reasoned that the teen may have offered herself to authorities as a sacrifice for her parent. Perhaps, concluded the court, it was Nancy who would do "anything" for her mother. There was no evidence to suggest that Nancy's confession was made on her mother's behalf, nor was there any evidence to implicate anyone other than Nancy in the killing.

In acquitting Nancy of the homicide, the court told the girl: "I don't know who did this, you or your mother. But something happened in that apartment that night that resulted in the death of an infant, and everyone in this family is covering for everyone else."

The court, however, did not acquit Nancy of all charges. The judge found her guilty of conspiracy and of tampering with the evidence. Even though this was a felony adjudication, it was a defeat for the prosecution. No loss is as great for a prosecutor as seeing a murderer leave the courtroom clearly guilty but not beyond a reasonable doubt. In this case it was especially troubling because it reinforced the family's belief that they could control their own destiny by taking whatever actions they deemed appropriate. It taught the Ruiz clan that it is best to lie and appropriate to kill.

The court ordered the Department of Probation to do an I & R, and ordered an MHS as well. The court noted that Nancy had been pregnant during the time the case was being investigated and that the pregnancy had terminated via an alleged miscarriage. The court also noted that Nancy had just given birth to another child and that the child protective services agency should investigate that matter as well. Despite the court's willingness to acquit Nancy of the homicide, the judge was not eager to trust Nancy with another baby. Reasonable doubts did not prohibit imposing reasonable precautions.

The pictures painted by the I & R and by the MHS reports reveal much to suggest that Nancy was in fact capable of killing and surely did kill Baby Boy Ruiz. Although Nancy had given numerous accounts of the night the infant was killed, she told the court's investigators that she could no longer remember anything. She claimed she was now in "complete shock," and that she had absolutely no recall of the events. With a homicide acquittal behind her, Nancy had beaten the system.

Nancy further told the probation officer that she remembered telling detectives that she had no memory of the offense but that she was coerced into making statements. She claimed no memory of her family's actions following the birth of Baby Boy Ruiz, but she did know that they were all in the apartment when the child was born and when it died. She had no explanation for her refusal to get off the toilet and for the layers of toilet tissue that hid the infant's body. Everything pertaining to the incident was lost in a shadowy past.

Interestingly, Nancy was assertive about her new role as a mother. She volunteered that she and Manny were now married and, therefore, she now "had no reason to kill."

The court's psychiatrist found Nancy to be unreliable and hard to believe. The doctor indicated that Nancy was guarded, withholding and, when confronted with inconsistencies or implausibilities, able to supply only superficial rationalizations. Nancy told the examiner that she was an "A" student. In fact, she had virtually dropped out of school and was failing most courses. She told the doctor, just as she had told the probation officer, that she could not recall any of the events the night her son was killed. Yet this failure to recollect the facts did not prevent Nancy from proclaiming her innocence of all wrongdoing and from excusing the actions of her family. They had assured her of their innocence, and this satisfied any questions the teenager had about the death of her child. She saw no reason even to look any further into the matter because she believed the inquiry would distress her mother. She sought to bury the inquiry—along with Baby Boy Ruiz.

Nancy saw no reason for psychiatric help or for counseling because she saw nothing wrong in her actions. She did not view herself as being in any emotional distress, despite the fact that her child was dead. This lack of concern for the dead infant, she asserted, in no way represented her ability to love, care for or raise the new baby. Nancy recognized that empathy was lacking, but she didn't think that was important.

The best insight into Nancy's character came from the psychologist who tested her several times. Nancy continued to be evasive during the interview and made overt gestures during testing to present neutral material about herself and her family. She displayed no evidence of psychosis, but she continued to display an inability to empathize with people. Her present-sense orientation made her unable to plan for the future, and her inability to delay gratification guaranteed that she would never fulfill her goals. The psychologist concluded that all these events, from the killing of the baby through the trial, were evidence of a "characterological disturbance and that she may be prone to the use of denial in her everyday life."

The court placed Nancy Ruiz on probation with the strict condition that she get psychotherapy and that she no longer live with her mother. She would have to live with her husband in Brooklyn; the progress of the family would have to be monitored. Although Nancy had been referred for counseling in the past by protective services, and she had always refused to go, the court told her that this time it would have to be different. She would follow the order of the court, she was told, or face incarceration.

Counseling cannot change people who do not want to change. When the patient sees nothing wrong in his or her behavior, any attempt to modify that behavior is wasted effort. Within eight months of the matter concluding, Nancy had moved away from her husband and was back with her mother. If her probation status is violated, she will not go to jail. Courts do not like to separate mothers from their children, even when there is a killing in the family. The newspapers are filled with stories of child protective cases that "fell through the cracks."

Nancy Ruiz is living proof that being fertile is not the only prerequisite to being a parent. She is also proof that the judicial and social welfare systems can be manipulated through lies, cheating and even murder to accomplish whatever a family deems important or to avoid that which they deem unimportant. EMS could easily have been called earlier that fatal evening to take the pregnant teen to the hospital when labor pains started. Nancy could have left the child in the nursery and never turned back. The system would have taken in the abandoned child, supported him and perhaps found him a pre-adoptive home. Instead, Nancy Ruiz made her choice, and the system buried a little boy.

Not one note in Nancy's social services record reveals any consultation with the teenager about birth control. There are referrals to "parenting skills" classes and suggestions for counseling, therapy and related services. By age sixteen Nancy Ruiz has already miscarried at least once, killed one infant and is raising another. She has rebuffed all services offered her and has ignored her court-ordered conditions of probation. With at least another twenty-five years of fertility ahead of her, Nancy has yet to be taught and encouraged to use contraceptives. Of course, such a lesson is not needed. Nancy Ruiz knows that any child she doesn't want she can kill.

When do we get the body of Baby Girl Ruiz?

7.

In New York's Assembly the Speaker makes the rules. As majority leader of New York's lower legislative house, the Speaker controls the items that pass through the committees and finally make it to the floor for a vote. An item without the Speaker's blessing is forever stalled "in committee." In true dictatorial fashion, the membership may only vote on those items that the Speaker allows them to consider. The concept of representative government is lost on New York's legislature; only the Speaker "speaks." The members follow in silence. Even the most popular issues remain captive to the Speaker and staff. Juvenile justice reform has been a longtime hostage of the Speaker's office.

For more than a decade, a majority of New Yorkers have been asking for comprehensive juvenile justice reform. Although some changes had been made in the late 1970s allowing certain cases to be prosecuted in the adult criminal system, the bulk of the Family Court Act's juvenile justice sanctions remain untouched since the time they were adopted in 1962. Before the epidemic of juvenile violence swept the nation in the late 1980s, the state legislature was asked to   prepare New York for the upcoming crime wave. Prosecutors in the city of New York, along with the state's District Attorneys Association, knew that the existing juvenile justice code was insufficient to meet the need for public safety. The State Senate, mostly hard-nosed Republicans and conservative Democrats, immediately embraced the idea for common-sense change.

The Assembly, dominated by liberal Democrats from the cities, rejected the reforms outright. They had historically rejected fingerprinting offenders arrested on charges such as gun possession, sexual abuse, felony assault and certain robberies. They also opposed longer terms of incarceration for muggers, robbers, arsonists, sex offenders and even for juvenile killers. As the Assembly leadership stared down the barrel of the upcoming crack epidemic and violent wave of youth crime, they pretended that everything in the juvenile justice law was fine.

When a white jogger was raped by a group of black juveniles in Central Park in 1989, America began a serious reevaluation of its criminal justice processes. Kid violence got a new name—"wilding"—and the calls for reform finally began to drown out the slogans of the advocates who had used the past 25 years to erase accountability and polarize urban America. Suddenly, people were no longer willing to be liberal when it meant sacrificing their safety and the safety of their children. Crime had come out of the ghetto and onto the doorstep of middle-class America. Violent crime was no longer just a social affliction of the poor that could be debated at parties, barbecues and in college classrooms. It had finally gotten the attention of the taxpayers, and they wanted action.

The New York legislature in the late 1980s, however, turned a blind eye to this emerging crisis. Even the state's liberal governor, Mario Cuomo, asked for major reforms of the juvenile code; but the Assembly leadership was not listening. Fingerprinting the expanding class of offenders who were carrying guns still brought cries of "stigma," "racism" and "discrimination" from many of New York's elected representatives. The acts of violent predators were still being addressed by members of the Assembly's minority caucus as a need for "prevention" and "alternatives to incarceration." The oxymoron "minority over-representation" became the dominant issue for many advocates and policy makers within New York's criminal justice community. For the Assembly leadership, and for their supporters, studying racial composition in the jails was of greater urgency than meeting an immediate need for public safety. The issue was not whether Rome was burning; the issue was whether it was burning in an egalitarian fashion.

The Assembly leadership, however, was smart enough to know that failing to appear "tough on crime" could cost them their jobs. Public sentiment about violent crime became a premier national issue in the early 1990s and continues to dominate the debate today. If Willie Horton could crush the national Democratic Party, the state's Assembly leadership had nowhere to turn to seek support for their ideals. They knew they had to demonstrate an anticrime position to the voters, while still remaining true to their philosophy that deflected individual accountability in favor of blaming societal ills. In short, the Assembly needed to look as if they were doing something, when in fact, they would do nothing. It was politics as usual, and of course they succeeded.

In 1994 the New York State Assembly introduced legislation called the Comprehensive Criminal Justice Reform Proposal at the request of the Speaker (and others in the leadership). The bill promised to offer a three-pronged attack on crime: **"Getting Tough, Getting Smart and Getting Realistic."** They announced their proposal in a fanfare that included two round-table discussions in the Albany legislative offices. One discussion focused on the reform of the adult criminal system and the other was intended to address the long-awaited Assembly proposal on juvenile crime.

Prosecutors, defense attorneys, judges, and social workers, along with a crowd of child advocates, were invited to participate in the discussion on juvenile justice. Of course, getting experts from every philosophical corner in the system may have filled the room with authorities, but it guaranteed inaction. Every legislator and lobbyist knows that the best way to move an agenda forward is to gather the proponents and limit the discussion. Likewise, the best way to kill a proposal is to hold endless meetings, discussions and follow-up studies. Dialogue breeds delay, a legislative specialty. As the name implies, a round-table discussion suggests circular reasoning with no beginning and no end. The Assembly leadership had taken enough steps to go home and tell their constituents that they had drafted a proposal and had discussed it with every major player in the juvenile crime system. They could blame its failure to pass on the Senate or on the governor and would still feel comfortable to continue their electioneering as crime fighters. Only their fellow legislators, the lobbyists and the experts knew that their efforts were a sham.

A review of the juvenile justice sections of this 108-page proposal disposed of any notions that the Assembly had gotten any "tougher, smarter or more realistic." It was clear that the former Legal Aid lawyers who filled the staff counsel positions in the Assembly's leadership office had written a bill that did more to enhance crime than it did to deter it. Punishments were virtually left unchanged; protections for offenders, however, were enlarged on almost every page. It was clear that the "tough, smart and realistic" approach was an unworkable hoax on the public and certainly incapable of dealing with the violence of someone like Luis Omar Perez.

Luis Omar Perez sat still as the Family Court judge ordered him into *DFY* placement following his *dispositional hearing.* The court made the required finding that Luis needed treatment, supervision and confinement, and it followed that statement with a soliloquy on the inability of the law to effectively deal with predators like Perez:

This juvenile is before the Court with one of the worst antisocial histories this Court has seen. It is mere chance that there has not yet been more seriously hurt victims, as a result of this Respondent's anti-social conduct. . . . Even if the Respondent's mother was Mother Teresa, she would not be able to provide supervision for him, since he is, because of his severe antisocial personality, beyond the control of any reasonable parent. . . . [He needs] psychiatric treatment, to the extent that such treatment can deal with his severe antisocial personality disorders. . . . More significantly, however, he needs confinement, since he is a clear danger to the community. . . . I consider this Respondent to be one of the most dangerous. . . juveniles who has ever appeared before me. . . . While the law does not permit me to focus more intensely on the danger issue, and confinement issue, that is, I lack the power to place him in a more secure facility than otherwise allowable by law, the maximum I can place him in is a so-called limited secure facility with the Division For Youth. . . . However, this case is an illustration, among other cases that appear before this court, that the Family Court Act, Article Three, though laudable in its rehabilitative purposes, may well be inadequate in its application to very, very severely antisocial juveniles who, despite their ages, constitute a clear, clear danger to public safety. This is one such juvenile.

In the early morning hours of June 15, 1993 Luis Omar Perez and his friend Opal Lind needed money to buy heroin.

Luis had recently arrived in New York from Puerto Rico to live with the mother he had not seen in ten years. Although only fifteen, Luis had become streetwise beyond his years while growing up in the streets of Puerto Rico and now in New York. He had not attended school since he was six years old, and he could not read or write, in English or Spanish. Now that his father was in prison, his drug-addicted mother was supposed to provide supervision. Instead of supervising the boy, his mother allowed Luis to remain out all night, something the teen had been doing with regularity. As dawn was beginning to break, the two young thugs approached their middle-aged victim as he sat waiting for a bus on Manhattan's Lower East Side. Using his finger inserted inside his coat to simulate a gun, Luis ordered the man to turn over his money. They shoved him to the ground, kicked him and threatened to crush his skull with a bottle if he did not hand over his money.

Opal and Luis were too stoned to combat their victim when he started to fight back. When it became apparent to their intended prey that the youths did not have anything more than a finger in their pockets, the man started swinging wildly at his attackers. Rather than risk injury, Luis and Opal decided that they would look for another victim.

Before the two bandits could leave the scene, a police officer pulled his car in front of the bleeding victim. The man told the cop what had occurred and pointed to his fleeing attackers. Luis and Opal were arrested for attempted robbery and felony assault.

When the case was referred for prosecution, and even during trial, it seemed very similar to many of the cases that make up the bulk of juvenile practice. Group robbery is the most commonly charged offense in New York City's juvenile justice system, and felony assault follows as the second most often charged crime. Yet the extent to which violence had become a regular part of Luis's life was hardly appreciated by court or prosecutor until the case was set for disposition. Besides a subsequent arrest for car theft several days after this robbery incident, Luis was unknown to New York's criminal justice system. The judge, the prosecutor and the police had no idea that this fifteen-year-old was one of the most violent and dangerous predators in New York City. The criminal justice system was ignorant—and would have remained so— because of the kinds of protections that have been provided and extended to violent young offenders by New York's Assembly and hundreds of other misguided American apologists.

Luis Omar Perez had been convicted of attempted murder in Puerto Rico. Luis had taken a knife and sliced the throat of another youth while the two were in a public bathroom. Medical science, not lack of criminal talent, was the only factor that prevented the case from becoming a completed murder. Because he was a first offender, Perez was released by the court and placed on community supervision. Within weeks of his release, he was arrested again for firing a gun (which he admitted stealing) into a crowd in a public park. He was incarcerated for a short time and then escaped from a facility he described as "just like Spofford."

New York authorities knew nothing of this history when Luis was arrested for the attempted robbery shortly after his arrival from Puerto Rico. Like the legislative leaders in Albany (and in other state capitals), the politicians of Puerto Rico were concerned about the hardship and stigma suffered by an offender because of a juvenile court history. There were no fingerprints on file with the FBI to provide New York police, prosecutors and judges with an accurate view of the youth known only as Luis Omar Perez. In fact, like New York, Puerto Rico would not supply information about juvenile thugs to foreign state officials even though the perpetrator represented a threat to the safety of citizens. Puerto Rico, like so many other jurisdictions in the United States, would not violate the confidentiality of Luis Omar Perez—which apparently is more important than the safety and well-being of the citizens he places at risk.

Even if Puerto Rico had been willing to share the information with police and prosecutors about Luis Omar Perez's past, New York's Family Court Act guaranteed that law enforcement and the courts would remain ignorant of it. Perez could not have been fingerprinted for the attempted robbery. No record search could have been performed, and no rap sheet could have been generated. New York's Division of Criminal Justice Services (*DCJS*), the state's repository for all criminal justice records, had no history of this violent boy, and the FBI had no data about his crimes. Luis Omar Perez, firearm thief, gun-wielding maniac and seasoned throat-slitter was a first offender in the state of New York. Any subsequent arrest would not have revealed his violent past in the Caribbean or in New York. Had he not been as dumb as he was dangerous, Luis would never have told his history to the court psychiatrist, and the legislatively endorsed ignorance would have been perpetuated.

Many advocates for confidentiality of juvenile records are often the same people who represent young offenders in court or, in the case of the staff counsel in the Assembly leadership's office, are former defense attorneys. To these advocates, accurate criminal histories are the enemy. Keeping a court ignorant may be the defense attorney's paramount objective in the dispositional process. Opponents of information-sharing often say that confidentiality is important because mistakes in the records can cause irreparable harm to youngsters who may be seeking a job or credit approval sometime in the future. Yet such an argument is directed at accurate record-keeping, rather than the slippery theories that prohibit the sharing of data. Disallowing a sentencing court from having the full record of an offender is a matter completely unrelated to confidentiality.

The Speaker's tough, smart and realistic proposal for juvenile justice would have provided no protection for the community from Luis Omar Perez. In fact, it is likely that the Assembly's approach would have worsened the problem. Instead of enabling record-sharing between law enforcement and the court, the Assembly's proposal sought to tighten access to information. Only one piece of the legislation addressed the fingerprinting of people like Luis Omar Perez, and that was the circumstance of an officer mistakenly taking the fingerprints of the youth and then distributing them to law enforcement agencies. The Assembly proposal held the officer and the municipality liable for triple damages for violating the confidentiality rights of Luis Omar Perez (or any other violent felon coming under the protection of the Assembly's confidentiality umbrella). Clearly, such a proposition is designed to inhibit the ability of police to track violent offenders and virtually guarantees that the whole truth will never be known by the court.

Even worse, under the Speaker's bill it is unlikely that the matter would ever have been seen by the prosecution or the court. According to the Assembly's tough, smart and realistic proposal, first offenders, except for a few selected cases, were to have their cases *adjusted* by the probation service. This meant that Perez's attempted robbery—along with the bloody victim therein—would never get to the prosecutor or inside a courtroom. This *"tough, smart and realistic"* approach would have taken an offender, whom a judge labeled "one of the most dangerous juveniles" he'd ever seen, and required diverting him and his case into a social service regimen. Of course, diverting Luis Omar Perez, a youth with "severe personality disorders," from court and into a community-based program is wholly inconsistent with public safety. But then the *"tough, smart, and realistic"* proposal from the Speaker had less to do with public safety than it did with the philosophical views of bunker-mentality idealogues. Any adjustment of Luis's case would not only put a throat-slitting offender back into the community, but it would also make sure that the robbery that was the basis for the adjustment would forever remain sealed. No reference to the case could be made at a future sentencing, thus allowing the Speaker of the Assembly to ensure, once again, that Luis Omar Perez, upon a subsequent arrest, would enjoy first-offender status.

At the same time that the Assembly was holding its useless round-table meetings in 1994, the Governor's Commission for the Study of Youth Crime and Violence headed by former New York City Council President Andrew Stein was releasing its first report about the condition of New York's Juvenile Justice System. The report, based upon nearly one year's study of juvenile crime all around New York State, had concrete recommendations about the need for reforming the present juvenile justice process. These recommendations, based upon hard data, interviews with judges, attorneys, DFY workers, and upon the testimony of the politicians and the experts, rejected the Assembly's philosophy as a continuation of past failures. Instead, the commission looked to increase penalties, to give more power to prosecutors and police, and to break down the wall of confidentiality by increasing the sharing of information among law enforcement agencies and the courts. Fingerprinting people like Luis Omar Perez was a common-sense necessity that only seemed to elude the Assembly leadership. Similarly, the need for rational sanctions for violent offenders was the centerpiece of the commission's report—yet that suggestion was virtually ignored by the round table's promoters.

It is impossible to understand the Assembly's consistent opposition to common-sense changes in the criminal justice field. For ten years, the lower house had been the only stumbling block to imposing reform in the juvenile justice code that would clearly have met with the approval of the vast majority of New Yorkers. As crime continues to ravage neighborhoods and schools in New York City, mostly in poor neighborhoods predominantly populated by black and Hispanic people, it is alarming to find that the strongest opposition comes from the representatives of the people who are suffering the most. Whom do these legislators represent if they work so long and so hard to minimize the actions of very predators who imperil their community? Why have violent felons established a strong constituency in the Assembly when every other sector of every community has refused to sympathize with their list of excuses? How does the Assembly manage to pass a death penalty bill—which has already been enacted into law in New York State—but remain steadfast in their opposition to juvenile fingerprinting?

There is one individual who can answer these questions, and he is the same person who makes the rules in the Assembly. He is the leader who has opposed fingerprinting juvenile felons, has opposed increasing incarceration for juvenile felons beyond their minimal limits, and has led the crusade to protect the rights of Luis Omar Perez at the expense of the safety of New York City. He calls this philosophy **"tough, smart and realistic."** But that description, along with all the rhetoric and promotion surrounding the Assembly leadership's bill, only obscured the fact that responsible reform was again blocked by *one* person—and that juvenile justice remained hostage another year in the office of the Speaker.

Perhaps the autocratic nature of representative government in New York is what the Speaker really means by "tough and smart." Similarly, if preserving this power is his goal, then his tactics are selfishly "realistic." For all the victims, and especially for the victims to come, it is politics as usual.

8.

The new spirit of cooperation among the perps has been an honest citizen's nightmare.[8] Bands of boisterous young males are dreaded by virtually every New Yorker. Whether it's an angry group of drunken youths in Howard Beach, an armed trio stealing bicycles in Prospect Park or a "high-fivin'" band of rowdies on the A train, these loosely knit gangs spell fear for those they encounter.

Group crime has become an uncontrolled menace in the City of New York. You can call it "Wilding," "Wolf-Packs," looting, or just plain "Flippin' Herbs," the end result is the same. Teens are roving throughout the city stalking victims for fun or to "get paid." Each may appear to be the ordinary boy-next-door when alone, but in a group they feel free to display their predatory nature. Make no mistake, these offenders are capable of unlimited brutality. Their victims (or the surviving friends and families) know this all too well.

The beginning of December usually brings the holiday spirit. Moods tend to be uplifting, and almost everyone tries to smile. Having fun was exactly what Tarion W. and his three friends had in mind. Only fun at the expense of others is not in keeping with holiday cheer.

It happened on a downtown #1 train. The local was pulling out of 34th Street at about 7:30 P.M. The second to the last car wasn't crowded. In fact, it was surprisingly empty for an early weekday evening. As the train headed towards the 28th Street stop, the ubiquitous rumble of the subway was shattered by the slam of the door leading from the last car. Four youths yelling obscenities burst in. The near-empty train gave them the chance to jump on the seats, kick at the windows and doors, and to swirl around the poles. They laughed loudly, they screamed, and they shoved each other. It was all part of the plan, and it was working. They had instilled fear in every rider.

As they started their rampage, everyone on the car pretended to look away. New Yorkers know that eye contact is dangerous and has even proven fatal. So each passenger looked down, away, or pretended to read. But Tarion and his friends had these people right where they wanted them.

The perps focused their attention on a young couple seated in the middle of the car. The offenders had no way of knowing that these two were on their first date, but it would be a night they would not forget.

It always starts with the tease or the provocation.

Sometimes it's "Hey—what are you lookin' at?" Other times it can be an insult, racial epithet or other words of instigation. Tonight the surrounding perps were placing their hands on a woman's purse. They would touch it, pull it away. It was all part of the razz. The cat had the mouse, and it was time to toy with it. The kill would come later.

Suddenly one of the youths yelled "Do it!" In an instant the young man was thrown from his seat to the floor of the subway train. The four youths kicked him about the head and body and beat him with their fists. Tarion jumped on the seat across from the victim, who was attempting to protect his face and eyeglasses from the blows. His cries for mercy only fueled the frenzy of his attackers. As he raised his head and body to beg them to stop, Tarion W. took his chance. He grabbed the overhead horizontal bar that commuters cling to during the rush hour, and he swung forward. He drove his boot with the steel toe through the lens of the victim's glasses sending shards of glass into his eye.

As the blood began to pour out of his eye, the young man fell to the floor screaming. The train was now pulling into 28th Street and the doors were opening. The four kids ran out of the car laughing. They slapped each other, reveling in their victorious moment. In the short time it takes a train to go six blocks, they had changed a man's life forever.

The attackers hadn't taken any property. This was not about stealing. It had nothing to do with needing money to feed a hungry child or a sick mother. Their purpose was summed up in their delight as they disembarked from the train. This was entertainment. This was recreation. It was city kids having fun, and it was a prime example of the new style in kid crime for the '90s.

Group crime has become the staple of Family Court

prosecution. By the end of the 1980s the most common   serious charge brought against offenders in New York City's Juvenile Justice System was group robbery. By 1991, *felony* assault by groups had outpaced loaded-gun possession as the fastest-growing crime in the Juvenile Justice System. Yet in 1992, 1993 and 1994, when the New York State Assembly was asked to enhance the penalties for group assaults, they failed to pass the bill. They also refused to pass a bill that would have allowed for the fingerprinting of offenders like Tarion W. Instead, the elected representatives of the People of the State of New York were apparently satisfied with the maximum initial penalty which Tarion received: eighteen months in a limited secure facility. In fact, most felonies in the juvenile system share this same result.[9] The legislators, by rejecting fingerprinting for assaults of this type, have also given their approval for keeping offenders like Tarion without a criminal history. When Tarion commits his next violent crime, he will still enjoy his first offender status.

What seems like common sense to most New Yorkers has been traditionally absent among the lawmakers in Albany. Common sense can't be taught—unless the next victim to feel Tarion's steel-tipped boot in his eye is an assemblyman. Victims are fast learners.

9.

In the spirit of black humor it would save lots of time, and it would make life much easier if those who rationalized crime simply made lists instead of indulging in courtroom oratory. Those who feel compelled to place the blame on anything or anyone but the person actually responsible are good at writing reports and proffering summations that contain the same worn apologies from case to case. Court resources would be saved, and realists would be spared the rhetoric, if the excuse-makers would categorize all their justifications and would then provide the court and opposing counsel with simple numbers corresponding to same. Swift and certain summations could be followed by swift and certain justice.

For instance, the majority of the excuse-makers list **poverty** as the number one rationale for the proliferation of criminal activity. Choosing to ignore the millions of hardworking honest people who live below the poverty level, politicians and rabble rousers habitually name poverty as the root of crime. Curiously, these same philosophers blame poverty for the crime-riddled neighborhoods that make trapped victims of the working poor. No explanations are offered to suggest why poverty makes one the predator and the other the prey. Urban philosophers don't want to find flaws in their dreams by condemning the lawbreaker. Individual responsibility is discounted in favor of the theory that poverty, like a contagious virus, spreads crime.

Second on the list to justify violent felony by young people is **the breakdown of the family unit.** Included as subcategories, or as related causes, are divorce, single mothers, deadbeat dads, domestic violence and teenage parenthood. Certainly these reasons may explain antisocial behavior, but when offered as rationales for crime, they fall short of their intended purpose. In any event, many of the violent offenders today are generations removed from the traditional notion of the nuclear family. In some cases, no such family unit ever existed. [10]

It is impossible to develop a finite list to satisfy the excuse-makers. Surely the proof that one item on the list is no longer acceptable, or politically correct, will generate more excuses for the list. Every year some new urban philosophy finds a variant of racial discrimination, ethnic intolerance, religious zeal or homophobia to add to the list of excuses. Yet the most common excuses (which remain forever popular) reduced to numbers would make the practice of law faster and more efficient. Counsel could appear at disposition to offer a succinct "1, 6, 10, 14, 34 and 42" in defense of their client. The reasons are as worn as the people who proffer, oppose and determine them.

Perhaps the list would look like this:

Excuses for Violent Felony Conduct

1. Poverty
2. Family breakdown
3. Victim of drug addiction
4. Family member a victim of drug addiction
5. Mother neglects family
6. Father neglects family
7. Victim of child abuse
8. Victim of sexual abuse
9. Victim of alcohol
10. Mother in jail

11. *Father in jail*
12. *Father unknown*
13. *Victim of HIV/AIDS*
14. *Family member a victim of HIV/AIDS*
15. *The schools failed him*
16. *The media made him violent*
17. *Video games made him violent*
18. *Slipped through the cracks in the system*
19. *Is a victim of the foster care system*
20. *Is a victim of the welfare system*
21. *Is in special education*
22. *Needed to be in special education*
23. *Didn't belong in special education*
24. *Was left back*
25. *Was promoted without passing by the schools*
26. *Hangs out with the wrong kids*
27. *Is a follower*
28. *Has a low IQ*
29. *The juvenile justice system failed*
30. *Needs counseling*
31. *Needs therapy*
32. *Needs a new kind of therapy*
33. *Needs a role model*
34. *Needs a father*
35. *Needs to be away from his father*
36. *Needs a social worker*
37. *Needs a psychiatrist*
38. *Needs a psychologist*

39. Needs a job

40. The streets are mean

41. Is a drug addict

42. Is a recovering drug addict no longer in remission

43. Was a crack baby

44. Is a victim of fetal alcohol syndrome

45. Is a victim of incest

46. Is a victim of police brutality

47. Is a victim of the drug wars

48. Is a victim of sexism

49. Is a victim of racism

*50. **IS A VICTIM***

Stacy Logan[11] would have the distinguished honor of having one of the longest—if not *the* longest—list of possible excuses for his violence. Certainly there was no dearth of legal, social and psychological offerings by his defenders to suggest excuses for one of New York's most dangerous predators. The crime novelist who describes the cruel street urchin, or the television screenwriter who creates the savage mugger, had the likes of Stacy Logan in mind. He is the prototype offender of whom most New Yorkers are afraid. He is black, he is young, he is angry—and he likes to get physical.

Stacy and several comrades in crime were in the vicinity of Lincoln Center on a warm June morning looking for a victim. Two young white teens had the misfortune of being at that location. Stacy and his accomplices grabbed the young boys and started beating them about their heads and bodies. The five young blacks were larger and stronger than their two white victims, but Stacy was not interested in a fair fight. As the attackers took turns holding their victims, they systematically punched and kicked the two helpless boys. Stacy slammed his fist into the mouth of one youth, making sure to chip and remove teeth. He jammed the same youth's hand into the sidewalk, breaking the boy's wrist in four or five places. Stacy then turned to the next victim and rammed his fist twice into the trapped teen's right eye. The youth fell to the ground unconscious as Stacy drove his shoe into the young man's head. With that last blow, Stacy temporarily satisfied his thirst for blood. An accomplice rummaged through the victims' pockets, taking a few coins as his prize. Leaving their battered quarry in the street, Stacy and his friends ran off toward Central Park.

It did not take the prosecution long to convict Stacy Logan. Both witnesses easily identified their attackers (the other youths were not juveniles, and thus were tried separately in the Criminal Courts). The lengthiest part of their testimony concerned the description of their injuries. Besides the mounds of hospital records and medical reports that were admitted into evidence at trial, the two battered victims spent hours describing their wounds and their prospects for recovery. One of the young men had suffered permanent memory loss along with the probability of a lifetime of blurred vision in the right eye. The other boy will require several operations to repair a wrist that will never function quite as well as the one he had prior to his meeting with Stacy Logan.

Stacy did not testify at trial, but his interviews with the investigating probation officer who prepared the *I & R* and with the doctors who provided the Mental Health Studies provide revealing insight into the ways to create a sociopathic monster.

Stacy was raised by his mother until her drug habit

became so bad that she could no longer care for the child. Stacy's father and mother were never married and never lived together; the father was not a resource for the boy in any case because of his incarceration eight years earlier for murder. Stacy was raised by his maternal grandmother, who was also caring for Stacy's mother (presently in a relapse of her drug habit and suffering from the first stages of AIDS). Stacy's grandfather was no longer in the home because of his drinking problem, and he rarely sent support to help with the family's expenses. Stacy's grandmother was working a full-time job in addition to her caretaker duties, so there was virtually no supervision for the boy.

Stacy provided the court clinicians with a detailed behavioral history. He told the doctors and the probation officer that he had problems in school from about the third grade. He started fighting with peers at about that time, and he was suspended several times for hurting other children in his class. Regular suspensions continued through junior high school, as the violence in his character seemed to escalate. Despite his periodic attacks on other students, school officials never called police. Instead, they sought to protect the reputation of their schools before protecting the safety of their students. Looking to social workers and guidance counselors to treat the violent deviants of the student body, they preferred to settle matters outside the criminal justice system. (After years of violence resulting in murder, rape, robbery and assault in New York City schools, too many officials would still rather counsel a problem than remove it.)

Naturally, hindsight proved that the school officials did Stacy and his future victims a disservice. There was no accountability demanded by the school, just suspensions of a youth who already saw little reason to seek an education.

As time passed, Stacy got more aggressive and the schools got even less responsive. He was "kicked out" of his first high school and was moved to an alternative school. There he was placed in special education classes, where teachers assured his grandmother that Stacy would thrive. And thrive he did—on predation. He was arrested by a school safety officer for carrying a razor in school and attempting to cut the guard with that razor. When the guard testified at the school suspension hearing about the attack, the hearing officer dismissed the case. Instead of a suspension, Stacy was offered another chance by the system. No punishment was exacted for carrying the razor to class, and school officials decided not to prosecute the case in the courts.

Shortly thereafter, Stacy was arrested for possession of a pistol while trespassing in another high school. He was again suspended from his own school for five days, but the case was not referred to the police or prosecutors. The schools did not inquire about where Stacy got the gun, why he was carrying the gun, or why he was in a school where he was not enrolled. They did not look into—or ask the police to investigate—whether Stacy was implicated in any of the recent armed offenses at the school or in the vicinity of the school, nor did they bother to check whether the youth had a feud with any student at that high school. When the clinicians from the court asked him about his reasons for carrying guns and knives, he told them he does it because he "wants to," and that he "likes guns."

Stacy told the interviewers that he used marijuana, stayed out beyond his curfew, even all night, and that he enjoyed inflicting pain on other people. He liked violence, even if it meant violence against himself, and he dreamed about suicide. He told the psychiatrist that he hated school because they "ask too many questions" and that psychiatric guidance was useless because "I know what I'm doing."

Stacy gave the court workers a sugar-coated version of the events that brought him into court. He tried to justify his vicious attack against the two white teens by suggesting that they had made a racist remark that resulted in their beating. The clinicians were quick to point out that the two small victims were hardly likely to provoke an attack by five larger males. Stacy did not address this apparent inconsistency, other than to point out that he thought the white boys got what they deserved.

Stacy faced three years of *restrictive placement* because he was found guilty of a *designated felony* act. His counsel at the *dispositional hearing* tried to use Stacy's history as a way to excuse the youth's violence. What could be expected, he rhetorically asked the court. The failure of the school to act in a timely fashion and the failures of the social service providers were mentioned as other examples of the youth's slippage "through the cracks." The defense sought leniency for its client because, they said, a youth should not be punished for acts that resulted from societal ills.

The defense and the probation department were quick to list the reasons that made Stacy Logan the predator he had become. His *I & R* read more like a textbook in social work basics than an evaluation for the court. Rather than preach to the judge, and ultimately to the appeals court, counsel and his witnesses could have chosen to offer a list—not unlike the one above—to describe and excuse Stacy Logan.

In this case and in others, there is error on the part of the schools, the justice system and the social service providers. Had they reacted promptly and appropriately, a young man would not face a lifetime of blurred vision and memory loss, and another would not have lost the use of his wrist. Rather than blaming society for the monsters it creates, the government ought to be held accountable for the victims it begets. Everyone knows there are no valid excuses for Stacy Logan's violence. There are reasons for his behavior, but there is no justification for his victims' pain and permanent damage.

The truth about Stacy Logan is as clear as it is cruel. The truth rejects the philosophies of today's urban "scholars," and focuses on the source of the violence. The truth is that Stacy Logan is a lost soul. He is sure to die young and violently unless he is caged. In any event, the final truth about Stacy Logan is that the list of his victims, certain to include innocent husbands, wives, mothers, fathers, daughters and sons, will surely run longer than the list of his excuses.

10.

The current rage in the criminal justice system is ATI. Legislators, governors and mayors embrace Alternatives To Incarceration as the way to balance budgets in fiscally tight times. They reason that through the 1980s and early 1990s more people in the United States were incarcerated than in any other time in history—and violent crime continued to increase. ATI advocates point out that despite the growth in prison space, there is more violence than ever before. Thus, they say, putting people in prison is obviously not the solution to the problem of violent crime.[12]

Such an argument, of course, lacks as much sense as it does logic. Crime is not out of control in New York because there are too many people in prison; it is out of control because there are not enough violent people incarcerated. Surely, the advocates for ATI have yet to explain how keeping violent offenders in the community will make life in the cities safer. Likewise, labeling the violent crime epidemic as a public health crisis may be a clever way to warn the public of the dangers of "infection," although proponents of this theory fail to follow it through to a logical conclusion: Quarantine the carriers of the infectious disease.

Some advocates are quick to point out that they seek only to remove the nonviolent offenders from prisons. They point to felony laws that crowd jails and prisons with low-level drug dealers. These proponents of premature parole choose to ignore the people who have died in "drug-related shootings" or in fights among street dealers to maintain turf. In any event, many advocates of ATI rarely practice what they preach about nonviolent offenders. Instead, those in this "alternatives" crowd, wedded to the ideology of the classroom and social engineering textbooks, continually seek the rehabilitation of hard-core, dangerous offenders. They do not pursue ATI programs for car strippers, shoplifters and other minimally violent offenders. The zeal and idealism of many in the alternatives arena drive a desire to redeem the souls that most of the population recognize as beyond redemption. Felons such as robbers, assault defendants and sex criminals are a favorite among those who believe that crime is a behavior in need of modification. The youngest offenders, presumed to be more malleable because of their age,[13] are the preferred target of those who believe that therapy, counseling and trust can overcome the personality flaws and negative nurturing that breed violence.

The *Family Ties* program, run by New York City's Department of Juvenile Justice (*DJJ*) in the early 1990s, was New York's model for ATI in the juvenile justice system.★ By any measure, it was a resounding failure. In DJJ's quest to gain the trust of the offenders in their programs, they assumed a militant advocacy role that rivaled the late William Kunstler in his most loquacious moments. DJJ's Family Ties staff viewed the court and especially the prosecution as the enemy, and they were willing to lie or cover up all facts that would likely cause a youth to be incarcerated. DJJ said that Family Ties saves New York City millions in tax dollars.[14] Unfortunately, this kind of debt always gets paid with public blood.

The program is designed around the Homebuilders model, a program originally developed for foster children in Seattle, Washington. The theory is based upon the assumption that children need a solid family structure to develop and that service providers can provide intensive in-home assistance to meet the family's needs. Based upon initial assessments by Family Ties staff, the worker (called a "Family Preservationist") provides both parent and child with a contract for behavioral changes. The worker then remains on call twenty-four hours a day for the next several weeks and makes visits to the home to ensure compliance. After a successful completion of this program, the youth is then placed in an intensive probation program.[15]

While it may be easy to understand the use of a family preservation program as an alternative to placing children in foster care, the expansion of this model to the world of criminal justice requires a considerable leap of faith. Rather than

★ The Family Ties program was reorganized by DJJ commissioner Maldonado in 1994. All comments regarding Family Ties pertain to the pre-1994 program.

focusing upon the preservation of the family, the juvenile justice system is geared toward rehabilitating the offender. Even if the breakdown of the family structure contributed to the cause of crime and delinquency in a particular case, does the short-term supervision of the family address the delinquent acts that have already occurred? Surely six or seven weeks of services, no matter how intensive, cannot unlearn the behavior that an unsocialized individual has experienced throughout his or her thirteen or fourteen years of life.

The case of the Wright brothers makes clear that the preservationist's role in Family Ties is dedicated first to the preservation of the program. Max Wright was charged and subsequently convicted by the Family Court of drug possession. Both the probation *I & R* and the Mental Health Service *MHS* report recommended placement, but the Family Court judge chose to refer the youth to the Family Ties program. Within weeks, Montez's brother, Kyle, was arrested for selling narcotics. Kyle's case was picked up by another prosecutor and was assigned to a different judge. Neither court, nor the prosecutors handling the two matters, were initially aware of each other's case.

Max did not cooperate with the basic contract provided by the Family Ties preservationist. He was a truant, and there was little family cooperation that was likely to cause a change in behavior. Yet while this failure was in progress, the court referred Kyle Wright to Family Ties. The family preservationist did not tell the judge or the prosecutor about the family's lack of progress in the matter relating to Max but indicated a willingness to accept Kyle (and thus the same family) into the program. By the time that acceptance had been achieved, the two prosecutors had compared case files. They informed the court that the Family Ties program was accepting a family that within the past several weeks had failed to cooperate with the referral. An angry judge did not appreciate the program's willingness to accept a family for services that had just rejected those same services two weeks earlier. Surely, opined the court, the money spent on such an endeavor was wasted. The amenability of Family Ties to accept the Wright family seemed to serve only the program and its statistics, not the offender, the family, the justice system or the community. Family Ties had conclusively demonstrated that the measure of its achievement was in the number of those served, not in the number of its successes. The court reprimanded the worker and expressed an unwillingness to trust the program again.

It is that factor, trust, that makes alternative sentencing programs pass or fail judicial and prosecutorial scrutiny. It is easy for a court and a prosecutor to embrace a program that works. But the program has got to work by standards that are universally acceptable, and not be based upon the hopes and dreams of an ideological social engineer. Nor can a program mask the truth to preserve its funding stream. Sooner or later the courts, the prosecutors and then the budget people will get the facts. Only honest providers will survive that kind of scrutiny.

Trust is much easier to lose than it is to gain. When the Family Ties workers do not tell the court that a particular youth has not been seen for a month, they lose credibility forever. When they defy court orders, they lose the ability to appear in front of that judge again. When workers refuse to read probation records and mental health studies relating to a potentially violent offender because they feel that such knowledge may be prejudicial, they prove themselves fools.

Augie Serrano, another youth served by Family Ties, is violent and crazy. He is beyond the control of his mother and anyone else who has tried to supervise him. He had been confined to a psychiatric hospital because of his violent nature and was before the Manhattan Family Court because he had attempted an armed robbery with a pistol. Augie also had a warrant history on his previous cases, which helped the court decide that the youth needed to be detained at Spofford pending final disposition.

The *I & R* and the *MHS* both indicated that Augie needed to be placed. The probation department had determined that the boy's mother was incapable of supervising her son, especially in light of the youth's history of leaving home for extended periods of time. Augie's father had recently brought the boy to the police in a futile attempt to control the youth's aggression. For all practical purposes, Augie was out of control.

Despite the obvious need for incarceration, the Family Ties program was asked by counsel for Augie Serrano to consider the youth for the community-based program. His violent crimes, his psychiatric history, his repeated absences from home, and his parents' admitted inability to control him did not deter the court—over the prosecutor's objection—from paroling Augie to the Family Ties program.

Within one week of the youth's release to the program, he had violated his curfew. The prosecutor asked the family preservationist to come to court to file proceedings to revoke the status, but the worker did not come. Instead, the prosecutor had to ask the judge to order the Family Ties program to produce Augie Serrano. At that time the family preservationist admitted that she had not seen the youth for over two weeks and that the boy had left home sometime during that period. Apparently, the intense supervision of the Family Ties program did not require the worker to know the whereabouts of the youth. In any event, the family preservationist did not deem the boy's absence important enough to share with the court until she was ordered to do so by the court.

DJJ was proud of its Family Ties program. Among prosecutors and most of the judiciary, DJJ stood alone in this respect. Perhaps their claims for money saved can be measured as the dollars not spent on the deferred incarceration of people like the Wright brothers or Augie Serrano. Yet the money not spent on their incarceration is surely a postponement of placement costs rather than a savings. Within weeks, Augie Serrano was arrested again. Along with his fondness for weapons, he also displayed a craving for narcotics and the quick profits that they offered. For this, Augie was placed with *DFY* for the maximum allowable period of eighteen months. The money spent on his diversion via Family Ties was therefore wasted, along with the money spent on his latest arrest and prosecution. Had DJJ and the court acted with their heads rather than their hopes, the youth would have been jailed for his community's own good. DJJ's financial report on Family Ties does not mention these costs to the city. According to that report, failures like the Augie Serrano and Wright brothers' cases are not an appropriate part of the budget analysis.

What price is paid by the next victim of crime for the foolish decision to consider a violent offender for community-based supervision? What does a neighborhood save when drug dealers are allowed to remain in the community, and continue to sell drugs, as a social experiment that has failed in the eyes of everyone except the service providers? How much cost is saved by the justice system when an Augie Serrano is arrested, prosecuted and placed in confinement?

Questions like these are never answered by the alternatives crowd. Success is the most elusive aspect of community-based sentencing. Clearly this is so, because advocates of these policies would otherwise continually point to their many successes—if they existed—to justify the expansion of the programs. There are, however, no press conferences held by advocates to explain the quality and large-scale achievements of their program. The press, admittedly, would rather seek out the gross failures than point out the positive victories. But the absence of any self-promotion by the advocates for alternatives to incarceration on behalf of their growing industry should suggest to those in control of the public treasury, that a dollar spent is probably two dollars wasted.

Family Ties, in its original form, will likely disappear[16] along with the myriad of other social service failures that have come and gone. There will, undoubtedly, be another program to take its place. It will be run by the same tireless advocates who refuse to accept the simple truth that everyone in America appears to know—but refuses to believe: *The real alternative to incarceration is a society plagued by crime.*

11.

The kid couldn't believe it. It had never happened before. There had been a few threats, suggesting that he was in trouble, but generally he seemed to come through unscathed.

Yet this time was different. From the moment she opened her mouth, he knew that this time the court could not be fooled.

On the surface she seemed like all the others. A "lady" judge. Therefore weak. No woman could take *him*. Her petite frame and white lace collar on the robe belied her tough disposition and "street smarts." She did not smile. She did not talk to him, she talked *at* him. She glared. She raised her voice. There was no pity. She seemed so out of place.

The judge had just convicted Tyrone of robbery. She had listened to the testimony of the witnesses, and she believed them. They accurately described how Tyrone and his friends had surrounded the couple and had taken their money. They told of the fear—no, the *terror*—and Tyrone had enjoyed listening to it. It almost felt as good to hear it today as it had felt when he had done it. For a moment the power was back with Tyrone. But when he saw the judge's face, the power was gone. Now *she* had the power, and she was going to use it. He was going in.

The probation officer didn't help him much. He wasn't as understanding as the probation lady who accepted his excuses for missing appointments. This probation officer told the judge about the other case. If the officer had known the whole truth, he would have told the judge more.

"You seem to think this is a game," the judge said. He kept looking down. She was nasty.

"Look at me, Tyrone."

He lifted his head up but he didn't look at her.

"I can make it a game. Is it a game?" she asked.

"No." He meant that. It was more than a game. But it still was fun.

"Do you know about video games? Do you know about losing? The sign flashes 'GAME OVER'—you know that? That's your life now, 'GAME OVER.' And I push the buttons."

He wanted to lie to her, but she wouldn't let him speak.

She even cut off his lawyer. Maybe he could go home with a curfew. It had worked before. Maybe the *ATD* school. He had done that before as well.

"The respondent is REMANDED"—the word echoed through his body—". . . to the Commissioner of Juvenile Justice—secure detention only." Spofford. Jail.

In seconds the Court Officer had his hands behind his back. The cuffs were going on when he heard his mother's screams. They were escorted out of the courtroom and into the well. The last thing anyone heard was his mother mumbling something like ". . . this ain't no fuckin' arcade."

12.

The public thinks that the police and the prosecutors work hand in hand. After all, they're on the same side. Both want to catch the criminals and send them to jail. Even the judges assert that the prosecution and the police are one unit for the purposes of the Criminal Justice System. Nothing could be farther from the truth.

Prosecutor/police relationships vary from fair to terrible. Cops don't like to be second-guessed by young law school hotshots with no idea of what goes on in "the street." It is not uncommon for the seasoned and cynical patrolman to have his stop or search challenged by some twenty-five-year-old idealogue from Long Island. Textbook sociology does not make it with an NYPD veteran.

On the other hand, cynicism rules over objectivity, and the officer may *know* that the perp is carrying a gun, but his threshold for probable cause won't be accepted by any court in America. As painful as it sounds, the case stinks, and only because of poor police work. The little "hotshot" may be right—even if he is a liberal. The cop will be told by his supervisor that the case will be tossed—if the cop gets told anything at all.

Relationships between the prosecutors and the cops don't get better on up the brass ladder. The overweight desk jockeys at 1 Police Plaza (who know as much about the street as the new assistant district attorney) make policy that inures only to the benefit of the policy makers.

Here's one example: A former police commissioner decided to require parental consent for all "fillers" at juvenile lineups. A lineup is an identification procedure in which a perpetrator is placed in a row of similar-looking people. The victim then sees the display and may make an identification. The non-perpetrators are called "fillers" and usually get a few dollars from the police for their participation. When the lineups involved juveniles, the police commissioner wanted permission from the parents of the "fillers."

At first blush, this may seem fair. Maybe parents wouldn't want their kids in a lineup. But the kids actually learn from the procedure and may even feel good about helping the cops catch a "bad guy." Think of it as public service for kids—like jury duty. Besides, it seemed weird to impose a parental consent requirement in the same city that had just sanctioned the distribution of condoms to high school students *with or without* the consent of the child's parents.

The NYPD parental consent rule had been part of the Police Patrol Guide for a long time. Like many department rules that restrict the ability of a police officer to function, the rule was ignored. No detective could expect to find five or ten kids of a particular description, locate their parents, have them agree to participation of the youths, and then have them sign a consent form. Instead, kids were asked to participate, usually on their way home from school, and they were promised money and pizza. The system worked.

Then a not-too-bright detective screwed it up. He went to a local high school and pulled a mentally retarded kid out of his special-education class to be a "filler" in a lineup. The kid's mother said that the youth suffered trauma as a result and naturally brought the expected lawsuit. The commissioner said that he could understand the reluctance to having a child placed in a lineup, even as a filler. As a result of the lawsuit, the police commissioner started to enforce the rule requiring parental consent of all "fillers" to appear in lineups. After all, almost every NYC police commissioner thinks public relations are just as important as solving crime. Good press beats a good record when these guys go job-hunting.

The net effect of that decision was virtually to shut down juvenile law enforcement in the city of New York. Detectives could show photos of suspects, but there could be no physical identification, and since New York law prohibits a police photo as evidence of identification at trial, there could be no case.

Instead the former police commissioner decided that the precincts would keep lists of all youths cleared for lineup participation.★ Patrol units would travel around their precincts with consent forms and would get parents to sign a release for

---

★ Commissioner Bratton developed a procedure to develop a procedure to develop a city-wide "filler-pool." All these youths have supplied parental consent forms, and the program is off to a good start.

the participation of their children in lineups. Even though manpower was low, the commissioner wanted the cops to go get signed releases from parents, in addition to the already unending routine a patrol cop has to go through.

Of course the program failed, and lineups were not conducted. When a kid known as the "baby bandit" was picked up for a string of armed robberies in midtown Manhattan, the cops spent two days trying to get "fillers" for lineups. Two detectives traveled the city with consent forms, trying to get parents to sign waivers for their kids, while simultaneously attempting to pick up the same kid immediately after the parent signed the form. When no lineups could be arranged, the suspected "baby bandit" was released—courtesy of the New York City police commissioner.

I guess he's a better father than he is a commissioner. Judging by his program, that's not too hard. Unfortunately, he wasn't getting paid to be a father.

13.

A few of the kids who come through the juvenile Justice System are really stupid. And I'm not talking about the kids with failing grades—because grades are only one indication of intelligence. I'm talking about kids with no sense about themselves or the world around them. Of these few, none were as dumb as the Cemetery Vandals of Staten Island.

In 1988, prior to the time "bias crime" was a fashionable

term, and prior to the time it even had a name, a group of kids in Staten Island found joy in the desecration of graves in a local Jewish cemetery. These were the cocky punks every cop hates. They deny all wrongdoing, relying on the fact that mom and dad will believe them and eventually bail them out of their troubles.

When this particular case of vandalism came to Family Court, one of these perps denied participation. Unlike his buddies (who had already pled guilty), he steadfastly maintained his innocence. He told his parents and the high-priced lawyer they had retained, that *he* was not one of the guys doing this kind of stuff. Knowing their son could do no wrong, the parents insisted upon a trial. They wanted public vindication of their son, and they would not even consider a guilty plea.

Sometimes these kids are just *too* cocky. This perp forgot to tell his parents about the video camera. He forgot to tell them that kicking over headstones and marking up epitaphs was so enjoyable that he wanted to preserve these moments forever. So he and his buddies took one of their parents' camcorders and taped the whole incident. Drinking the beer, pissing on the graves, knocking down the headstones, etc., with a few anti-Semitic remarks for a special touch—all this was permanently preserved as his special "Kodak Moment." Each event had been recorded by the video camera the boys had dropped when the police chased them through the cemetery. And guess who had the starring role?

As a courtesy, the prosecutor chose to play the tape for mom and dad in his office. He figured that it might save them some embarrassment at trial and might also facilitate an acknowledgment of guilt. It might also help the parents to learn more about the kid that could do no wrong. In fact they did learn a lot that day: Cameras don't lie; perps do. Then they take pleas.

14.

Angela Darpa Calandra is a class act. She is one of a handful of people in the NYC Department of Probation who really understands the system. She runs the Juvenile Intensive Supervision Program (JISP) and, prior to that, ran the Probation Department's Community Service Program through the Department of Parks. She is a tough taskmaster for the kids as well as for the probation officers she supervises.

JISP is the best community-based dispositional program in New York City. Angela made it that way. Unlike traditional probation, which has a kid report as infrequently as possible, the JISP program keeps after the kids. Officers know about the school progress of their probationers, and they make surprise visits to check on curfew violations. Unless a kid really wants to turn his or her life around, he or she is virtually sure to violate probation status. But Angela takes no crap from *anyone*. When you violate the JISP program, you *go in*.

The JISP program is new in the city. The Probation-Parks Program was its predecessor, and it also had good results. Kids would have to get up early on weekend mornings to clean up and maintain the New York City parks as a condition of probation. If you met your community service requirements, everything went well. If you were a wiseguy, Angela had you in Spofford.

No one is perfect, and that includes Angela. At age fifteen, Lee S. was a cold-blooded killer. He was riding a bicycle in Starrett City, Brooklyn, when he spotted an elderly woman walking. He fixed his gaze on her purse and accelerated his approach. He grabbed the bag and dragged the elderly woman to her death along the concrete as he attempted his getaway on his bike. Whatever time this woman had to live, Lee S. took away in pursuit of a few dollars.

Sometimes the combination of the "right" judge, "right" lawyer and other "right" factors guarantees the wrong result. Everyone, except the prosecutor, thought Lee S. would benefit from the Parks program instead of full-fledged confinement. They thought he had shown sufficient remorse and was interested in becoming a good citizen. Translation: He was a good liar.

Enraged at the outcome, the prosecutor described this miscarriage of justice as: "Kill an old lady; rake some leaves." Probation violation was predictable, and Lee S. lived up to our expectations. And he was shipped upstate after his first known violation.

Following the violation proceeding, Angela "took her lumps" like a professional. She told me that she had made a mistake, and that she felt badly about going out on a limb for Lee S. In the Criminal Justice System, people never acknowledge mistakes—appeals courts acknowledge them for you. I had always respected Angela for her work, but that time she earned respect as a person.

15.

The woman was full of it. She could have passed for twenty-three or twenty-four, but there was no way she was fifteen. Yet each time the judge asked her to state her age, she claimed that she was fifteen years old. The arraignment on the petty larceny charge was postponed until someone could verify her age. The case was adjourned for two days until the defense attorney could produce a relative. The "kid" was locked up.

There was a sure fire way to see if she had a record, and that was to fingerprint the woman. Any "hits" would verify the suspicion that she was in fact an adult. The court, however, refused to order the thief to be fingerprinted, because the New York statutes only allow for fingerprinting in serious felony cases. Some idiots in the legislature have been more concerned about "stigmatizing" people than about running a criminal justice operation. It doesn't matter to them if perpetrators can't be identified

Of course these concerns about fingerprinting and stigma don't center on the adult shoplifters who think that the Family Court will provide them an easy walk. The concerns are over fingerprinting the robbery, burglary, sex crimes and weapons offenses that don't allow record-keeping. For instance, the State of New York has no way of knowing accurately who the kids are who have carried guns to school. Loaded-gun possession is not a "fingerprintable" offense. The same is true for the kid who shoots you in the arm, leg or shoulder, causing you physical injury. That kid has no "hard record" with the state. So too, the kid that attacks and injures the cop. He can't be printed either.

It's not as if the prosecutors haven't been trying to change the laws. Since 1986, the City of New York, the State District Attorneys Association and even the governor have been trying to expand the ability of law enforcement to fingerprint these offenders. Each year the same rhetoric is heard about stigma, racism and the other buzzwords of the politically correct. And each year fingerprinting gets lost in a blaze of liberalism via anarchy.

In fact, some of the state assembly people have said they would agree to fix the fingerprinting mess in the juvenile system. Naturally, they want a trade-off. That is, the prosecutors would have to give something up (preventive detention was once suggested) in order to fix a procedure that is fundamentally flawed. This is the business of the state assembly: trade to keep everyone happy—even the crazies. Of course, in the end no one is happy. Since the price of the trade has been too high, a system that can't identify its offenders is still in full force. For all practical purposes, the true identity of many violent people is a mystery—courtesy of elected officials.

After three weeks in Spofford, the unidentified "fifteen"-year-old finally came forward with some straight answers. She had heard that the juvenile system was easy and that release would be immediate. Since she already had a criminal record for shoplifting, she didn't want to spend a few days in the pen. So she lowered her age and thought she could present herself as a first offender. Instead she got more time from the Family Court than she would have received from even the toughest judge in the criminal court.

By the way, she was thirty-five.

16.

Computer hackers are the smartest offenders. In one case a couple of kids got into a lower-level security section of the Pentagon's computer. The Feds got all hot and bothered and raided the kids' houses. The case came to Family Court—no Federal Court would take it—and we gave the kids an *ACD* on the condition that they turn in all their computer equipment to us. That probably wasn't legal, but it made everyone happy. The kids also promised they would not buy new equipment for another six months, and they assured us it would never happen again. I don't know if the Feds were happy—but what could we do with these kids anyway?

Another set of hackers lived on Staten Island and committed their crime solely to prove a point. It seems that some big company had promoted a free poster for all who sent in a special form. When the company ran out of posters, they apologized and said that all the posters were on a first come–first serve basis. You don't tell that to hackers with modems.

The kids called the company and found their way into the voice-mail system. They screwed up the mail order department beyond repair and then really took their revenge. When they found the right code to record voice-mail messages, they got into the president's line and recorded the following piece:

> Hello. You reached the office of_____,
> president of _____. I can't come to the phone
> right now, because my secretary is under my desk
> giving me a blowjob. Leave a message when you
> hear the beep, and when she is finished, I'll call you
> back. Thank you.

The attorney handling the case said that he probably learned a better lesson than anyone else in the courthouse: Don't piss off people with modems.

17.

The victim was a homeless guy with all the visible signs of an alcohol problem. Everyone wondered why the kids wanted to "mug" him. Clearly, he had little to offer anyone. Additionally, he was one of the meanest-looking suckers anyone had ever laid eyes on. Big, scowling, missing teeth—he was the picture of hostility. His personality did not betray his looks.

During final trial preparation in the prosecutor's office, he sat with a cop (it made everyone feel good) and his daughter. She was a deeply religious woman with the voice of an old "fire-and-brimstone" preacher. She could look at her father in the same nasty manner that he looked at everyone else. This was not a Norman Rockwell scene.

The prosecutor explained to the victim that she would have to bring out his drunken state at the time of the attack. It was better to bring this out rather than have the defense raise the issue. The prosecutor wanted to take the "sting" out of this part of the testimony. After he was advised of this fact, his daughter bellowed in the most religious of tones: "I don't approve of your lifestyle. You shall repent." She settled it. She was *not* coming into the courtroom.

At trial the garbled speech of the complainant made it more difficult to understand than we could have anticipated. Maybe it was the years of alcohol abuse or maybe the years on the street. The missing teeth didn't help either. Whatever it was, he was so hard to understand that the prosecutor was repeating the answers as she believed them to be: "And after they hit you about the head with the stick, what happened next?" Nobody objected to this type of examination. Nobody wanted to mess with this guy.

On cross-examination the defense attorney wanted to make the most of the victim's inebriation at the time of the event—as well as his blood alcohol level at the present time.

LAWYER: You said you started drinking when you got up. When did you get up?

VICTIM: At eight o'clock.

LAWYER: In the morning?

VICTIM: Yeah.

LAWYER: How much did you drink?

VICTIM: About a pint of wine. But it wasn't too bad 'cause I shared it.

LAWYER: How much did you drink up until the time of the alleged crime at 11:30?

VICTIM: About four quarts of wine, five quarts of beer—and a $3.00 vial ("crack" cocaine).

At that point the homeless man turned to the court and said, "It ain't that bad, judge. I can hold my liquor."

As the cross-examination continued, it was clear that the victim's speech was not understood by the defense counsel. Finally, in frustration, the attorney asked the scariest homeless man in the world to speak clearly. It was viewed as a challenge.

The victim stood to exhibit his larger-than-life frame. He leaned toward the defense counsel who stood a mere 10 to 15 feet away. Raising his index finger on his left hand, he motioned for the attorney to come closer. "Maybe you can't hear me. Come a little closer, and I'll tell you in your ear." The smile was as wicked as he could make it, and the silence that followed seemed to last forever.

"N-no th-thank you," stuttered the defense lawyer. "I have no more questions." He sat down.

Cross-examination is the lawyer's chance to challenge the opposing witness. The rules of cross are as varied as the number of attorneys who attempt this most difficult of trial arts. It is a tough curriculum, but one thing remains clear—*the lawyer must never let the witness get the upper hand.*

The moral of the story? Being homeless and helpless on the streets has very little to do with one's ability to control the courtroom.

18.

In the Juvenile Justice System, extradition is governed by a complex set of laws called the Interstate Compact on Juveniles, which most states, as of 1994, had adopted. Few people understand or are familiar with these rarely utilized statutes, including some of the most experienced juvenile court attorneys and clerks. The new assistant in the office knew nothing about extradition when he was handed the file and told to arrange the return of the youth to his home state.

The youth was wanted somewhere down south for murder, attempted murder and rape. It was alleged that he abducted a young couple at gunpoint, killed the man and raped the woman. He shot her as well, and left her for dead in a quarry. The woman miraculously survived the shooting and, half-alive, crawled out of the quarry. She was found the following day and was able to identify her attacker as a fifteen-year-old boy who lived nearby.

The youth, who left the jurisdiction right after the crime, took a bus to New York City and was picked up as a "runaway" by the Port Authority Police at the 42d Street bus terminal. The Port Authority has a policy of questioning young-looking people who loiter about the bus terminal in Manhattan. Kids from all around the country run to New York to see the big city, and most are disappointed. These kids are a feeding source for the pimps and drug dealers who also seek out the kids who loiter at the Port Authority facility. This kid was like so many others, and when the police found him, they immediately did a warrant check. The murder warrant from "down south" fell, and he was arrested.

The extradition paperwork was easier than expected, and the arrangements were set for the return of this alleged teenage murderer. The actual return, however, was not easy at all.

On the scheduled day of return, two *very* large police officers from the requesting jurisdiction showed up in the prosecutor's office with their "bubba-type" hats and the largest forearms in the civilized world. They were not too happy to drive up north (to the city that they described as full of "liberals and communists") to pick up this little murderer. They wanted their man, and they wanted to be on their way as soon as possible.

The youth was taken down to the lobby of the Manhattan Family Courthouse in handcuffs. He was turned over to the two sheriffs, who quickly shackled his wrists and his ankles. For added security and humiliation, they ran a chain from the ankle bracelets to the wrist shackles. The officers bade the prosecutor and an escorting police officer a short goodbye and promised that the youth would get what was coming to him.

The youth hobbled out of the building as one of the officers dragged him toward the double-parked police car. The other officer went around the back of the car and opened the trunk lid while the officer escorting the teen grabbed the vertical chain and hoisted the young offender into the trunk. The trunk lid slammed down, and in a moment they were southbound.

Some people think that violent juveniles ought to be treated like adults. Others appear to believe they should be treated like cargo.

19.

The judge looked down from the bench over the tops of his glasses. He was humming—only because he wanted to make the little robber uncomfortable. He would have been uncomfortable—if he had more than a refrigerator IQ. His lawyer had just stepped out of the courtroom to discuss a few details with the next witness. The perp was alone in the courtroom, except for the prosecutor, clerk, one court officer (seated behind the perp) and the judge. No one was there from the perp's "side."

As the judge looked down from the bench, his humming got louder and louder. The perp began to squirm, and the judge started to smirk. It was time for the kill.

"You see that guy over there?" bellowed the judge as he pointed at the perp. The judge was looking at the prosecutor. "You see him?" he asked again. The judge started nodding his head. "Don't you worry," he said to the prosecutor. "That guy is gonna get a fair trial. Yep, a fair trial. Then we're gonna hang him."

Very few things can "wake up" a perp in a courtroom. Despite their constitutional right to be present at all stages of a proceeding, their attention span sometimes limits their presence in the courthouse. This time the perp got excited and tried to tell his lawyer about the judge's humming and promise to hang. Unfortunately the perp had about as much credibility with his lawyer as he had with the court. The lawyer tuned him out and the judge locked him up.

Of course with an 80+ percent recidivism rate among violent juveniles, and with the reinstatement of the death penalty, we may get to see him hang yet.

20.

The three kids got onto the train looking for trouble. The worst of the bunch was Philip. He had the gun, and he played the leader. Philip was the by-product of a foster care system that had gone amuck. Kids got shuffled from house to house, while their parents were continually absolved of all responsibilities, except for the part that makes more babies. The end result in many cases were kids like Philip, although even the failing foster care system could not be held completely responsible for his behavior. Philip was rotten to the core.

These three guys were going to carry out a robbery. Philip had decided that this was a good train because it wasn't too crowded. All the passengers were seated when the boys entered the car, and Philip was staying with his plan to find and rob the biggest dude on the train. Philip knew he was tough, and he wanted to prove it to his buddies, the passengers and to the world.

The victim stood out like a sore thumb. He had to be six-three and about 250 pounds. Philip walked over to the big guy and stood directly in front of him. The youth reached behind his coat and into his waistband to pull out the pistol. The gun was revolver style, black with a long barrel. The mere sight of this large weapon would have scared almost any individual. Anyone except the intended victim.

Philip had picked poorly. The large parole officer was familiar with guns, and he saw immediately that the kid was displaying the meanest-looking starter's pistol ever made. It shot nothing but blanks.

Philip pointed the gun in the officer's face and said confidently, "This is a stickup."

The officer stood up to his full height and looked down at Philip and his unreal threat. He pulled his own gun out, shoved it into Philip's nostril and said, "No. It isn't."

Philip's bravado faded into his youth and once again he was a boy of fourteen. He showed fear and begged the officer not to shoot as the crowd on the train applauded the parole officer. Philip was under arrest.

While in Spofford, Philip was arrested again by detectives for a vicious sexual assault. He had used the starter's pistol on at least one prior occasion. The victim in that case, a teenage girl, was not as knowledgeable about guns and did not fare as well as the parole officer. Philip and his friends gang raped this girl and, while she lay screaming for help, Philip shoved the barrel of his starter's pistol in and out of her vagina. He justified his brutality by suggesting that his own culpability was diminished since he propped up her head during the attack. This, he thought, would make her more comfortable while he and his friends completed their assault.

The worst part of this tale is not Philip's brutality or his failure to recognize his own culpability. It is that there are hundreds of Philips walking around New York, and there is little there to provide the average citizen with protection. Sooner or later we all are challenged. . . . Is the gun real or is it a starter's pistol?

21.

Sometimes interrogations of juveniles yield more than just confessions. You often receive insight into the kids' minds—as well as their educational background.

Most good detectives will talk with a kid prior to taking a statement. It lets the officer know if the kid understands reality (confessions from psychotics and from retarded youths aren't worth much in court), and it helps create an atmosphere of familiarity and trust between perpetrator and policeman.

Cops usually ask kids questions. New York City offenders tend to get asked very simple questions. Anything beyond the third-grade level is probably unfamiliar territory.

Consider the fourteen-year-old robber being questioned by the seasoned transit detective. When asked to give his address, he was right on the money. When asked to name his state of residence, he knew that too.

"Name another state, kid."

"Uh, uh. . . Jersey," said the perp.

"Okay, name another state," said the cop.

"Chicago," came the reply.

Another product of our multicultural education program. Geography must be Eurocentric.

22.

Most trials are boring. Real-life trials have nothing in common with *L.A. Law* or *Matlock*. Even the most mundane evidentiary groundwork can take longer than the hour-long television drama that contains opening statements, examination, summations and all the related investigation. Trials are often tedious attempts to introduce evidence. Laying the "foundations" for the evidence is dull, repetitious and a guaranteed cure for insomnia.

Most people tend to let their minds wander when the

tedious questions seem to go on forever. The lawyers half-listen (most will deny it, but it is true), the court officers move about, and the clerks grab a cigarette in the hall. The judge, poor slob, is stuck. Each chair in the courtroom faces the judge, and he or she must appear to be paying attention.

Then of course, there are those judges who reject tradition and turn their chairs to face the wall behind the bench. They fall asleep and wake only at the sound of "Objection!" Even Vito Titone, of the Court of Appeals, the highest court in New York, was caught napping by the press. Even an important case can induce sleep.

Other jurists are more brazen. One Family Court judge used to walk out of the courtroom into the small "robing room" behind the courtroom and flap his arms under his robe to stay awake. These batlike maneuvers caught unsuspecting attorneys off guard. Some giggled, some choked and some just sat down. It certainly moved the trial along. The regulars in the building hardly even noticed.

The late Nanette Dembitz could read the *Law Journal,* write an opinion and listen to the testimony at the same time. One guardian of the law in the midst of a hearing made the mistake of questioning whether the court could listen, read and write at once. Judge Dembitz repeated the question *verbatim* and told the lawyer never to challenge the court on the record again. From that time on, however, Judge Dembitz rarely heard a thing that attorney had to say.

Of course, nothing beats the Brooklyn judge who routinely walked off the bench in the middle of a trial and into the toilet behind the courtroom. "Keep your voice up, counselor, I'm listening to everything you say," came a voice from afar. No one knew if he really was listening. No one wanted to find out.

23.

After his client had been released at the arraignment, the attorney handed the young man his business card. "Call me," he told his client. "We have to discuss some issues regarding motions I have to make. This case and your future depend upon these motions. Do you understand me?" asked the lawyer. His client gave a nod, but the blank stare told the attorney otherwise.

It did not surprise the lawyer when the client failed to call. Weeks went by, and the young man never contacted his counsel. The motions were not made. The lawyer figured the kid was in the wind, and the adjourn date would be fast and easy. The court would issue a warrant, and the whole "spiel" would take two minutes.

Imagine the attorney's surprise when his client arrived in the courthouse on the scheduled return date. "What are you doing here?" asked the lawyer of his client.

"It's my court day," replied the kid. His diction was right off the street.

"Yeah, I know. I didn't hear from you. I thought you weren't going to show."

"Gotta show," said the client.

"Right," said the attorney, realizing that his client's speed-limit IQ governed their conversation. "You were supposed to call me. We were going to prepare a motion," lectured counsel.

"Don't know the nummer," said the kid.

"I gave you my card."

"I lost it," said the client.

"I'm in the phone book" replied the attorney.

"Don't got no phone book," replied the kid.

"So call information," said the lawyer, trying to impart

some logic upon the young offender.

"Info-mation," said the client. "That's four-eleven on the phone. Right?"

"Yeah right," said the lawyer, not expecting the next retort.

"Couldn't find no eleven on my phone," said the world's dumbest client.

24.

It is said that confession is good for the soul. Perhaps that is why the kid in Queens chose to inculpate himself like no other.

The trial testimony of the complainant was about to conclude. She had described the attack, the force and the theft down to the smallest of details. She was a good witness, and the upcoming in-court identification was going to be easy. The prosecutor, using the technique of "double-direct" examination, asked the witness the standard identification question:

Q: Do you see the person that ran up behind you, pushed you down to the ground, grabbed your bag and punched you as he took the purse in the courtroom today?

Before the witness could point out her attacker to the

court, the perpetrator slowly raised his hand and stood up. It was as if we were watching television in the 1960s and the question was raised "Will the real . . . please stand up."

Everyone in the courtroom had a chuckle. The Assistant Corporation Counsel asked the judge to take notice of the youth's voluntary confession in open court. Opposing counsel had little to argue on behalf of his client's recent admission.

The kid was found guilty, and he was placed. Confession may have been good for his soul, but some judges aren't that forgiving.

25.

It's always interesting to watch the dynamics at the defense table when the accused is about to testify. Everyone knows a wild story will be told when the defense attorney argues with his client about testifying or when counsel reluctantly advises the court that the respondent will testify in his own defense. Just like the adult criminal system, the juvenile justice system is bound by the Fifth Amendment right against self-incrimination. The youth need not testify, and no adverse inference can be drawn from the silence. The prosecution has the burden of proving all the charges beyond a reasonable doubt. When the kid testifies, however, you can usually count on him to fill in any of the missing elements of your proof. Perps are usually a prosecutor's best witness.

The chain-snatch case was cut and dried. The perpetrator grabbed a gold necklace from the woman on a midtown street. The victim saw her attacker approach and grab the chain from her neck. She testified credibly that she saw his face, his multicolored jacket with a "TROOP" logo on the back, his blue jeans and white and black sneakers. But most of all, she would never forget that gold tooth that seemed to dominate his smile.

When he grabbed the chain and ran, the victim screamed. She pointed to her attacker as two police officers gave chase. The youth turned the corner, and the pursuit continued. Suddenly, the victim saw one officer drag the perp back around the corner. The cop was holding the young thief by the collar in one hand, and the gold chain was raised in the officer's other hand. The complainant rushed over to the cops and started screaming at the perp. The identification was clean, and the case was airtight.

Against his lawyer's advice, the perp wanted to testify. His attorney told the court that he was opposed to his client's decision but that the youth was insistent about testifying. The client claimed that the whole thing was a matter of coincidence (pronounced by the youth as co-in-sa-danse). He claimed he was walking down the street minding his own business when the cops grabbed him. The fact that he matched the description of the actual perpetrator was a co-in-sa-danse. So too, was his being in possession of the same type of chain, also broken, that was owned by the victim. An additional coincidence was that his clothing perfectly matched that of the perp, at least as much of the clothing as the victim could recall.

On cross-examination he was asked about the remarkable number of coincidences that he was alleging. (Asking him to reflect upon the probabilities of such an event would have been pointless.) He insisted that the case was a matter of "co-in-sa-danse." Each question got the same answer:

> Is it your testimony today that you just happened to be wearing the same kind of (a) shoes; (b) jacket; (c) pants as the perpetrator?
>
> Is it your testimony that you just happened to have the same kind of chain as the victim? And that it was broken, just like the victim's? And that you happened to be carrying it (a) that day; (b) at that same location; (c) while running away from the scene of the crime?

Each of the above questions was met with the same answer: A co-in-sa-danse. He repeated that word over and over, as though he were wedded to a new learning experience.

Finally he was asked about the most glaring co-in-sa-danse of all: the gold tooth that he shared in common with the perp. "You are also telling the court, that in addition to the supposed coincidence of sharing the same jacket, pants, gold chain and description with the perpetrator, you also have a *gold tooth?* Is that also just another coincidence?"

His look changed. No longer did he display that lying perp face, the one conveying that the truth is whatever is convenient. He now looked at the prosecutor in a perplexed and incredulous way. "Aw man," he said, "everybody in Brooklyn got goad teef."

When the laughter subsided, the youth looked around the courtroom. He couldn't understand what had been so funny. In any event, he now had the opportunity to spend his time with other people equally innocent and detained. Another co-in-sa-danse.

26.

The three kids followed the prosecutor onto the train. They had followed her from the argument in the appeals court where they heard the case against their good friend (and partner in crime). She was an assertive advocate, and she had said many things about their buddy that seemed offensive (although all true).

She sat down for the long ride back to New York City. The trip from Albany via Amtrak takes about two and one-half hours. It is a scenic ride along the shores of the Hudson River, and it gives every appellate lawyer the chance to unwind. These three guys were determined to interfere with this particular lawyer's rest.

They seated themselves behind the woman and started immediately with the insults. "White bitch." "She be fuckin' with the wrong homeboy." "Her white ass." The epithets just kept coming.

After twenty minutes, the train made its first scheduled stop in Hudson, a small city at which very few passengers come aboard. As the train pulled out, the insults kept coming. The woman squirmed uncomfortably, but what could she do? The other passengers were also annoyed, but fear prevented them from challenging the obviously street-wise young men.

About ten minutes out of Hudson the prosecutor had had enough. "Are you guys going to cut it out, or will I have to get the conductor?" she asked. Their answers indicated indifference, and they kept the comments going with more than a touch of male chauvinism. She stormed away.

Ten minutes later the train pulled into Rhinecliff. The woman had not returned to her seat, and her young torturers were enjoying their success at scaring the "dragon lady."

Suddenly their joy was replaced with a fear that was obviously familiar. As their anxiety increased, the other passengers began to feel relief. A group of Amtrak Police officers and local Rhinecliff cops boarded the train and approached the three young men.

"You got tickets?" asked one cop as his three or four comrades stood over the seated trio. They showed their tickets. They were quiet now, even polite. These were upstate police, and they don't take kindly to city shitheads.

Being polite didn't help. As the female prosecutor appeared with the trainman, another cop said, "I hear you're harassin' people on this train." The statement was conclusory.

"We ain't harassing people," said one of the three, "we harassin'" *her!*" He pointed to the prosecutor as he offered this defense. He didn't know why everyone in the train started laughing.

The cop continued. "You can't harass *her*—and you can't harass anyone."

Having just been in court, one of the young men now suddenly felt armed with legal knowledge. "I can say what I want. You check it out. It's in chapter one of the constitution. It's in the first commandment."

That was the last thing any of the kids said. In seconds they were off the train and likely to learn the most important lesson of all time: The first commandment doesn't apply in upstate New York.

27.

Jack Maple may be the smartest cop in New York. He started as a tough, street-wise transit cop with Brooklyn running through his veins. His philosophy about the job is simple: Police are supposed to be catching crooks. Sensitivity training and intellectual policing are for the college boys. Jack Maple can smell a gun at 100 yards. Policing is instinct, and it is his life.

Jack is a character. He is overweight—but regularly on a diet. He works out "on the heavy bag" he keeps in his office—but only intermittently. His bowler hat and bow-tie are his trademark, and they pale before his black and white wing-tipped saddle shoes. If you ask him how he can walk about New York looking like he got dressed in the dark, his answer is simple: I carry a Glock. [17]

For a guy with only a high school education, he knows more than most of the top police brass in America. Jack has innovative ideas about policing in New York City. These are not the global ideas that get discussed in classrooms in Cambridge and New Haven. These are concrete ideas designed to catch felons. When a Maple plan is implemented, crime goes down.

Jack Maple is the expert in decoy policing. He is the man responsible for the infamous (televised and celebrated) Transit Police decoys. His plan is simple: Put a fake drunk on a train or in a station with an attractive—and obvious—gold-colored chain. A perp will find your decoy and grab the chain. When the perp takes off, the backup team moves in and makes the collar.

The theory behind decoys is that perps love an easy score. The cops just make it even easier for a guy who is probably responsible for multiple robberies and larcenies. The case has no civilian complainant, and therefore the prosecutors don't have to worry about reluctant witnesses and civilian schedules. A decoy case is a conviction in the bag.

Jack is the master of the confession. Take Jack Maple to the Dakotas and he'll get four solid statements from Mt. Rushmore. Because he is a street guy, and because he can relate to the perp, Jack can get him to talk. He may put his arm around the young lad to play "Uncle Jack."

"C'mon. Tell your Uncle Jack. You can talk to me. Tell me about your girlfriend, tell me what you do with her, all right? Your Uncle Jack understands. Now tell me about what you did." As he utters those words, Jack Maple has his arm around the young man. His voice is sincere. The kid forgets about the *Miranda* warnings and throws whatever sense he has to the wind. The perps talk to "Uncle Jack." All the time.

Jack's ideas are even better than his professional deeds. Jack is the moving force behind the "Perp Channel." Because most law enforcement people know that perps commit felonies again and again (it's their job), they only get caught on a small percentage of their crimes. But eventually most of the criminals get caught. So Jack wanted to make sure that every criminal upon arrest gets the opportunity to be viewed by *all* (or at least many) of his victims.

Enter the modern world of television. Jack Maple dreamed up the "Perp Channel," where victims of crime could watch arraignments twenty-four hours a day. Cameras would focus on defendants at the time of arraignment, and anyone recognizing this person could call a toll-free number to identify the perp. In addition, stolen items could be displayed for return to their rightful owners. When a perp confessed to more than one offense, the "Perp Channel" would broadcast the time, place and type of crime in order to locate the victims and to have them come forward. In effect, television would become a tool of the police. Clearly, the recent proliferation of "real-life" police dramas are a good indication that the "Perp Channel" would do well on the Nielsen charts.

Unfortunately, the court system and legislature in New York, wanting to keep the public ignorant of their misdeeds, have consistently refused to support cameras in the courtroom. And when they finally allow them, some civil libertarian will find a compelling reason to keep the first amendment at bay in order to protect the privacy rights of some scumbag.

When Bill Bratton became Police Commissioner in New York he did the unthinkable. He took a street cop who had been a mere lieutenant and made him a deputy commissioner. Bratton, also a smart cop, knew that he was a lot smarter with Maple in the front office. Within a year of Bratton's appointment, the city saw five new major police strategies accompanied by a double digit drop in violent crime. The strategies had Jack's signature all over them, and the folks at One Police Plaza knew that Maple was beginning to control crime in New York. Now, all the big brass who used to think that Jack was nothing more than some crazy upstart were sucking up to him at cocktail parties and asking him, "Excuse me, commissioner, can I get you a drink?"

But Jack Maple, even with top cops serving him drinks, is most comfortable hunting down some perp with a squad of decoys, or sitting in a squad room looking over pattern sheets. Jack knows what everybody but the politicians seem to know: *The cops are there to do one thing: Catch crooks.* Now, what will happen when they make him Commissioner. . . ?

28.

The woman got on the elevator, and it was apparent that she was crazy. Not crazy in the eccentric or neurotic sense, she was crazy in the psychotic sense. The Family Courts of New York get a few of these every day. Getting in the elevator, however, means that you have to get close.

She was angry. Lots of the "Hotel Hysteria" crowd (patients or those who ought to be patients at Bellevue Psychiatric Hospital) are angry. She walked into the elevator and said **"FUCK."** Everyone else heading down tried to avoid eye contact.

"SHEEET! I say FUCK-SHEEET. Them mo'fuckers don't know who they be fuckin' wiff. Be takin' my chil'ren. Don't be takin' no chil'ren from no big-time drug dealer. They don't be takin' my chil'ren—they messin' wiff a big-time drug dealer."

The chore for the other elevator occupants was to keep from laughing. The woman had about as much in common with a big-time drug dealer as Nancy Reagan has in common with Madonna. But you couldn't laugh. She was too fucked up to laugh at.

The elevator settled at the main floor. The doors opened and the psycho looked out. She was lost. The elevator was a challenge—the subway had to be a marathon event. No one wanted to pass her—she was *still* an unpredictable nut case— so everyone stood still. Finally, somebody from the rear yelled, "This is the lobby—all big-time drug dealers off."

"SHEEET."

29.

Sometimes it's harder to take a plea in the Family Court than it is to try a case. Often this is a lawyer's doing. Other times it may be due to the perp. The rest of the time it's because the system is so screwed up.

Taking a plea on a case with Tom Curtis is torture. Curtis is a Legal Aid veteran who takes his role quite seriously. He works hard and leaves no stone unturned. It is not uncommon for Tom to make late-night trips up to the most unsavory neighborhoods in New York in search of a witness named "Clyde." After all, if the kid said Clyde saw it all, then Tom will investigate. Of course, the fact that Clyde is less real than Elmer Fudd never seemed to matter. Tom did his job. He checked it out, and that is the responsibility of a good criminal defense attorney.

Tom's determination and drive carry over into his plea negotiations. He wants to know everything about the case before the plea. Are you promising that the complainant really will appear? Did the witness really see all that he said he saw? Will he testify that way? If you were a defense attorney would you take the plea? Should he take the plea? Do we think it's malpractice to take the plea? Do we think any less of him as a lawyer because he took the plea?

In fact, when it comes to aggressive defense counseling, there is none better than Tom Curtis. The highly paid lawyers who come in representing drug clients and gang offenders have more to learn from the guy who beats the prosecution than any other Legal Aid attorney. At the same time, Tom is a realist: he knows when and how to plead out his client. Chances are his client, or most any other perp in the system, is a barely functional illiterate with a low IQ. Thus, it is imperative to prep a client for pleading guilty. Without careful preparation for the five or six simple questions the court is required to ask, the perp is destined to fail. In truth, many trials are conducted because the perp is too dumb to plead guilty. (So much for the ideologues who want to provide *job* training.)

Lots of times the attorney and client work out a system to plead. Counsel, in mode *sotto voce*, tells his client "Say 'Yes'" or "Say 'No.'" But sometimes a client's answers or lack thereof tell the whole story:

> **JUDGE:** I understand that you are waiving your right to a trial. Before I can accept your plea, I need to know certain things. These things concern your right to a trial. Now before I ask you about waiving your right to a trial, I have some questions. How old are you?
>
> **PERP:** Fit-teen. [For those of you not familiar with "street" math, FIT-TEEN is one more than FO-TEEN and two less than SEB'N-TEEN.]
>
> **JUDGE:** Do you go to school?
>
> **PERP:** Yeah. [Sure. No doubt his eloquence and charm are the result of his commitment to education and hard work.]
>
> **JUDGE:** Do you read, write and understand English?
>
> **PERP:** Huh?
>
> • • •
>
> **JUDGE:** I find that the respondent has knowingly, intelligently and voluntarily waived his rights. . . .

30.

Luis and Louie were an item. At least Louie seemed to think so. At thirty-five years of age, Louie was a homosexual pedophile who enjoyed the company and companionship of fourteen-year-old Luis. Luis terminated the relationship when he pumped eight shots into Louie and left him dead in a Manhattan SRO hotel.

It was a hot Saturday in July when Police Officer Jones of the Midtown North Precinct stood on the corner of 46th Street and Eighth Avenue. As he looked past the seedy hotels, hookers and the world's largest collection of adult entertainment establishments, he could see the Port Authority Bus Terminal four short blocks downtown. In his blue police uniform, Officer Jones stood amidst this iniquity as a symbol of law and order lost. Some see this area as a place to begin, others see it as the future for all of New York. Even the tourists know that once you're here, it is best to leave. Louie and Luis fit perfectly into this place.

Suddenly the cop was approached by a young man who calmly said that he had just shot a man in one of the local hotels and that he was giving himself up to the police. With that, Luis reached into his waistband and pulled out a .22 calibe revolver. The gun was empty but for one spent cartridge in the cylinder. Within a minute Luis was searched, cuffed and on his way to the Midtown North precinct.

The events that led to this encounter were the subject of the next several hours of interrogation at the Midtown North precinct. Luis had as many versions of the truc story as the police had questions. Time after time, Luis led the cops through a different rendition of the facts. It became clear that victim and offender led a symbiotic lifestyle. Both used the other to suit their own purpose. Only now it was clear that a cold-blooded killer beats a pedophile every time.

In his written statement for Detective Castillo, Luis said that Louie had called his house and offered him $1,000 for sex. He said that he found the gun in the hotel bathtub and that he killed Louie when the man tried to seduce him. He alleged that he was ignorant of the older man's intentions when he went with him to the hotel room, and he was lucky to find the gun in the tub at such a critical moment. His video statement a short time later was just as unconvincing, although by that time it was clear that Louie and Luis had been "hangin' out" for about three years. The pedophile had been buying the youth clothes, food and concert tickets—yet Luis insisted that there had never been a *quid pro quo* in the form of sex. Everyone at the Midtown North Precinct knew that Luis was holding something back. A rookie cop would have known that this was a well-planned homicide. Unfortunately for Luis, killing came easier than lying.

At 5:30 the following morning, everyone at Midtown North was ready to wrap up the case. They were charging Luis with murder, although the gun in the tub story seemed unlikely. The police were ready to let the District Attorney and the Grand Jury sort this one out. Another killer teenager. Another dead pedophile. Another day in New York.

While Luis was being fingerprinted, he turned to one of his questioners, Detective Chung, and said, "You didn't believe me about the gun being in the bathroom." The cop told the kid that nobody believed that story; the notion was that he probably brought the gun to the hotel.

"Yeah, you're right," said Luis. "I bought the gun about a week ago from a guy in Brooklyn for one hundred dollars. I knew he [Louie] had to go two weeks ago. Yeah he's been calling me up for the last month wanting me—you know—to take my clothes off and have sex with him. *So I knew he had to go because he was messing up my lifestyle."*

The new truth started to pour out of the young man. Maybe his will had been broken by the hours of interrogation, or maybe he just couldn't hold it in any longer. One thing was clear, this cold-blooded killer aged fourteen years was not feeling remorse.

The kid told the cop that Louie had called him in the morning and told him to meet him at the Port Authority Bus Terminal. Luis took the gun and met his pedophile friend. They walked north from 42nd Street to one of the myriad SRO hotels that blanket the city's "red light" district. Louie was angry because his young friend had just looked at a young girl on the street. This jealousy turned ugly when Louie slapped his young companion in the hotel lobby.

Upstairs in the room, Louie did not disguise his desire. He wanted sex. Recognizing his vulnerability, young Luis promised the pedophile a surprise if he took off his clothes. The soon-to-be-killer had his unknowing victim cornered. Luis had a well-designed plan and was ready to carry it out.

Without hesitation, the victim stripped down to his underwear. As the teenager pretended to disrobe, Luis told the man to cover his eyes. He had a surprise for him. The eager Louie complied with the youth's command. He was caught up in his own hormones and pedophilia.

Louie was on the bed with his eyes shut. His hands covered his face as he continued to play what he thought was a sexual game. Luis told Detective Chung, "I took the gun out and I pointed it at him. I said to him 'surprise—open your eyes.' And I started shooting as soon as he put his hands down."

Luis kept firing. He emptied eight bullets into Louie. He

was determined to get the job done. The guy "had to go."

Luis put the gun in his waistband and walked out of the room. He went down the stairs of the seedy hotel and out into the hot July sun. He walked over to Officer Jones and turned himself in.

When Luis was arrested, he was charged as a *Juvenile Offender.* Murder by a fourteen-year-old in New York automatically puts the matter initially before the criminal courts. Luis was arraigned in an adult court, surrounded by adult criminals.

But a fourteen-year-old who kills a pedophile is not always viewed as a criminal. Pedophiles are morally bankrupt by definition, and kids who are the target of a pedophile are always victims—even when they are cold-blooded killers like Luis. Unfortunately, the Grand Jury did not see the callous and deliberate side of Luis. They did not hear the same matter-of-fact tone that kept the Midtown North cops unconvinced. They didn't see the pleasure in his eyes that he derived from his description of the shooting. They did not feel "murder" in the presence of Luis. [18]

The Grand Jury voted to charge the youth with simple loaded gun possession (with intent to use same). The murder charge was dismissed, and the matter was *removed* to the Family Court. Through his own admissions, Luis had managed to get away with murder. Suddenly freedom was not that far away, and there was no Louie around to be "messin' up [his] lifestyle."

The Family Court found Luis guilty of the reduced charges and set the matter down for disposition. Although murder was no longer a legal issue, everyone knew what Luis had done. No judge or prosecutor wanted to make a mistake in this case. The Probation Department and the court's Mental

Health Service's Unit were ordered to prepare reports about Luis.

The court's agencies confirmed the obvious by talking to mom. This was a family in trouble. Both mother and father were unable to control the young offender, although mom was eager to lie for her son. It was easy for her. She had already lied on behalf of another son who had also been arrested and placed through the Family Court. So mom told the court that Luis was a good boy. She knew this because she searched his room daily and never found a gun or drugs. She also tried to convince the court that the pedophile was really an old family friend and that this whole incident was a big mistake. Finally, if her son had any faults, he was a bit depressed. But that, she said, could be treated at home. In reality, mom was concerned that an out-of-home placement for Luis would reduce the welfare budget—and put the squeeze on the other five kids who were part of her family.

When the agencies interviewed Luis, they saw a youth quite unlike the one described by mom. The teenager was characterized as hostile, angry and oppositional toward adults. Although Luis consistently blamed others for his troubles, he was moved to four or five different junior high schools because of his behavior. Luis had recently been suspended and subsequently transferred because he possessed a knife in school.

Luis' psychological profile was frightening. The doctor opined that Luis was a danger to the community and that the youth needed to develop *more appropriate social values* (as though any of his social values could have been deemed "appropriate"). The recommendation was that Luis be placed in a structured setting, out of the community, and away from all potential victims.

Furthermore, the data collectors found no evidence of

remorse. At one point Luis even told an evaluator that he thought the gun was unloaded (despite the fact that he fired nine times and bullet hit the deceased all but one of the times he squeezed the trigger). The probation officer and the psychologist disbelieved virtually all of the youth's self-serving accounts. It was clear that Luis had made violence and weapons part of his everyday life.

The court, in agreement with the experts, expressed concern about community safety and placed Luis for the maximum initial period allowed under the Family Court Act—eighteen months in a limited secure facility. With blood on his hands, Luis was headed for a short stay in the woods of upstate New York.

There is no equity in the Juvenile Justice System. All facets of the process ignore responsibility either for the victim or for the public. Community safety is a component of the statute, but it is missing in practice. The state's Division for Youth administers its own population controls because there is no independent review of prisoner release. When a facility gets crowded, someone is sent home. So the kid who killed a man in an SRO, the same kid that was called violent, oppositional, and unbelievable by the professionals, the kid that had made guns a part of his lifestyle, was released in seven months. No checks, no balances, no justice. Just risks.

At least DFY had a plan to prevent Luis from remaining on the streets. DFY worked hard to get Luis a summer job. The young man needed responsibility, and DFY was ready to take the chance. If only the people at the day care center really knew *who* was taking care of the children. . . .

31.

New York's Family Court is a closed book. The rules have been modified in the last few years to create an appearance of openness, but in reality the place is shut. Members of the public are routinely asked to identify themselves before being admitted to the courtroom, and promises of litigant anonymity are extracted from reporters prior to gaining access to the courts. With the exception of just a few Family Court judges, the courtrooms are nearly "air tight."

Closure of the court is a throwback to a time long gone. In days when children really *were* innocent, really *were* victims, the purpose of confidentiality was plain. When a youth's future could still be shaped, the need for anonymity was clear. When *juvenile delinquents* were kids who "hung out" on street corners, drank beer and maybe caused mischief, the belief that an errant youth could overcome his errant ways was a reality. In the old days, privacy was a kid's best protection from himself. It was his insurance for the future. Besides, juvenile delinquents of yesteryear outgrew their behavior.

Enter the '90s delinquent. Violent, predatory and lacking any sense of right and wrong, the typical juvenile criminal is probably involved in robbery-related, assault-related or felony drug activity. Whereas the juvenile of yesteryear (prior to 1987) was most likely involved in minor crime, this year's model has more than a 90 percent chance of being accused of a felony in Family Court. Today's violent teen will probably increase his criminal behavior before he is killed, jailed or ages out of crime.

Despite the change in the offender, the practice of shielding him or her has remained constant. As the escalating level of violence causes every hope for "rehabilitation" to fade into the background, the practice of anonymity/confidentiality still stands between the public and an effective criminal justice system. People who live in clapboard houses will never know about the junior arsonist next door, and parents seeking a babysitter have no access to the trial of the neighborhood's sex offender.

As the public voices concern and outrage over the juvenile justice system, it is clear that it has only piecemeal sources of information. Bits of relevant data mixed with speculation and rumor lead to conclusions about the system that are necessarily inaccurate. On the other hand, if confidentiality is no longer relevant in terms of today's offenders, whom are the courts protecting with their rules of closure?

Family Court judges enjoy a level of nonaccountability similar to the litigants appearing before them. The proceedings are closed in practice, the court record is "confidential," the probation record and reports are "confidential," the Mental Health Services records are "confidential," and the school records of the offender are also "confidential." Finally, if the case is dismissed, these confidential records are all *sealed*. Because the security of these records greatly exceeds the security at most facilities charged with the care and incarceration of these felony offenders, most Family Court judges decide every matter away from the scrutiny of the public and press.

When an eleven- and twelve-year-old were arrested with a youth in his late teens for a Queens rape and abduction, the case caught the attention of the local news media. These three youths had jumped into a car parked in the lot of a supermarket. Seated in the vehicle were a young woman and her two-year-old son. The boy and his mom were waiting for another woman, who had just stopped by the market to catch up on some last-minute shopping.

The teenager pushed the woman down onto the front seat and held her down. He covered her mouth so she could not scream. The eleven-year-old held the two year old child in the back seat and was told to muffle the small child's screams.

The twelve-year-old had the gun. As the teen held his victim down in the front seat of the car, the twelve-year-old put the barrel of the gun to the face of the victim. The youth laughed as he pressed the cold steel against the face of the woman. Meanwhile the teen tore at the victim's clothes in preparation for his assault.

As the rape progressed, the gun-wielding youngster twirled the gun around his forefinger in a callous display of power. He pushed the barrel again and again into the woman's face and laughed at the horrors to which she was being subjected. The teen's hand covered the woman's nose and mouth, but the twelve-year-old stared at the fear in the eyes of his victim. Her fear was his excitement, and at that moment he was on top of the world.

When the teen finished his attack, he moved into the driver's seat and sped out of the parking lot. A block away he shoved the woman and her screaming child out to the street. A passing police car, suspicious about this event, began a chase. Other police cars joined the pursuit, and soon a high-speed race throughout southeast Queens began. The youths ran the stolen car up onto a sidewalk and hit a telephone pole. The chase was over, and the young villains were caught.

Despite years of police experience, even the most senior investigators could not help but show revulsion toward this crime. Raping a mother in front of her child was bad enough, but the participation of the two preteens was too much to bear. Although the families of the two younger assailants were willing to take them home pending referral to the Family Court, the cops decided that these kids were in need of incarceration. Release not only seemed improper, it was unthinkable. The police officers never would have believed that the Family Court judge would have allowed such violent offenders to go home.

The two youths were brought to Family Court late in the afternoon. Since the Family Court does not have night arraignments, a case must be filed during normal business hours, or the matter is put over to the next court day (or soon thereafter). The Family Court Act provides for such an event by allowing for a prepetition hearing. In this proceeding, the prosecutor is supposed to prove jurisdiction over the case, and then the matter is adjourned. While release to a parent is preferred under the statute, there is room for discretion.

The press found this case irresistible. It had everything a tabloid needed to grab a headline. Yet the judge in this matter made the story even better for the reporters. Because the parents were present, and because *this was a first arrest for each youth,* she released the kids overnight to the custody of their parents. The police work was not yet done—the victim had not completed her medical exams—but the offenders were home with their families. This was the stuff that sells newspapers and, therefore, makes great news.

The next day, a story about the rape, car chase and the release of the offenders was big news for one of the tabloids. In keeping with their understanding of the confidentiality laws, the papers would not print the names of the two juveniles charged in the incident. They did, however, print the name of the judge who released the two youths. That set off sparks in the Queens County Family Court. A supervisor in the Corporation Counsel's Office was called by a court official and accused of leaking the story. In truth, that attorney was not responsible for the release of the information to the press.

The court official who accused the prosecution of leaking the story to the press protested the release of the name of the judge who handled the case. Weren't we aware, he asked, that these matters were *confidential?*

There are times when confidentiality is used more as a sword than a shield. At other times, we must ask ourselves, whom are we protecting? The innocence that confidentiality was supposed to serve has been lost for decades. Now the secrecy only benefits those whose guilt is their lack of accountability. When the court is finally open—*really open*—we will then see who and what has been safeguarded. Rest assured, it has not been the public interest.

32.

Kids are put into detention for two reasons. Either the court finds that, if released, the youth is unlikely to appear in court or that he or she is likely to commit a crime. The court must be certain upon the issuance of a *remand* order that all possibilities to avoid detention have been considered and that the detention is the least restrictive environment for the young offender. Only when all these standards have been met can the court incarcerate even the most violent juvenile criminals.

Thus **DAP** was most puzzling. The **D**etention

Alternative **P**rogram was an *ATI* (Alternatives to Incarceration) program brought on by the tough economic times of the early 1990s. It is a program administered by New York City's Department of Juvenile Justice *(DJJ)* and funded via the "Safe Streets—Safe City" anticrime program of 1991. Despite its origins as a law enforcement initiative, DAP had about as much in common with community safety as the Boston Strangler had with Gandhi.

The premise behind DAP was simple: It is cheaper in the short run to keep offenders out of jail. Therefore, the DAP program, playing hostage to the limited funds of the recession, advocated the release of offenders from detention. Kids were screened by social workers and caseworkers over an approximate ten-day period while in the custody of DJJ.[19] When the DAP staff believed that a youth made a good adjustment in detention, the youth was evaluated for release. In court, the DAP worker submitted a letter to the court suggesting that the respondent, whom the court had previously deemed dangerous or unlikely to appear, was a good risk for release. Jail overcrowding has forced prison and detention managers to exercise "creativity" when solving the high cost of the exploding prison population. Practically, the only result has been the release of people who simply have no business living outside of a prison environment.

In typical DJJ fashion, the administrators and workers in the DAP program wanted to prove that they were ready to accept the challenge. Rather than be sensible by limiting the first few cases to nonviolent offenders, the program workers wanted to put the system "on the map." These idealists had their heads in the clouds but their brains in their behinds. They chose to start big—with Marlando.

Marlando was a creep. He was a freshman at Aviation

High School in Queens, and everybody knew he was trouble. He proved this when he decided to bring a loaded semi-automatic pistol to school with him.

School officials were tipped to Marlando's gun, and the youth was searched and arrested. At arraignment his poor school record and the gravity of the charge caused him to be remanded into detention. Guns and schools have not fared well throughout history, and nobody needed Marlando—an acknowledged behavior problem—settling his "beefs" with the gun he kept in his bookbag.

In a few days, Marlando was tried and found guilty of the felony gun offense. His remand was continued pending *disposition* because the court found him a danger to the community. The people at DJJ had different ideas.

Sometime during the course of his detention, Marlando was interviewed by a staff worker from the DAP program. The youth, wise beyond his criminal record, told the counselor about his fine school performance. He indicated that he was not a behavior problem in school and that he was an "A" and "B" student. The caseworker, relying solely on the youth's representations, recommended that the court release the youth to the DAP program. Although the probation department, the prosecution and the defense had these records, the worker never called for verification. Instead, he chose to believe the guilty offender without any corroboration of his accounts.

Not surprisingly, Marlando had lied. He lied about his exemplary behavior and about his grades. The youth was failing most subjects, although he did manage a "D" in gym. Some of his grades were missing because he had missed ninety-five days of school within the first semester of that year. Yet DJJ, when confronted with this information (necessarily making Marlando a liar), chose to stick by their recommendation and seek the release of the gun-toting teen. They had become another advocate for a kid who needed a martinet more than a mouthpiece.

The prosecution, in opposing the release of the armed youth, expressed concern about his poor school attendance. Failure to attend school regularly, urged the prosecutor, was an indication that the youth was unlikely to remain committed to any program. Although ninety-five days of absence is the bulk of the semester, the DAP worker was not concerned. The caseworker attempted to excuse Marlando's attendance problems by explaining that a recorded absence only indicated that the youth missed his first-period attendance check. Such a student, he asserted, could therefore be marked absent for the entire day. The worker believed, *based upon Marlando's representations,* that the youth recorded ninety-five days of absence because he was really habitually late. (The only day of attendance that could be verified was the day Marlando appeared in school with his weapon.) The worker further suggested that even if the respondent did miss ninety-five days in one semester, it would make no difference in his belief that the youth should be released from detention. He justified this by saying, "... I have had kids that were absent for three years from school."

More disturbing was the DAP worker's disregard for the gravity of the underlying offense. Although the youth had been found guilty of carrying a semi-automatic weapon inside a public school, the worker said that Marlando posed a "... minimal risk to the community." He asserted that strict supervision of the young man would meet the statutory requirement for community protection and that this would not be the first armed offender brought into the program.

In reaching this assessment the worker did not seem to

think it important *why* the youth had the gun. No information was sought to determine whether or not Marlando was
looking to settle a "beef." No information was obtained by
DJJ to see if the youth was involved in other violent acts that
might have led to the need for a gun. There was no questioning of school officials to check whether they knew about any
"enemies" in the school who might be at risk. It didn't seem
important to the Department of Juvenile Justice that
Marlando's presence in school could result in the death of
another student, a teacher or any other person in the school.
Instead, the worker asserted that he would serve as the youth's
advocate to get him back into the high school he had rarely
attended. In keeping with the stereotypical image of the ideological social worker who places textbook faith over practical considerations, the DAP caseworker chose to believe in his
client rather than in the potential danger he had already displayed. Luckily, the court chose not to be so foolish.

Complying with the requirements to provide a least
restrictive alternative and utilize every option other than
detention, would mean the youth had to be released. The
judge, however, knew that guns and schools don't mix and
chose to place the youth upstate in a DFY limited-secure
facility before the kid could cause further trouble. Within a
few days Marlando was doing his time.

Kids and guns are an explosive combination. Teenagers,
by definition, believe in their own immortality. They are made
fearless by Mother Nature so that they can test their own limits. Yet the teen with a gun who has no concept of his own
mortality also has no appreciation for the vulnerability of his
fellow students, teachers, friends and strangers. A youth's
"immunity" from death makes him great with a gun when he
is a soldier, but very dangerous when he lives in the city with

the rest of us.

Within one month of Marlando's hearing, another youth with a pistol walked into a school in Brooklyn and murdered two students. The Family Court judge who placed Marlando upstate could not have foreseen this event, although common sense suggests that there is little use in carrying a weapon to school other than an intent to use it. Yet this simple proposition seemed to elude the DAP worker and his agency. In their zeal to institute their treatment program, they lost sight of the lives that were threatened by Marlando.

DAP is an abandoned program. Somehow funding a program that advocates the release of gun-toting offenders seems inconsistent with a policy called "Safe Streets—Safe City." The program died because those who advocate on behalf of such agendas are too willing to take chances on marginal people. Every time an ideologue takes a chance on a violent teen, he is risking an average citizen's life. The public should not come cheap. The people at DJJ did not understand that concept, and virtually all of DJJ's policy-makers were fired when the mayoral administrations changed.

While no one will know whether Marlando would have walked into Aviation High School and blasted away into a crowd, the parents of every student were possibly spared the anguish of a murdered child. The judge and the prosecutor saw this as self-evident. The caseworker from New York City's DAP program missed that point. Had the worst occurred, who would have acknowledged the blood on his or her hands?

33.

If the victim had died it would have been one of those "Misdemeanor–Murders." It was the kind of case that is only criminal by definition. Some may call it vigilantism and others may call it mob violence. The cops who arrested Prandy understood that it was merely getting even.

It started around Memorial Day when the summer unofficially calls everybody out into the street for nightly mixes. Up at the corner of 158th Street and Broadway, the mostly Dominican crowd was getting into the rhythm that blasted from the radios. Everybody was relaxed and all were having a good time.

Frank didn't fit into the neighborhood. Frank was a twenty-one-year-old black guy from the Bronx who came down to 158th Street with Jose to make a score. Jose, Frank's partner in crime, knew of a lady with lots of cash in her apartment. So Frank grabbed his trusty revolver and let Jose be his guide.

At about ten P.M. when the outside festivities were really starting to get hot, Frank and Jose knocked on Maria's door. Maria yelled something in Spanish, so Jose had to do the talking. She opened the door to feel the muzzle of Frank's gun shoved into her nostril. The two thugs then thrust open the door and began to ransack the apartment. Maria's protests were unheard as the outdoor party intensified to the beat of 120-decibel salsa music.

The two men searched for cash in every drawer and in every cabinet. They tossed furniture about the small apartment and tore clothes from the closets. When they didn't find the treasure they had expected, Jose asked Maria for the money. She said she had none in the apartment but knew where they could get some. Frank's gun was very convincing.

When Jose translated the bare facts for Frank, the black man told the others that they were going to "get paid." He put the barrel of the gun into the base of Maria's spine and walked her outside into the street party. Although Frank held Maria closely, he failed to conceal his actions. A bystander saw Maria's predicament and shouted to his friends to begin the rescue. Jose understood the message and took off. Frank, failing to understand anything the young men had said, continued to slowly walk Maria up Broadway.

In a flash, Frank was surrounded by twenty young Dominican men ready to prove their machismo and rescue the lady. Besides, a black guy was holding a Latino woman at gunpoint, in a word, unacceptable. Frank had no understanding that this present position was extremely hazardous to his health. But within seconds, Frank understood exactly what the crowd had been saying and what a fool he had been. He was thrown to the ground and felt the feet of twenty angry Hispanics smashing into his skull, ribs, kidneys and groin. That was the easy part. Next somebody grabbed his gun and he heard it go off. He felt a stinging in his shoulder as the joint shattered. About the same time as he heard the shot, he saw the guy with the knife. The knife cut into his back as he felt another boot smash into his skull. He heard the racial epithets, and he heard the warnings about staying away from the neighborhood and from Latino women. With each warning and with each threat came another blow to his head and again to his groin.

For the first time in Frank's life, the next sound was a welcome relief. The sweet sound of a police siren streamed into his ears as the blood seeped out of his head, shoulder and back. Before he saw the cop, Frank passed out.

The cops had received a call that a crowd was beating a man to death. With sirens blaring, they sped to 158th and Broadway. They figured they probably would be there several times that evening, since these big "parties" often require police to separate the merrymakers. As the sirens blared louder with the patrol car's approach to the corner, the crowd started to thin out. As the first officer jumped out of his car, he was just in time to see Prandy give Frank a final kick to the head. When Prandy was cuffed, the crowd began to cheer for the young man.

The reaction in the prosecutor's office wasn't much different. Should Prandy get a community service medal? Should the prosecution take it more seriously and charge the youth with littering? How about a Crime Stopper's pin?

Everyone in the complaint room—cops and prosecutors alike—felt a certain respect for what Prandy had done. Yes, he had broken the law, but maybe he (and the crowd) had prevented these guys from hurting Maria, and maybe he saved her life. Perhaps Prandy—like the cops and prosecutors, had felt a sense of frustration over the inability of the criminal justice system to provide swift and sure justice. Frank's injuries were nothing more than an occupational hazard for any *dirt-bag,* and their effect would last far longer than anything the system would dish out.

Nobody in the complaint room had to say it. Prandy had gotten even—for himself, for Maria, and for everyone in law enforcement. Now, how should Prandy be charged?

34.

There is no "sentencing" in the juvenile justice system. The legislature's nonstigmatizing euphemism for the normal concluding phase of delinquency proceedings is "disposition." This time, however, the lawmakers might be right by affixing a nonthreatening label. At disposition, most youths have little to fear, even from the maximum allowable sanctions. Yet before the *de minimis* maximums are applied, the offenders may once again challenge the state's evidence and seek a dismissal. Culpability determined at the fact-finding hearing is irrelevant. When phase two of the case commences, the burden rests again on the prosecutor. Guilt of the offender has already been established at the fact-finding hearing, but for the purpose of a juvenile delinquency proceeding, the "fat lady" has yet to sing.

At disposition, the state must still *prove* that the guilty youth needs treatment, supervision or confinement. There is no presumption that even the most violent offenders will end up punished. Community protection was a legislative afterthought for the Family Court Act.[20] Traditional priorities have always focused on the needs of the offender and the opportunity for (the elusive and ideological) rehabilitation. During the presentation of the state's case at disposition, the defense may challenge the prosecution's evidence and cross-examine the witnesses. The defense may then choose to put on their own case by offering witnesses and other evidence to challenge the recommendations of the state.

Should the prosecutor fail to prove that the offender requires some sanction, the case must be dismissed. Convicted armed robbers, rapists and killers must be shown to need the services of the juvenile justice system. Their crimes alone are not enough to trigger a sentence. In juvenile justice terms, the offender's actions never speak as loudly as his or her lawyer's words. With a statute as crazy as New York's Family Court Act, it is no wonder that Karim G. is still out on the street.

Karim is a violent felon. He is also manipulative, shrewd and willing to sacrifice anyone else for his own sake. He lies convincingly, and best (or worst) of all, his family is also willing to lie for him. In short, he has everything a kid needs to beat the dispositional system.

It was an early afternoon on a January weekday that Karim and his buddy Roshad got on the downtown "A" train. Roshad was the trigger man, and Karim was the talker. Karim could charm the skin off a snake and, even if he couldn't, Roshad was *strapped*. It was time to *"get paid."*

As the train headed south toward the 168th Street station, Karim saw Charlie—the *vic*—with the multicolored coat. Karim and Roshad walked over toward their prey to scope the situation. Karim really liked the coat, and he thought that the victim was just about his own chubby size. Karim sat down next to his victim to do some shopping. With his armed friend a few paces away, Karim told Charlie how much he admired his coat. He asked him about his coat size and then he told Charlie he wanted to try it on. Realizing that Karim's conversation was about more than admiration for the jacket, Charlie told Karim to get lost.

Karim demanded the coat as he signaled his backup to approach. When Charlie pushed Karim away, Roshad pulled out the gun and told him to give the coat to the youth. Charlie refused and Roshad ordered, "Now!" "Do it fast," said Roshad.

Charlie responded by pushing Karim. As they struggled, Roshad joined the fray by shooting Charlie in the abdomen.

All accounts differ as to whether the gun was fired once or twice, but somehow Roshad sustained a superficial gunshot wound to his hand. As the train pulled into the station, the would-be robbers ran out of the train and to the street, leaving their bleeding victim to stagger onto the platform.

The 168th Street station is often filled with cops, and that day was no exception. Charlie stumbled into the arms of a *Transit Police* Officer who radioed for an ambulance and for assistance in catching the assailants. Two cops on patrol gave chase, and Karim was apprehended on the street a few steps from the station entrance. Roshad was caught two blocks away, and his gun was found under the car where he had tossed it.

Karim pleaded guilty to the attempted armed robbery of the coat. The court appreciated the presence of both his parents in the courtroom,[21] and ordered Probation to prepare an Investigation and Report *(I & R)*. The judge said that the Probation Department should seek a mental health study if their investigation indicated that placement of Karim was likely. A mental health study is a precursor to placement, but the court was hoping that the eager and polite Karim would not require confinement. It was clear that Karim had already begun to work his charm on the judge.

When the I & R was completed, the court was inclined to leave Karim with his family—and within the community he had so deftly terrorized and wounded. Relying on the Probation Department's opinion that Karim was "a goal-directed youngster with strong family involvement" and that it seemed unlikely that the youth would get into further criminal activity, the court placed Karim on probation. Thus, as the victim healed from his abdominal gunshot wounds, the perpetrator walked out of the courthouse into freedom. Justice—

or its perversion—had been done.

It is instructive in Karim's case to look behind the conclusive parts of the *I & R* to illustrate the weakness in the Probation Department's dispositional recommendation. The probation officer, the school officials and the court were all taken by Karim's gift of "gab" and the unusual chance to hear from *two* parents exhibiting apparent concern. Looking carefully at the data, however, and drawing conclusions upon the facts rather than upon the charm of the interviewees, provides an obvious alternative to the recommendation for community-based supervision.

Karim's version of the events differed significantly from the statements of the victim and from the confession of his codefendant. Both Charlie (the victim) and Roshad (the shooter) confirmed the version of events that had Karim demanding the coat with Roshad's armed backup. Karim told the probation officer that he was with Roshad when Roshad spontaneously decided to steal the man's coat. Karim said that he had nothing to do with the robbery and that he only pleaded guilty because his lawyer forced him to do so. According to Karim's latest version of events, everything was Roshad's doing. Karim said he was sorry that the man was shot, but he couldn't have been hurt too badly. After all, asserted Karim, the man was able to stagger out of the train onto the platform as he pursued his attackers. The probation officer, however, failed to ask Karim why—if he was without culpability—he ran out of the station and to the street with Roshad. Karim did not stop when commanded to do so by the police but chose to flee from the pursuing officers. Nor did this young man stop to help the victim as he staggered his way out of the train. Instead, denying all criminal intent, he chose to run away from the crime scene together with the person he labeled as the lone offender.

Karim's "concerned and involved" family offered little credible information to the investigating probation officer. Yet somehow the young man's mother managed to convince the Probation Department that the youth should remain in the community. She said her son was respectful and did not present any behavior problems in the home. When she suggested that this incident had "set the entire family back," nobody asked her: "Back" from what? No one asked the mother if she was aware that Karim had been cutting school at the time he and his friend shot their would-be robbery victim. How did this jibe with the description of an obedient son who never missed his curfew?

More disturbing was the mother's assertion that her son was doing well in school. Was she pleased with the fact that Karim had missed well over eighty days of school for the first two-thirds of the present academic year? Was she upset with his chronic lateness (on the days he did attend)? Did she accept Karim's explanation for his persistent absences as a result of getting "lost" in his new school (although he had already been enrolled in that school eight months at the time the *I & R* was completed)? When she asserted he was doing "well" in school, was she satisfied with his 56 average? Was his satisfactory school performance reflected in his need to enroll in summer school to make up the classes he'd failed?

All third-person accounts about Karim must be juxtaposed with the offender's self-description. He told the investigating probation officer that he obeyed an 8:00 P.M. curfew. He said he had a good relationship with everyone in his family and that he had no gang connections. He hoped that one day he could open his own accounting business. (No one even considered asking Karim to describe an "accounting business.") It all seemed too good to be true. It was.

To satisfy the concerns of everyone in the courthouse about his involvement in a near-fatal robbery attempt, Karim brilliantly (and deceitfully) shifted culpability. "I was with the wrong person at the wrong time," he said. "I deserve probation, and I hope that's what the judge gives me," urged the young thug. He invented a story that had Roshad doing all the dirty work. Karim said he had to stand by helplessly as Roshad demanded the coat and shot the victim. Karim further stated that Roshad pointed the gun at the victim's head and fired, but the mechanism jammed.[22] He also claimed that he was surprised about Roshad's attempt to rob the man. The whole affair was none of his doing. None of these facts were corroborated by the police or the victim. Clearly this story did not jibe with Roshad's confession. Yet this shifting of blame was not picked up by the probation officer. She and the judge failed to consider whether a juvenile justice system designed around rehabilitation could meet its goal when the offender denied all culpability.

For reasons unknown, the court and the Department of Probation were not motivated at the hearing to look behind the obviously flawed data in the report. Instead, they chose to nod in agreement as Karim's lawyer reiterated the nonsense that permeated the *I & R*. He seized upon the language extolling the virtues of Karim's familial support and built a case around the youth's prospects for a law-abiding future. Every bit of misinformation was carried to its illogical end; advocacy replaced honesty; all truth was molded into legal fiction.

The *I & R* as written, containing the unexplained absences, poor academic average and the conspicuous lies about the youth's involvement in a shooting, was moved into evidence. Although the probation officer acknowledged that the underlying incident was "a very serious one," she concluded that ". . . it would appear that the Respondent may not be at risk for continued delinquency." The court celebrated these conclusions by pressing the prosecution for a consent to a *conditional discharge.* The judge even flirted with the idea of dismissing the petition. She questioned whether the youth really was in need of treatment, supervision or confinement. Forgotten was the armed robbery attempt on the subway. Lost in the rhetoric were the poor school record and the myriad of lies. Disregarded were the complainant, his gunshot wound, and the pain associated with the recovery from abdominal surgery. Pursuing a community-based disposition for Karim had become a crusade for the court. It had nothing to do with law or justice. It was all about hope.

A glimmer of reality moved the court otherwise. The prosecution was unconvinced by the canonization of Karim. He still was an armed felon, cautioned the prosecutor, and armed robbers needed to be watched. Those armed robbers who shoot people, urged the state, needed to be watched even closer. A subliminal reminder that community safety and approval were inextricably linked was enough momentarily to bring the proponents of ideological jurisprudence down to earth. Reluctantly, the court shifted one small inch from a position of total hope toward one based on reality. The judge placed the young felon on probation for the minimum period of one year.[23] It was not a good day for community safety.

Three months after Karim was placed on probation, the prosecutor's office sent a letter to the private agency that was hired by the Probation Department to help with the supervision of Karim. The prosecution, still unwilling to accept Karim's suitability for community-based supervision on faith, sought a status report regarding the would-be robber's adjustment on probation. Within ninety days of disposition, the mother who had sworn there were no behavior problems with her obedient and respectful son, threw him out of her home. He had suddenly become too much for her to handle. Karim was now living with his father at an address unknown to the Probation Department—the same agency that was supposed to be supervising the young man in the community. (There was no testimony at the dispositional hearing about the suitability of the father as a resource for Karim. Probation knew nothing about the man except that he was "concerned." In fact, Karim's unilateral move out of his mother's home may have been a technical violation of the terms of probation.) Further, the youth was implicated in a recent felony assault—once again *with weapons*—but this too was unknown to the Probation Department.

Thousands of kids throughout the City of New York are on probation for felony offenses like armed robbery, assault and weapons possession. Karim's case is not unique in the level of violence or in the system's failure to respond. The reason crime is abundant in New York is that people like Karim are returned to the streets and encouraged to continue their violent behavior. Wherever do they get that idea?

35.

Many of the lawyers with the *Legal Aid Society* have their priorities out of sync with the rest of humanity. The support for this proposition is not in their representation of the scum of the earth. The fact is these lawyers often attempt to justify their clients' sociopathic actions by displacing the blame. These ideologues have the term "prosecutorial misconduct" on their lips at all times. They suggest that the whole criminal/ juvenile justice process is a grand conspiracy against the help- less, homeless, and abused—or whatever label is chosen to apply to their criminal client. They say that the police, the prosecutors, the judges, the probation officers, and the shrinks—they're all prejudging the client. Explanations for conduct are offered as excuses. Lost in the shuffle is the client's deed—robbery, rape, drug dealing or even murder. These ide- ological defenders see every one of their violent clients as *vic- tims*—and society as the victimizer.

When the *Daily News* ran a story about recidivism among juvenile criminals,[24] there was a feature article on Benjamin Dent. The best guess is that Benjamin Dent is a killer-in-waiting. He was placed with DFY for eighteen months for a robbery and a grand larceny at age fourteen, and was sent home six months later via an early release program. While in DFY's *Community Care* program and at home less than one week, he robbed a street vendor. He was released on that case pending trial because the witness failed to appear at a pretrial hearing.

Awaiting trial on this new offense, Benjamin demonstrat- ed his full predatory potential at a neighborhood fast-food outlet. He showed up at the shop daily, terrorizing the owner and demanding free food. When the owner threatened to call police, Benjamin said he was a juvenile. He flaunted his immunity. This immunity became a sense of invulnerability as Benjamin visited the store again and again. Like a giant cat he stalked his prey and teased his victim. Once he brought along a stick and smashed windows. He continued to demand free food as he flipped tables and chairs. He urinated on the counter and demanded that the owner clean it up. Young Dent displayed all the telltale signs of a dangerous offender. Youthful innocence had been replaced by hard-core violence.

When the youth urinated on the counter, a store employee got angry. He ordered the youth out of the store, but the boy would not move. The employee, a recent immigrant who could not accept a young boy behaving this way, picked up a broom and ordered Dent out of the store. Benjamin grabbed the broom and beat the employee on the head. The man required emergency hospitalization and stitches to repair the gash in his skull.

The *Daily News* focused on Dent as a new breed of predator who should never have been released early from DFY's residential care. In preparing the story, the reporter spoke with people at the DFY facility where Benjamin had lived, as well as his mother, his sister, the victim, the store's owner, attorneys with the Office of the Corporation Counsel —among them the prosecutor in the Dent case—as well as unnamed sources.

This teenager's brutality, as reported by the newspaper, shook (but did not surprise) many people within the juvenile justice system. DFY personnel were not pleased with their decision on early release for Benjamin, and court personnel expressed disgust and frustration that he was only one of many to fit a new meaning for the acronym "YUPPIE"—Young Urban Predator. But it was the reaction from a Legal Aid lawyer that tells it all: In a courthouse corridor she told a prosecutor she was appalled that the office of the Corporation Counsel would supply the name of Benjamin Dent to the press. Juvenile proceedings and identities, she asserted, were confidential. She said that Benjamin Dent's name should never have been disclosed and the young man's privacy had been invaded. Another violation of someone's rights, asserted the Legal Aid lawyer, and another example of prosecutorial misconduct.

Priorities. The ideologues have warped priorities. Benjamin Dent—convicted by the Family Court of robberies and felony assault—had someone there to champion his privacy in the halls of justice. Benjamin Dent, a felon who terrorized his victims before striking near-deadly blows, had an advocate who expressed outrage because New Yorkers would know the truth about this client's character. Benjamin Dent, a recidivist who learned nothing from incarceration with DFY except that it was short enough to encourage the commission of more crime—had someone in the system ready, willing and able to paint him as a victim.

It is not clear how Benjamin Dent's name came to be used by the *Daily News,* nor is it important. Within a few days of publication his name was forgotten, likely to be recalled again the next time the media focuses on his unbridled brutality.

Benjamin Dent is dangerous. *Benjamin Dent* is a predator. *Benjamin Dent* will probably kill someone some day. So, despite an advocate's twisted claim for confidentiality, remember that name: Benjamin Dent. Benjamin Dent. Benjamin Dent . . . and remember him the next time his Legal Aid lawyer makes him out to be a victim.

36.

The criminal justice system is a crap shoot. Sometimes the bad guys go free. Sometimes the bad guys go to jail. When Judge Carmen[25] presides, sometimes the bad guys go free and the prosecutors go to jail.

In the mid-1980s the Family Courts still handled the cases that comprised traditional "juvenile delinquency." The "crack" epidemic had not yet hit New York, and the group violence relating to assaults and robbery were just beginning to emerge. Guns were not ubiquitous in the school system and "wilding" was a term still to be invented. Thus it was quite ordinary when Meredith, a new prosecutor in Family Court, filed a misdemeanor case charging Shawn with the sale of two joints (marijuana cigarettes).

Shawn was a street kid who had a history with the child welfare people. He had been neglected and had been in and out of foster homes and group residences all his life. When he sold the pot, Shawn had been AWOL from a Social Services shelter. The arraigning Family Court judge found him unlikely to appear in court and ordered Shawn into secure detention. Like all "jail" cases, Shawn's was returned to court in three days for a hearing.

Shawn's defense lawyer from the Legal Aid Society stated that she was not ready to proceed. She told Judge Carmen that she needed to resolve some possible suppression issues concerning the legality of the seizure of the marijuana. Therefore, the defense was requesting an adjournment. Meredith, the prosecutor, said she was ready for trial and asked to proceed. Judge Carmen correctly recognized that the defense was entitled to the adjournment and agreed to put the case over for a few days.

The Legal Aid lawyer then asked the court for a "probable cause hearing." Defense counsel said that, although she was not ready to proceed to trial, she had a right to a probable cause hearing if the court was going to continue the detention of her client. The prosecutor countered that the continued detention resulted from the *respondent's* request for an adjournment and that the prosecution should not bear the burden for delay occasioned by the defense. In any event, Meredith said, no probable cause hearing was authorized in misdemeanor cases. Both lawyers and the court looked to the ambiguous language in the statute to support their position on Shawn's right to receive a probable cause hearing.

It's easy to see that a legislature full of attorneys would often have good reason to write laws that are invitations to litigation. Vagueness and overly broad scope are synonyms for *billable hours*—at least when the ambiguity requires resolution on behalf of financially secure litigants. The language in FCA §325.1 is not likely to make anyone in the Family Court rich, but it is likely to leave everyone confused. The statute is supposed to define when a probable cause hearing is required in juvenile cases. Instead, prosecutors and defense attorneys argued their interpretations of this statute all the way to the United States Supreme Court.[26] For the next seven years, the courts remained split on the time of, or entitlement to, a probable cause hearing.[27]

Judge Carmen ordered Meredith to commence a probable cause hearing. Although she was a newly admitted attorney, the prosecutor was savvy enough to recognize that such a hearing only served the discovery concerns of the offender and his counsel. Additionally, the prosecution had no interest in doing probable cause hearings on misdemeanor cases, especially those relating to marijuana and other minimal offenses.

If the court was going to release this youth, Shawn's nonviolent record would not have compromised community safety. Thus, Meredith declined to proceed with the hearing and fully expected the court to release the juvenile joint jockey.

Instead, the court repeated its direction to commence the probable cause hearing. He advised the young prosecutor that she was facing contempt charges if she failed to proceed. At this point, Meredith's supervisor appeared and attempted to remove the novice attorney from the case. Defending her position on the probable cause issue, he informed the court that he would now appear as the attorney of record on the case. Judge Carmen, ever persistent, refused to allow the substitution and held both lawyers in contempt for their failure to proceed with a probable cause hearing. He remanded the attorneys to the custody of the Commissioner of Corrections, had them escorted out of the courtroom by court officers and placed in cells. The judge opined, "You cannot refuse to obey a judge's order. . . . I sentence them to stay incarcerated until they *purge* themselves of that contempt. . . ." Following that direction, Judge Carmen vacated Shawn's secure detention remand and put the boy back into a group home.

As the day wore on, it was clear that the judge would not retreat from his position. The prosecutors were to remain in jail until he was satisfied that they would be willing to commence a probable cause hearing against this minor offender. That stubborn posture was made clear when at 5:00 P.M. the judge visited the detention facility in the courthouse to check on his prisoners. Seeing that the attorneys were not in the cells but rather were waiting with the corrections guard in the vestibule of the detention facility, the judge was outraged. He ordered the guard to move the lawyers into the cells. He asserted that the "problem" in this case was that the prosecutors thought they were better than everyone else. Putting them into the cells, he suggested, would be an appropriately humbling experience.

The court remained open that evening until an order releasing the attorneys was signed and delivered to the Department of Corrections at 10 P.M. After ten and half hours behind bars, the two incarcerated attorneys, along with their colleagues and another six or seven attorneys from the Office of the Corporation Counsel, went home.

The following day the city began its assault on the mean-spirited actions of Judge Carmen. A case was filed against the judge seeking a vacatur of the contempt citation and expunging all records. Mayor Ed Koch, in a press conference at City Hall, awarded the two lawyers the City's Medal of Freedom. The mayor wasted no time pointing out that the criminal justice system was bound to suffer when the courts start jailing the prosecutors and releasing offenders.

It was clear to most of the civilized world that Judge Carmen had abused the power of contempt citations. He could have released the pot dealer or he could have dismissed the case.[28] Since the prosecutor is vested with the ultimate decision on whether to file a case, she necessarily retains the discretion to decide whether to proceed. The court is the arbiter of the case, not the controlling entity for presentation. Unlike many third-world countries, and apparently unknown to Judge Carmen, American judges are not empowered with the role of "Grand Inquisitor."

Judge Carmen did, however, receive a token degree of support. The Legal Aid Society, the same people who defend the actions of rapists, thieves, murderers and other lawbreakers, supported the jailing of the prosecutors. In papers submitted by one of Legal Aid's chief attorneys in opposition to the motion to vacate the contempt, the Society said:

> Summary punishment for contempt committed [by
> the two Corporation Counsel attorneys] in the
> Court's presence was clearly justified, as petitioners'
> [the two attorneys] defiance seriously compromised
> the Court's exercise of its authority.[29]

These harbingers of civil liberties concluded thus:

> Petitioners [Meredith and her supervisor] had an
> obligation to obey that order and have demonstrated
> no entitlement to [vacate the contempt] to counte-
> nance their wilful defiance.[30]

The tabloids recognized the commercial value of this
event, and every paper in town was ablaze with the story
about the prosecutors who went to jail. Condemnation of the
criminal justice system was everywhere, and the usual reformers were all about urging their usual reforms. What had begun
as a marijuana case with no possible press value had become a
major media event because a judge chose to use muscle over
brains.

The press missed the point, however, in reporting this as
another example of the criminal justice system gone awry.
Clearly, there is absurdity in a Family Court judge jailing a
prosecutor because there is disagreement over a point of law.
Equally clear, however, is that the court failed to achieve its
purpose. Contempt is the ultimate and final power of the
court. The court is vested with this power to ensure proper

respect for the authority of the judiciary. Power when abused, however, does not engender respect. Rather, Judge Carmen, by abusing his power, assured himself that respect will remain forever unattainable. Everywhere he goes, to the bar association, meetings, lectures, people continually whisper about the "incident."

Despite the mayor's media blitz, the press never saw—at least never reported—the real tragedy in this case. Judge Carmen crossed the line when he ordered the lawyers held in contempt and jailed, but he exceeded acceptable limits of civilized behavior when he visited detention and ordered the attorneys into the jail cells.[31] Discretion, on the part of the Corporation Counsel, prevented disclosure of those gruesome facts. As angry as the media and the mayor appeared, only part of the story surfaced.

Furthermore, the Legal Aid Society exceeded the bounds of fair practice and advocacy by defending Judge Carmen's order jailing the lawyers. While there was no quibble with Legal Aid's standing to support their client's right to a probable cause hearing, their call to enforce the contempt was vindictive. It bore no relation to their role as advocates,[32] but instead confirmed their leadership's ideological commitment to universally oppose the prosecutor without respect to the matter at issue. Those who routinely make excuses for the conduct of the worst offenders, suddenly supported incarceration and the firm hand of the law.

This case had nothing to do with a kid's right to a hearing. Instead, it was another example of unfortunate friction in an adversarial system. In this case criminal justice was no longer about right and wrong, it had become a personal crusade for retribution and vindication. Yet Judge Carmen made a colossal error, not by jailing attorneys, but rather by drawing the lines of battle where people could see them. He let his pride rule his courtroom, and he let his temper make the rules. He failed to protect his record, and he let the matter go on for too long. He erroneously assumed that because he was a judge, he had to be right, even if he had to force everyone to agree.

A short time later the contempt order was vacated on consent, and all references to the jailing of the attorneys were expunged from the Family Court documents. The official records relating to the motion to vacate the contempt were sealed. But courts can only seal documents; they cannot erase the memories of two lawyers who spent ten hours in jail because a man in a robe tried (and failed) to make a point. Nor will an adversary's attempt to punish remain within the corners of a sealed file. Two attorneys remember, and two attorneys are waiting, not for the day to get even, but rather for the ultimate in civilized behavior: an apology.

37.

The pundits are quick to point out that the breakdown of the family unit is the root of society's problems. Preservation of "family values" and a strong support system within the home will prevent crime. So say the experts. Unfortunately for the pundits, there is much anecdotal evidence to the contrary.

It is not the existence or the preservation of the family

that predicts the likelihood of delinquent kids. Dozens of violent predators come from intact families. The presence of a family for support is not the issue; rather it is the *quality* and *type* of support that often separates the offender from the law-abiding youth.

Jamiko Akbar[33] has a caring mother who came to court for every appearance. She gave her son unwavering support. She was not abusive and did not neglect her custodial responsibilities. Her contributions to his legal defense and her unwavering allegiance to his claims of innocence, however, guaranteed his placement with *DFY*.

The Akbar family used to be called the Feiffer family. Ms. Feiffer went to court to change her family's names because she wanted her identity to match her true heritage. So she went from Barbara to Naptali, and her son went from Jerome to Jamiko. Unfortunately, changes in temperament did not accompany the changes in title.

Jamiko had been a troubled youth growing up in California. His mother had been working for the railroad, when creative impulses told her to leave a $40,000.00 per year job to come to New York to be a writer and composer. Her play and her music did not sell, so she went on public assistance. All the while she did her best to convince herself, her friends and eventually the Probation Department that her truant, mischievous and irreverent son was a good boy. He just never got any counseling.

Jamiko's first arrest in New York was for car theft. Although the car in question was legally parked, had license plates both front and rear and had only one broken window, Jamiko asserted that he was just seated in a car he thought was abandoned. He, echoed by his mother, said he was in the wrong place at the wrong time. Culpability, despite all the evidence to the contrary, was denied.

Shortly thereafter, Jamiko was arrested again, this time for felony assault, menacing and sexual abuse. He and several friends saw a woman leave a neighborhood supermarket with a wagon full of groceries. The youths threatened the woman with broken glass bottles as Jamiko lifted her skirt and fondled her genitals. As the woman tried to escape she was hit and cut with several of the bottles wielded by the boys.

Jamiko's version of the events varied significantly from the findings of the court. He suggested that the lady exited the supermarket, pulled out a "blade" and "cut him" for no reason. He was arrested, he claimed, because the police believed the lady. Once again Jamiko and his mother attempted to excuse the behavior as a result of being in the wrong place at the wrong time. The youth denied remorse because he asserted that he did nothing wrong. His mother later explained that remorse was inappropriate since guilt was not in issue.

Following the court's fact-finding against her son, Ms. Akbar recognized that placement of Jamiko with *DFY* was possible. In defense of her son, and far exceeding the responsibility taken by most parents of young offenders, she sought out various agencies to deal with the boy. She contacted several community-based programs that were designed to cope with kids in trouble. The program administrators wrote letters of recommendation to the court on behalf of Jamiko and asserted that the youth was, or would be, enrolled in their program. Each director or coordinator (of these publicly funded youth programs) assured the court that Jamiko would be a great candidate for their group, so long as he remained in the community.

The letters of recommendation on behalf of Jamiko are more entertaining in their omissions than informative in their

content. They depict a youth who did not fit the profile painted by his criminal history; nor is it clear that any of the half-
dozen agencies had information correctly reflecting Jamiko's
status with the courts. Instead, the court received a small stack
of general references whose worth was easily measured by the
brevity of their praise and the obvious inattention to detail.
For instance, in one letter to the court, the program director
wrote that after meeting with Naptali Akbar (there is no indication that the director met with Jamiko), he could "attest"
that the offender was a "fine young man . . . [who] had some
bad experiences." Of course, describing Jamiko's crimes as a
series of "bad experiences" was a minimalization of maximum
proportions. One wonders whether the "bad experiences"
referred to Jamiko's acts, his arrests, or unknown events that
may have precipitated his delinquency. In any event, the
phrase tends to suggest that blame and accountability should
not attach to a youth simply because of an involvement in the
criminal justice system. If the experiences were bad for
Jamiko, how should the program director have described the
effects of the event on the woman the youth assaulted and
violated?

Another agency's letter to the court described the program as aimed at "enhancing abilities." The specific abilities
the program sought to enhance were not mentioned in the
letter. What was clear, however, was that Jamiko had become a
"devoted member" of the program and that he had "progressed tremendously since he became apart [sic]" of the program. In fact, Jamiko's subsequent arrests attest to his progress,
and probably elucidate all ambiguity about specific abilities
that were enhanced by the program.

Ms. Akbar also sought out letters of reference from family
and friends. Jamiko's aunt in California described her nephew

as "reserved and disciplined." She said she spoke with Jamiko "in depth" about the incident and found out that the young man did nothing wrong. She asserted that Jamiko did not run from police at the scene because he had nothing to fear. Naturally, she wrote, this was conclusive evidence of Jamiko's innocence and the court should therefore dismiss the case.

Furthermore, the aunt referred to a robbery case that had not yet come to the attention of the court. She asserted that this robbery arrest, along with the previous cases, was evidence of a pattern of police harassment. She said the youth was being "railroaded" in an attempt to put him in prison. Clearly, she advised, such action is contrary to the facts before the court.

Ms. Akbar solicited a memo from a family friend, who wrote, "Jamiko is an intelligent and well-disciplined child, and has never shown any signs of delinquency." The friend further stated that placing Jamiko in a juvenile institution would be "extremely detrimental" and "very damaging" to the youth. Of course the memo fails to speculate on the effects in the community (in terms of future crime) by keeping Jamiko at home in the care of his mother.

These recommendations, along with several others, were presented to the court on behalf of Jamiko at the *dispositional hearing*. The purpose of moving these reports into evidence was to counter the well-researched and—contrary to Ms. Akbar's evidence—accurate reports from Probation and the Mental Health Services. Both the *I & R* and the *MHS* painted a very different picture of Jamiko Akbar from the one presented by his mother and her letter campaign. Both the *I & R* and the *MHS* told the truth.

Jamiko and his mother had a rationalization for every event that reflected poorly on the youth's adjustment. He consistently asserted being with the wrong people at the wrong time, so that it was evident there was little time spent in the right places with the right people. Since every negative event in his life was not his fault, he brazenly asserted that he felt no remorse. Why should he feel regret for an event that was not his doing or was the result of outside factors?

While disposition was pending, Jamiko was arrested again. This time the charge was an attempted armed robbery of a taxi driver. Although he and his accomplices were caught by police at the scene, he again denied culpability. Jamiko asserted that the other apprehended youths were the responsible parties and that *he* never displayed a weapon, threatened the cab driver, demanded the money or ripped up the back seat of the cab. In typical Akbar style, he told the probation officer, "I did nothing wrong."

Despite Jamiko's new arrest and his continued denial of responsibility, the court ordered a term of probation supervision in the sexual assault case. The judge was taken by the mother's commitment to her son and said that the solid family foundation would keep Jamiko and his mother together. The letters were an indication to the judge that the mother was taking steps to deal with the delinquency. The court was not interested, however, in exploring *why* the mother had failed to seek out this help prior to her son's arrest. Nor was the court interested in reflecting upon the clear escalation in the severity of Jamiko's crimes. Instead, the court stated that it was mandated to impose the "least restrictive alternative"[34] at disposition. Although the prosecutor argued that community safety required placement and that placement was recommended in the *I & R* and the *MHS,* the judge wanted to take a chance on Jamiko. Unlike true games of chance, however, the judge who gambles on an offender rarely puts his own interests at risk. The judge here risked the safety of the people of New York City—and, of course, the city lost.

In effect, by keeping Jamiko Akbar in the community the court rewarded his mother for her presentation of the misleading letters and affidavits. While these offerings did little to present any relevant evidence to the court, the judge unwisely accepted their generalizations and recommendations over the precise accounting and predictions in the *I & R* and the *MHS*. The judge chose to accept fantasy as proof while disregarding the reality of Jamiko's escalating violence. Naptali's letters describing her son as "reserved and disciplined" or as "a fine young man" were either lacking in adequate histories or full of lies. In any event, common sense should have suggested that a description of Jamiko as "well disciplined" and "without any signs of delinquency" should have been rejected. By keeping Jamiko in the city, the court not only added to the youth's record, it also encouraged the Akbars to promote deception and manipulation in future proceedings.

While the taxi case was pending, Jamiko and a friend robbed a man of his cash at a gas station. They attacked the middle-aged victim, beat him to the ground and dragged him along the asphalt before they ran off with the loot. As the thieves ran from their bruised and bleeding victim, a passing patrol car scooped up the boys with the stolen money in their hands.

Jamiko and Naptali once again claimed that this was another case of police misconduct and institutional racism. The youth and his mother told court officials that other boys were the actual thieves and that Jamiko was merely at the wrong place at the wrong time with the wrong people. It never occurred to Jamiko himself, or to Naptali Akbar, that he had already become one of the *wrong* people.

Over the protests, screams and tears of his mother, the

court ordered Jamiko detained at Spofford for the duration of the proceedings. He had demonstrated an inability to steer clear of criminal activity and needed to be contained. The support and encouragement offered by his mother were finally seen as an obstacle to reality. Her protestations of innocence had changed from the cries of a caring mother to the rage of a fanatic. It did not matter to Naptali that the system's view of her son had changed. Despite the obvious concerns about the court's duty to protect the citizens, the Akbars seemed astonished at the decision to detain. Perhaps such surprise is understandable in light of the previous ability of the Akbars to avoid incarceration by the constant proliferation of fiction. It was hard for them to understand that even a gullible society eventually runs out of patience.

Naptali, on behalf of her son, declared his innocence in both robbery incidents. When the taxi case went to trial, the evidence of guilt was overwhelming. Jamiko was found guilty and placement seemed inevitable. Both mother and son needed a new strategy, so Jamiko and Naptali went on the offensive. They fired their lawyer (who was provided free of charge through a community legal project) and retained a woman whom Naptali thought could ensure the ultimate exculpation of the guilty. Ms. Akbar told the court, and later the probation staff, that all the previous attorneys had deceived her and that she would be appealing the prior "illegal" convictions. To Naptali, the presumption of innocence applied as a matter of fact to her son, and that presumption was irrefutable. Anything short of exoneration was the institutionalized racism of a "kangaroo court." Any attempt to place her son in jail for the acts upon which he stood convicted was "genocide." Fantasy and reality had become inseparable, and the truth was not important to Naptali Akbar.

On the scheduled date for the trial of the gas station robbery, Ms. Akbar tried to fire the attorney she had recently
retained on behalf of her son. Ms. Akbar came to court, and
prior to the commencement of the proceedings, informed the
judge that she no longer wished to have the young female
lawyer serve as Jamiko's legal counsel. She asserted that since
her child was male he could not have a good working relationship with a female attorney. She wished to adjourn the
matter until she could find a suitable male attorney to represent her son.

Unfortunately for Ms. Akbar, the too-forgiving tolerances
of the juvenile justice system have limits. Although these limits are wide and usually extend beyond the scope of reason,
Ms. Akbar had already worn out her institutional welcome.
She told the judge that this attorney was not effective because
as a female she could not be effective with a male client. She
told the female judge that prior counsel had violated Jamiko's
"states [sic] and federal constitutional rights." She vociferous-
ly assumed the role of advocate by invoking the Constitution,
common law and her distorted perceptions of their applica-
bility (and violation) to her son's case.

When the court denied Naptali's application to relieve
counsel on the basis of her gender, the angry mother threatened, "I will be compelled to go to Federal Court to seek
relief." The judge told her to go anywhere she liked, but the
trial would begin.

Naptali refused to accept court-imposed limitations as
anything other than racism. She had always known that the
government—especially the court—responds to agitation and
a charge (grounded or otherwise) of "racism." What may have
been politically correct, however, in the early to middle 1980s
has often become politically ineffective in the 1990s. This

time Naptali leveled her charges at a judge who would not be
fooled by her letters of reference or intimidated by her threats.
Naptali and Jamiko were going to be judged on the merits,
and they didn't like it.

In the courtroom, mother and son began to shout their
protest:

> *NAPTALI:* I mean, why do we have a trial?
> *JAMIKO:* We're not having a trial.
> *NAPTALI:* He has already been sentenced.
> *JAMIKO:* Give me a trial now.
> *NAPTALI:* He has already been found guilty and
> sentenced. There is no law.
> *JAMIKO:* There is no trial, give me time . . . I know
> I'm going to be guilty. Give me time.

The demands, as unintelligible and conflicted as they
appeared, were far too raucous to be consistent with accepted
courtroom decorum. After several warnings, Naptali was
dragged out of the courtroom, all the while asserting, via her
screams, the innocence of her son and the racism in the system.

> *NAPTALI:* This is the People's court. . . . It's racist,
> institutionalize [sic] racist. There is the People's
> court, this is not your court. This court was made for
> the People. . . . Let the record reflect . . . show that
> it's for the People and by the People and this injus-
> tice must stop.

As a mother shouted her militant protests, her son the
perpetrator predicted his certain future. "Give me time now. . . .
She is going to put me guilty," yelled Jamiko. And find him

guilty the court did. After appointing a male attorney to serve as a guardian *ad litem* (a stand-in for a parent), the court found Jamiko guilty of all counts in the robbery petition. Based upon his display in the courtroom and based upon his mother's performance prior to trial, the issue of release or detention was academic. Family support and bonding assured Jamiko's remand to Spofford.

The updated *I & R* told the true tale of Jamiko and his mom. The youth was bounced about from school to school to cover up a hostile and aggressive personality. He was sent to private schools, in and out of New York State, and failed to meet the minimum requirements for academic success. Jamiko Akbar took failure as a way of life. However, he always had his mother to make the right excuses for him.

When the cases concluded, the respondent was placed with DFY for a period not to exceed eighteen months—the maximum allowable placement for a youth whose time in prison is only beginning. Yet Jamiko and Naptali are as persistent in their pursuit of exoneration as they are in their supply of additional excuses. The two filed petitions in the Federal Court seeking damages for violation of civil rights and for a release from placement based upon illegal convictions. Mother and son alleged, among other things, that the illegal convictions caused the youth stress that translates into $350,000.00 in damages. Similarly, they alleged that the youth never received "Mirander"[35] warnings although no confession was extracted from the youth.[36]

The pundits need to be corrected in their bold assertion that family breakdown is the root of America's crime problem and that it holds the key to a solution. The biggest mistake that the experts can make is to suggest that through family unity there is a global solution to the individual problems confronting the juvenile justice system. An intact family was clearly not the answer in the case of Jamiko Akbar. No one will ever know if the youth would have fared better in a foster home away from Naptali Akbar, although her influence on his life helped make him the person he is today.

All that is clear is that somewhere Jamiko and Naptali learned that they could make excuses for criminal behavior. Somewhere they learned that they could blame "the wrong people," or that they could yell "racism" and wait for the system to flinch. At some point, Naptali learned that she could manipulate the judge, the lawyers, the police and everyone else in the name of the federal and state Constitutions. She also learned that terms like "genocide," even in a context of non-applicability to the facts at hand, evoke the fear of alienating the politically correct values of a system gone amuck.

Jamiko Akbar is a common criminal. He may not be New York's next serial killer, but he needs to be told in no uncertain terms that he is the only person who will pay for his criminality.

The key to solving the problems of Jamiko's criminal conduct is not his intact family. Nor are "parenting" classes or family therapy a workable solution. A parent may be loving and giving, but the failure to teach responsibility for a child's own actions is a mother's or father's primary obligation. Failing in this duty, the intact family takes a back seat to the broken home every time.

38.

As Dwayne Jones[37] swallowed, he could feel the lump in his throat. It was there because Dwayne was more afraid now than he had ever been. He had grown up in the rough and tumble neighborhoods of the Bronx, but this was something far more terrifying than the usual encounter with the punks on the corner.

Dwayne could feel the pedal of his bicycle digging into his back as he lay sprawled on the sidewalk. One of the surrounding perps moved behind him and lifted the bicycle up from underneath his body. As he fell to the pavement, Dwayne did not shift his gaze from the gun barrel that was inches from his face. He didn't bother to watch the thief ride off with his bike because he knew these guys meant business.

Just moments before, Dwayne was riding his bicycle at the intersection of Barnes Avenue and 221st Street. The four perps seemed to come from nowhere as they threw him to the ground and demanded the bike. Like stagecoach bandits in a grade-B western, the youths waved their guns in the air as they made their demands. One of the armed youths fired his revolver into the air. The shots rang loudly in Dwayne's ears as he watched the youths hoot and scream with their pistols. This was the best of the Wild West in the Bronx, and unlike the folklore of Dodge City or Bat Masterson, this was real. These kids were the *real* young guns in a society not trapped within the celluloid frames of a Hollywood movie. These adolescent robbers were capable of killing and their victims would really be dead.

Dwayne's fear peaked as the smallest of the boys pushed a revolver into his face. The gun-wielding youth giggled as he watched Dwayne squirm and sweat. Dwayne's face was so close to the snub-nosed handgun that he could see that several of the chambers in the cylinder were empty. But Dwayne still did not move. He wasn't sure that *all* the chambers were empty, and moments earlier, he had seen another youth fire his gun into the air. Besides, a third youth with a semi-automatic pistol in his waistband was still present. Dwayne had no choice but to lie back and stare into the barrel of the black revolver.

Randy Nicholas loved the feeling of power that the gun provided. He stood over his nervous victim and pushed the weapon into his face. He laughed as his teenage prisoner jerked every time he shoved the gun closer. Randy laughed out loud as his young captive squealed the first time he squeezed the trigger of the empty gun. He squeezed the trigger again, and again his hostage flinched. Even an empty weapon brings chills to a begging victim who is never quite sure if the next turn of the cylinder will discharge the final bullet. The victim whimpered as the gun clicked again, and his tormentor reveled in the domination.

The deadly silence was shattered as the first youth fired his weapon into the air again. For a moment Dwayne was not sure whether or not that bullet had come from the revolver that was inches from his face, but the fear quickly turned to relief as his torturers fled the scene.

Dwayne, still in a cold sweat, recognized that he was lucky to be alive. Armed robbery is frightening for every victim and it is even scarier when the perpetrators fire their weapons—even in the air. In Dwayne's case it was far worse because the robbers chose to torture and intimidate. But what was most terrifying about the whole thing, and what frightened Dwayne more than anything else, was the fact that the guy who held the gun in his face could not have been any more than twelve years old. Dwayne knew it was time to move out of the Bronx.

Kids with guns eventually get caught, and Randy was no exception. He was brought before a Family Court judge, who saw the innocent face of a twelve-year-old boy without any criminal record. As the prosecutor told the court of the serious nature of the charges, the court looked down at the short and slight frame of the respondent. "Parole to the mother," said the judge, and Randy Nicholas was free.

Just three weeks after the robbery of Dwayne Jones, Beverly Harper was out shopping in her Bronx neighborhood. It was a warm sunny day in late September, and Beverly wanted to get out in the sunshine to do a few chores. At about 1:00 P.M. she crossed White Plains Road in the vicinity of 225th Street, and headed towards the commercial district with her purse on her shoulder. It was just another day filled with mundane responsibilities. That, unfortunately, was about to change.

As she crossed the street, she saw a young man leaning up against the fence. He was tiny and did not appear threatening. He wore a leather jacket and seemed to be no older than twelve or thirteen years. She noticed him looking at her, but she paid little attention to his stare.

As she approached the young man, she could see the traces of a mustache beginning to form on his adolescent face. When the youth said, "Give me your pocketbook," Mrs. Harper could barely believe that a boy so young would actually attempt such an act. Yet his words became a dark reality when he pulled a silver pistol from his waistband and fired directly at Beverly Harper. There was no further demand. There was no larger threat. He did not even provide sufficient time to turn over the purse. Randy Nicholas just drew his weapon and fired.

Mrs. Harper felt a stinging in her arm and a growing

numbness in her hand. The pop had sounded like a fire-cracker. It was not like the sound she expected to hear at such close range. When she looked down and saw the blood on her arm, Beverly Harper realized that the innocent-looking youth with the baby face had just tried to kill her. While Mrs. Harper felt shock and pain, her attacker ran off.

The juvenile justice system is not equipped to deal with people like Randy Nicholas. Despite the mandate in the Family Court Act that the court shall consider ". . . [T]he need for the protection of the community," the legislature never expected the Family Courts to deal with the homicidal ideations of Randy Nicholas.

The dispositional sections within the juvenile delinquency portion of the Family Court Act are clear and convincing evidence of an impotent statutory scheme. The laws that were designed to rehabilitate as well as protect allow for a maximum initial period of placement of up to eighteen months—on any felony.[38] While the period of placement can be renewed up to an offender's eighteenth birthday, the overcrowding within DFY ensured that a youth like Randy would probably be released prior to serving even one-half of the initial eighteen-month term.

If justice requires that the punishment fit the crime, then the Family Courts of the State of New York are without the power to dispense justice. Under New York's juvenile justice laws, a fifteen-year-old who assaults an elderly victim, or a twelve-year-old who murders for fun, or a youth who attempts to stick up a bodega with a sawed-off shotgun all face a maximum initial "sentence" of a year and a half. It is not beyond the realm of possibilities to have a perpetrator released from *placement* before his victim's wounds have healed. Accountability and level of offense are irrelevant for most prosecutions (and subsequent incarceration) pursuant to the Family Court Act. The felon who kills faces the same initial term of incarceration as the offender who possesses a stolen credit card. Yet the legislature—with either humor or incredulity—has mandated that at disposition the Family Court must consider the need to protect the community.

The absurdly brief placement periods that are supposed to rehabilitate the youth and also provide community protection are, in fact, incapable of accomplishing either objective. New York's Assembly, ever willing to protect those people from whom the rest of society requires protection, has repeatedly refused to lengthen the initial placement periods for the bulk of the juvenile criminals sentenced in the Family Courts. The eighteen-month maximum has endured as the choice of the Assembly since 1962.[39] Thus, the courts have operated with a dispositional scheme that reflects the New York society of more than thirty years past. With all the changes that have taken place in three decades, the Assembly has refused to acknowledge the vast changes among the juvenile criminals before the Family Courts. Unlike the 1960s, today's juvenile delinquency profile is no longer limited to beer-drinking, cigarette-smoking truants who break windows or steal hubcaps. The juvenile delinquent of the 1990s is more likely the gun-toting offender in a city school or the angry adolescent who settles his fights with a firearm instead of a fist. The 1962 laws were—for the most part—focused on the pranks of a teen like the *Happy Days'* "Fonz." They are helpless in affording the courts an ability to confront the challenges posed by the criminal behavior of a Randy Nicholas.

The short periods of incarceration in limited secure facilities[40] are a stark contrast to the recommendations made at Randy Nicholas' dispositional hearing. In an unusual, if not unprecedented, step concerning a recommendation for a twelve-year-old offender, the Department of Probation in the *I & R* recommended that Randy Nicholas be placed in a secure facility.[41] The Probation Officer wrote that Randy ". . . displayed a depraved disregard for human life by recklessly shooting his victim for no provocation during his act of robbery." The officer urged that a secure facility was the least restrictive alternative at disposition because Randy's "prognosis [for rehabilitation was] extremely poor" and that Randy ". . . displays no positive values, goals or motivations and his lack of respect/regard for others makes him a menace to those in the community."

The condemnation in the probation report, however, was mild compared to the recommendations of the forensic psychologist in the *MHS*. The senior psychologist who interviewed Randy Nicholas concluded that the youth ". . . should be considered dangerous. Extreme prudence is advised on the issue of his possible [release from custody]."

The doctor reported that Randy was unable to account for the court's serious finding of guilt against him. He showed no remorse for the shooting and attempted murder of Beverly Harper. The doctor wrote that Randy Nicholas minimized the victim's injury because she did not die. In fact, Randy chose to "flatly" blame his present legal conditions upon the woman he shot because "she got me into all of this."

Regarding the bicycle robbery where he terrorized the victim by repeatedly squeezing the trigger of the unloaded revolver, Randy again displaced his criminal responsibility. He told the psychologist that only one co-perpetrator had a gun and that he ". . . just showed up at the wrong time." He further denied ever possessing a weapon of any kind, at any time, and suggested that he had not been involved in any altercations within the past year.

Like so many of the youths who pass through the juvenile justice system, Randy tested as functionally illiterate. While his intellectual abilities were charitably described as limited, Randy separated himself from the bulk of his peers by an inability "... to anticipate the consequences of his actions." When these features are coupled with Randy Nicholas' "[I]ntolerance for frustration," the result, especially when Randy has a gun in his hand, is all too clear.

After interviewing Randy's mother, the psychologist was sure that placement in a secure facility was the only intelligent option at disposition. The mother, a hard-working single parent, had convinced herself that her son was "... [T]he victim of a judicial process gone awry." She claimed her son had no involvement in the violence of which he stood convicted and that he was a good boy who obeyed curfew and attended school. Although the mother was unable to tell the doctor the name, number or address of her son's school, she was emphatic about the boy's regular attendance. Further, Randy's mother said her son was not in need of therapy, counseling or any support services. He was just fine the way he was.

Unfortunately, all the expert recommendations, evidence and good intentions could not place this pint-sized predator in the appropriate place—prison. Although the juvenile justice laws of the state of New York require that community safety be a factor in the court's decisions, the legislature did not provide for secure facilities to incarcerate the gun-wielding offenders who consistently threaten community safety. Instead, the power of the Family Court is limited to sending a dangerous predator like Randy Nicholas into an open setting. These limited-secure facilities have no locked fences, armed guards or barbed wire. They rely solely upon the "eyeball" supervision of state youth counselors to prevent youths from strolling off grounds. Furthermore, after several months in residential care, violent youths are sent home for unsupervised weekend visits. DFY relies upon the good will of the offenders to voluntarily return to the facility following a weekend pass to the old neighborhood.

Even those who argue in favor of limited-secure facilities for violent adolescents like Randy Nicholas remain unimpressed by DFY's ability to provide custodial care, rehabilitative services and community safety. Violent offenders are released when facility staff believe that "He's as good as he's gonna get."[42] There is no independent parole-type review, nor is there another executive or administrative agency officially charged with overseeing the confidential release policies of DFY. Although charged with the responsibility of community protection, DFY has yet to regularly notify prosecutors, police or civic leaders about their intention to return a violent offender to the community. Availability of bed space alone drives the release policy of DFY. Those charged with the custodial care of the offenders are also charged with population control and parole policy within the facility. Community safety has thus taken a back seat to an intra-agency budget watch and DFY remains unchecked in its ability to return violent offenders to the streets of New York.

During Governor Mario Cuomo's "Decade of the Child," DFY actually lost funding. This led to the early release of offenders who were far from ready for return to the community. The net result is that people like Randy Nicholas, not yet five feet tall and still in early adolescence, will be back sooner on the streets of the Bronx. Perhaps he still has the silver gun that almost killed Beverly Harper. Maybe he knows where to get another black revolver like the one he used to terrorize Dwayne Jones. Despite his low intelligence and severe behavioral problems, Randy Nicholas will probably be released early from DFY to the Bronx neighborhood where he played with firearms at the expense of the residents. The odds also favor that another gun will find its way into the hands of Randy Nicholas. Perhaps next time he steals a bicycle, Randy will make sure the gun is loaded; perhaps the next time he robs a purse, Randy will make sure to leave his victim dead.

The sad and painful truth is that Randy Nicholas will be back before the courts in the very near future. While his reappearance will only show up as another point on the recidivism charts, he will be sentenced for ruining the life of another innocent victim. That victim (or the family of the victim), likely to come from the community where Randy has lived and hunted, can blame the offender as well as the juvenile justice system that should have held Randy in an appropriate facility for an equally appropriate period of time. The early release of an offender with a history of using firearms, and with a diagnosed low level for frustration, is a recipe for robbery, assault and murder.

The best insight into the violent world of Randy Nicholas and into the juvenile justice system that cannot protect the community from him came from Dwayne Jones as he lay sweating on a city sidewalk following the flight of his tormentors. It was time to move out of the Bronx.

39.

Rehabilitation is a bad word. When used in the Family Court, it assumes a fact that is rarely in evidence. In order to *re-habilitate* someone, it is presumed that the person was **"habilitated"** at some previous time. A more appropriate term for purposes of the Family Court is **socialization.** But if the court or the legislature, or any of the myriad of miscellaneous do-goodniks, were to adopt a word like **socialization,** the impossibility of the task would become self-evident. If people running the juvenile justice system were to accept the fact that the bulk of the violent young felons in the courts today need to be **socialized,** from the ground up, then the billions of dollars wasted on counseling and therapy could be properly spent on imposing some kind of structure. Sooner or later, however, when structure through **socialization** becomes impossible, structure through **incarceration** needs to be imposed to protect the community. Juvenile justice experts have yet to accept the simple but sad fact that some offenders are beyond salvation.

Ronald and Ricky needed $10,000. The criminal court judge had ordered $100,000 bail for their friend Sam and had authorized a $10,000 cash alternative. Although Ronald and Ricky testified before the Bronx grand jury that it was they, not Sam, who had robbed the bodega at gunpoint on Christmas, the grand jurors disbelieved their testimony. When the grand jury indicted Sam for the robbery, the judge locked him up in the Bronx House of Detention.

At fifteen Ronald was the youngest of the three boys at Charlene's Bronx apartment that evening. Charlene was Sam's cousin, and she missed him while he was in the Bronx jail. She spoke daily with Sam's wife, Shana, about his incarceration.

Both women talked about getting the bail money for Sam's release. Ten thousand dollars was, however, a large sum of money for two women used to relying upon a public-assistance income.

Charlene had a plan to get the bail money together. Her seventeen-year-old godson, Jamie, had just been released from prison for robbery and possession of drugs. She knew that she could rely on Jamie to help Ronald and Ricky raise the cash. Charlene told the three teens that a dealer on 111th Street in Manhattan always had lots of cash on hand. If the boys could get the money from Buckwheat the dealer, Sam would be released.

At about 10 P.M. the three youths left the Bronx and headed into Manhattan. To arrange the "loan" with Buckwheat, Ricky carried his favorite sawed-off shotgun and Ronald carried a 9 mm pistol. Ricky thought that the shotgun was too heavy to carry on the subway and across town, but his .25 caliber revolver was taken by the cops when he had been arrested the previous week. Ronald's .25 caliber pistol had also been seized during a recent arrest, but he preferred the power and feel of the 9 mm anyway.

The three youths left the subway and walked to East 111th Street. Then they turned west and walked across town toward Buckwheat's place near 8th Avenue. Ricky walked on the north side of 111th street, and the other two took the south side. The neighborhood was dangerous, and these guys knew better than to stick together like one easy target.

As they crossed Seventh Avenue, Jamie saw a familiar figure, an old friend called Crum, run toward him. Crum grabbed Jamie by the collar and demanded his new coat. Recognizing his old partner in crime, Jamie said, "Yo, Crum it's me." When Crum's accomplice appeared from the building at 212 West 111th Street, Crum told Jamie that the past was nothing more than history. He wanted the coat. But Ricky was there to help out. He walked into the middle of 111th Street, opened his long coat to display the shotgun, leveled the weapon at Crum and directed the would-be coat thief to take his hands off Jamie. Ricky's finger slid to the safety on the shotgun, and he let it click to warn Crum that the weapon was ready to shoot. Crum stared into Ricky's eyes and took the challenge. Crum shouted to his accomplice, "Yo, pull out."

It is amazing that the street urchins who continually contribute to the decline of New York are willing to jeopardize their own lives for the price of a coat. Perhaps it is the thrill of a dare or the recognition of their own worthlessness that confirms the trivial value of their existence. In this case, Crum's request to "pull out" was a direction, recognizable to every denizen of doom on the street, to display a weapon. Before the accomplice could reach into his own waistband, Ronald had joined in and held the 9mm pistol 20 inches from Crum's head.

Crum was a veteran of street wars. He didn't even flinch at the muzzle near his neck. His rap sheet was a collection of armed robberies, although his record reflected less than 5 percent of all the felonies he'd committed. He was a brave dude of nineteen who'd had two kids by two women. No fifteen-year-old with a pistol would come between him and the coat he wanted.

Crum's accomplice, hardly as bold or streetwise as Crum, ran into a nearby doorway and disappeared from view. Disregarding his friend's cowardice, Crum demanded that Jamie "Give it up" as he jerked the jacket by the collar. Crum grinned at Ronald and then at Ricky. He wanted the two gun-toting teens to know that he controlled 111th Street and that if anyone was going to do a robbery, it would only be Crum. This gamble would be Crum's last. Coolly and with precision, Ronald squeezed the trigger of the 9 mm. The shot whizzed past Crum's ear as Jamie broke free of Crum's hold and hit the pavement. As Crum turned to run, Ronald took aim again. From less than three feet away, he fired a shot into Crum's left temple. The bullet tore through Crum's brain and exited the other side of his skull. Later, as Ronald bragged to Shana about the killing, he described Crum's last sounds as "screaming like a bitch." Twenty minutes after Ronald fired a 9 mm slug through his head, Crum was DOA at St. Luke's hospital.

As the boys fled from the scene, Ricky wanted to know why Ronald had been so eager to pull the trigger. Ronald explained that although no one had seen Crum move, he was sure the guy was going to "come at [him]." Ricky accepted Ronald's explanation and even said that Crum was stupid to do a robbery without a gun. At seventeen, Ricky spoke with the voice of experience.

The case appeared to be an easy one for the cops. Crum's frightened accomplice knew Jamie from the street, so the detectives had him in the precinct for questioning within hours of the shooting. Jamie, recently paroled from prison, was in no position to bargain with the cops. Any sign of non-cooperation and the cops would have him back in prison before he had finished dialing his lawyer. Jamie told the cops everything he knew about Crum's murder and about their attempt to raise the bail money from Buckwheat. Jamie emphatically told the cops that Ronald was the shooter. He wanted to distance himself (and his tenuous parole) from Crum's killing. It did not matter to Jamie that Ronald had shot Crum to prevent the theft of his coat. One perp's loyalty to another is measured in minutes.

Within twenty-four hours the cops knew the whole story. They did not, however, have enough evidence to convict Ronald at trial. Jamie and Ricky were Ronald's accomplices, so their testimony alone could not convict him.[43] The cops needed to build the case against Ronald by finding other witnesses to the murder of Crum. Since no other witnesses from 111th Street would come forward, the police turned their attention to Shana and Charlene. Rumor had it that Ronald had made incriminating statements to both women. These statements, if they existed, along with the physical evidence would be sufficient to file a provable murder case against Ronald.[44]

The detectives took statements from Charlene and Shana and then got a search warrant for the guns. Unfortunately, the 9 mm that killed Crum was already missing. The cops found the shotgun and some ammunition, but Ronald had gotten rid of his 9 mm pistol. Ronald understood that it's not smart to keep a gun with a "body on it." Despite the fact that he was the youngest among the suspects in the slaying of Crum, it was clear to the cops that Ronald was the one with the most savvy. One of the cops described Ronald as the "scariest little bastard in New York." Ronald would have liked the title.

The detectives were relying on Ronald and Ricky to confess under the pressure of experienced investigators. Ricky, at seventeen, was easy prey for the seasoned detectives. A few minutes into the interrogation, he gave a complete account of the incident. Ronald, on the other hand, proved more difficult. He refused to give a statement to the cops, and despite his youth and inexperience, signed a statement that he refused to answer questions. A team of seasoned detectives with over eighty years of combined investigatory experience could not get the fifteen-year-old punk to waive his rights. His response was short, to the point and better stated than any well-trained criminal defense lawyer could have suggested: "Go fuck yourself." Ronald was released.

The case against Ronald continued to fall apart in the weeks following his refusal to talk to the police. Shortly after her conversation with the police, Shana was murdered in an alleged robbery attempt. While there was no evidence to suggest that Ronald had killed Shana, Charlene would no longer talk to the police. The cops had heard that Ronald had made a videotape for Shana and Charlene detailing his account of the homicide. Supposedly he bragged about the killing and about Crum's squealing immediately after the bullet ripped through his brain. With Shana dead, however, the cops could not find the videotape and were unable to build a provable case against Ronald.

While the murder case was pending, Ronald was arrested for driving a stolen car. He was locked up by the Family Court and was found guilty of a misdemeanor offense. Since the court was aware that the murder investigation was pending, the judge asked for an *MHS* to accompany the usual *I & R*. Placement for Ronald was an unqualified certainty.

The probation officer sat with Ronald in the interview cell, trying to keep the young man's attention. The youth tapped his feet, looked around and displayed annoyance at having to waste his time with the interview. He denied most of the allegations in the car theft petition, although he did acknowledge having been arrested while driving the vehicle. Ronald knew that he was too young to get a driver's license, but he said he "likes to drive." He saw nothing wrong with a fifteen-year-old driving a car through city streets and expressed remorse only for his arrest. While Ronald's mother told the officer that the boy was out of control and in need of placement, the youth was quick to disagree. He thought that he should remain at home to continue to do "whatever he wanted."

Ronald was able to justify everything about his life. When questioned about another recent arrest in the Bronx, the youth happily told the probation officer that a neighborhood teen had said something derogatory about his mother. Thus, he believed he was justified in running up behind the youth and smashing an empty liquor bottle into his skull. If Ronald had had one of his guns with him at the time, he would have settled the matter with more finality. The assault case did not go forward because the victim chose not to appear in court.

Noting that Ronald's "maladaptive" behavior was escalating, the probation officer said that the youth ". . . impresses as a youngster with absolutely no concept as to the seriousness and inappropriateness of his actions." Perhaps that statement is as insightful as anyone could be about Ronald and about his chances for success. The probation officer was careful to point out that when the mother requested placement for Ronald she also asked that none of his friends be allowed to visit him while he was upstate.

The conversation with the psychologist who prepared the *MHS* foreshadows the inevitable failure that will fill Ronald's life. The youth blamed his problems on his parents' divorce and his hanging around with "the wrong crowd." When asked about his legal history, he was able to account for several arrests, but he said nothing about the murder of Crum. When the psychologist raised that incident with the youth, he said he had forgotten all about it. Ronald said that it had happened a long time before—and the murder had just slipped his mind. Besides, he asserted, the cops were going to drop that case for lack of evidence. Ronald then suggested that the real killer of Crum was someone that looked like him.

Both the probation officer and the psychologist recommended residential placement with authorization for a secure facility. The youth, however, stood convicted of "joy riding," only a misdemeanor. Yet the court, the experts and the prosecutor all knew that Ronald was a danger anywhere but in a secure environment.

Ronald was sent to *DFY* and placed in a locked facility. He awaits his release, just one year following the date of his placement. This short period is the maximum initial "sentence" for a youth found guilty of a misdemeanor charge. Somehow the legislature expects the Family Court and the placement agencies to take the violence within a youth like Ronald and convert it to positive energy within twelve months. Either the legislature of the state of New York believes that the court can do miracles, or, more likely, they remain out of touch with the realities of juvenile justice. The results they expect in twelve *months* probably could not be achieved in twelve *years*.

Can Ronald be **rehabilitated?** Only a dreamer or a legislator would suggest such a possibility. Although he still possesses the alleged malleability of youth, Ronald has adopted a criminal lifestyle and street-savvy that would only have been expected of an older, and more hardened, offender. Ronald at fifteen is as hardened as most offenders ever get. He defies the police, terrifies potential witnesses and is able to shoot another man in the head at point-blank range. He is able to laugh at the death throes of a man he has wilfully executed, and he is as comfortable with a high-powered pistol as most youths would be with a baseball bat or roller skates.

The advocates and the legislature will not accept the fact that Ronald is beyond all hope of rehabilitation. His indifference to the pain and killing of others is proof beyond all doubt that Ronald is not—will never be—nor does he want to be—socialized.

DFY is filled with kids like Ronald. Some of them may not have his street-smarts, and many have yet to kill another human being. But most view human life as cheaply as Ronald views it. They cannot be taught the value or sanctity of another person's life—that has to be understood. That understanding comes via nurturing, not via a therapy session in a DFY residential facility.

Perhaps all the money spent on therapy and counseling ought to be diverted into programs that could teach the advocates and the legislators of New York that **rehabilitation** is not a process of mass production. They need to understand that the redemption of an individual comes from within, and that people like Ronald, who have no interest in their own rehabilitation, will never achieve it.

Rehabilitation is an illusion for the advocates and the legislators who have defined a society by postulates on paper rather than by principles of practice. It is quite likely that after Ronald's rehabilitation is finished at DFY he will again walk the streets of New York with another 9 mm pistol in his hand. As once before, he will raise that 9 mm to another man's head and pull the trigger. In fact, having done it before, this time it will be easier. When this occurs, the community can rest assured that New York's legislature will have laws on the books to protect the citizens. They will make sure that Ronald gets sent away for **rehabilitation**—again.

40.

In any proceeding under this article, the court shall consider the needs and best interest of the respondent as well as the need for protection of the community.[45]

. . . [T]he historic purpose of rehabilitation in accordance with the needs and best interests of the child remains a significant (if not primary) factor in deciding delinquency cases.[46] [parentheses in original]

An arsonist is a different breed of offender. There is something very creepy about someone who gets a thrill from watching a building being devoured by flames. Along with pedophiles, serial rapists and animal torture freaks, the arsonists have carved a special niche for themselves in the domain of the depraved.

Arsonists need what the Family Court cannot and will not provide—caging. Attempting to fulfill the mandate of the Family Court Act by attending to a fire-starter's best interests likely ignores the parallel purpose of community protection. Surely a youth who experiments with matches or fireworks is not beyond redemption and may outgrow his affinity for fire. In that case *rehabilitation* occurs with or without the assistance of social service providers. There may be no need for incarceration, and where it is required, that need is removed upon the passage of the violent phase.

But what of the hard-core arsonist? How do we treat the offender who draws energy from the flames he has ignited? What of the youth who stands before the burning building watching the fire engines spray their water and foam on the doomed structure, who feels invigorated and sexually charged by the smell of smoke, the intense heat and the crackling flames?   Do we attempt his *rehabilitation* at the expense of community safety?   Is he a good risk for a community-based program? Do the people of the neighborhood living in wood-frame houses have a lesser expectation of protection because the Family Court's purpose places their safety equal to, or less important than, the arsonist's best interests?

The Family Court Act draws no distinctions among felony offenders in terms of the law's overall purpose. Rehabilitation of the offender is the duty of the state, and that goal must be accomplished within definite (and quite short) periods of time.[47] The serial sex offender and the arsonist are within the same spheres of treatment as the car thief and the pickpocket. To the law and to those who eventually service the offender, the magnitude of the perversion is curiously immaterial. New York State has mandated *rehabilitation* via the assembly line. For each offender beginning *rehabilitation,* there is another being released. Quality control, of course, has been abandoned. Perhaps some lip-service is occasionally paid to special needs via group therapy or "rap sessions," but when overcrowding or expiration of placement forces an offender's release, *rehabilitation* is not a consideration. The public lives and dies with its government's abdication of the public safety obligation.

Michael Abruzzi★ is an arsonist. He is not a kid who merely plays with matches. He is one of the few real arsonists to come through the Family Court system. Michael Abruzzi enjoys fire, and he enjoys watching buildings burn. As far as anyone knows, Michael's arson has not yet killed anyone. He

★ Name and places have been altered.

has caused hundreds of thousands of dollars worth of damage, and it is only a matter of time until he burns a building in which a resident gets trapped. Maybe he will kill an elderly resident who cannot escape the searing heat and smoke. Perhaps an infant will die in the flames as a mother stands helplessly outside her home screaming at firefighters for help that they cannot provide. Maybe he will light a fire and kill himself. One of these events is as certain as tomorrow's sunrise.

It was a cool March afternoon when Richie Lagrima saw Michael Abruzzi on the sidewalk outside his home in Baychester, an upper middle-class community in the northeast corner of Bronx County. The neighborhood is almost all white and Asian, and it is comprised of small neat Cape Cod or colonial-style houses on well-kept lots. At first Richie tried to avoid eye contact with his longtime friend. Richie had seen current changes in Michael that frightened him. He knew about the recent fires in the neighborhood and had heard the rumors that Michael was an arsonist. He also had seen some scary changes in Michael's behavior since he was arrested for the arson at Baychester High School. That was Richie's and Michael's school, and there had been serious damage. Luckily no one had been hurt, but Richie was sure that the circumstances could easily have been different, even fatal.

Lately, Richie had been avoiding Michael partly because his parents did not want him associating with the accused arsonist but mostly because Richie had become afraid of his old friend. So when Michael suggested that they sneak into the public school down the street to "check it out," Richie refused. Instead, the two boys went to the house of another friend to listen to some music and talk. Within an hour, Michael wanted to go out again. The two boys went outside and down the block to the public school Michael had mentioned earlier that afternoon. Michael showed Richie an entrance he had made through a construction fence at the school and dared his friend to enter. Richie refused but promised his friend he would wait outside. About ten minutes later, Michael emerged from the building. He told his friend that nothing had happened inside, but Richie suspected trouble from Michael's grin. As the boys walked through the schoolyard, Richie saw flames oming out of a second-floor classroom. He screamed at Michael about the fire, but the young arsonist fixed a deep stare at the burning building. Richie later told investigators that he heard his friend laugh, in a tone so chilling it was as if the devil himself were laughing. The boys then ran toward the back fence and climbed out of the schoolyard as residents began to shout for the fire department. They ran several hundred yards down the block when Michael told his friend that he wanted to go back and watch. Michael left his friend on the sidewalk and headed back to the burning school as the sirens of the approaching fire trucks blared through Baychester.

The fire caused extensive damage in one classroom. Books and shelves were destroyed, along with the personal property of the children in that class. The room had a stench of smoke that would make the classroom unusable for nearly a year. The walls were smoke-blackened, and water damage was everywhere. The entire room had to be gutted and rebuilt, all to the delight of Michael Abruzzi.

Within minutes of extinguishing the blaze, investigators had determined that this was an arson fire. Neighbors were questioned, and soon the police were looking for Michael Abruzzi. Witnesses put Michael and Richie in the schoolyard at the time of the fire, and another witness saw the two boys as they were climbing the fence out of the schoolyard.

Furthermore, Michael was a suspect in several arson cases, and residents were eager to have the young fire-starter removed from the community.

The next day, fire marshals came to Richie Lagrima's house. Richie wanted to make sure that the police knew he was not responsible for the crime. He told investigators about Michael's forced entry into the school and recounted every detail he knew about the fire. Most of all, he focused on the laugh, Abruzzi's macabre laugh as the flames he initiated shot skyward. Richie would remember that evil sound for the rest of his life.

Despite his initial willingness to talk to investigators, Richie Lagrima was a reluctant witness by the time the case went to trial. Like all the people in the neighborhood, Richie wanted Michael out of Baychester, but also like everyone in the community, he was afraid to testify against Michael. No one wants to cross an arsonist, and Richie and his family were no exception. They could not sleep at night for fear that they would wake to the smell of smoke and the crackling of flames around their house. Michael, they knew, would seek revenge, and they did not want to become his first recorded fatalities.

Michael's father indicated very early on that he refused to authorize his son to plead guilty. The Abruzzi family hired a well-known criminal defense attorney to defend the boy as a last-ditch effort to clear Michael's name via a trial acquittal. They were confident that Richie Lagrima would refuse to testify against his friend. Unfortunately for the Abruzzis, they were wrong on all counts. Police and fire marshals took Richie to court under the threat of a *material witness order*, and the prosecution answered "Ready for trial," to the surprise of everyone seated at the defense table.

Competent counsel can provide a solid defense but cannot change the facts. Richie Lagrima reluctantly told the judge about his friend's forced entry to the school and about seeing the flames in the upstairs classroom. He further described Michael's fascination with the fire, and he gave detailed accounts of Michael's subsequent admissions regarding the blaze. All the while Richie testified, his former friend glared at him from the defense table. Richie nervously shifted about the witness chair, often wondering whether Michael was planning a fiery revenge for his cooperation with police and prosecutors.

The court found Michael Abruzzi guilty of arson and burglary in the torching of the Baychester Elementary School. Despite hours of cross-examination by defense counsel, the evidence presented by the witnesses, especially Richie Lagrima, and by forensic experts, guaranteed proof beyond any doubt that Michael Abruzzi set the fire.

Following the trial, the judge was informed about the pending arson trial relating to the fire at Baychester High School. He was also told of an earlier case that was *adjusted* at *intake*—although the intake report did not make it clear that the matter related to the distribution and possession of fireworks. Nor was the court made aware of the universal fear of Michael Abruzzi in the Baychester community.[48] Such a statement by a prosecutor as grounds for detention, without evidence of individual events to support that claim, would have been improper argument. The court did, however, have the opportunity to evaluate the fear on the face of Richie Lagrima as he testified about his former friend's arson.

The prosecution asked that Michael Abruzzi be *remanded.* The courtroom went silent when this request was made. No one expected that this middle-class Italian boy would go to Spofford. No one really expected the prosecution to ask.

Somehow the reality of his acts, the violence, the damage and the potential for death, did not jibe with the white kid at the defense table. So when this request was made, a mother started crying, a father lowered his head in shame and a defense attorney feigned disgust and disbelief.

Michael's lawyer argued that there were no grounds to remand the youth. The adult court where his other case was pending had released the youth, so that status, he argued, should remain unchanged. Never mind that the circumstances had now been altered by a guilty determination on an arson matter. Instead the lawyer stated that Michael posed no risk to the community and that he was regularly attending school. He failed to point out, however, that the school his client regularly attended was the same school he stood accused of damaging by fire.

Michael, the convicted arsonist, was released by the court. His history of arson was brushed aside because of his roots in the community, his privately retained and well respected attorney, and his pleading parents of middle-class Baychester. Had Michael been poor and black, his ass would have been in *Spofford*.

The juvenile justice system deludes itself daily by pretending to be primarily designed for the rehabilitation of youth. The baseline theory of juvenile justice proposes that no youth is beyond rehabilitation and that a positive change in a youth's direction will start the offender back toward a productive lifestyle. There is no youth that is beyond rehabilitation, so goes the theory, because every youth sentenced in either the Family Court or in the adult criminal system is headed for the rehabilitative services of the Probation Department or DFY. Kids are pushed into schooling, counseling, therapy and/or drug treatment. They are told that they have to overcome the inner violence that was created by a society that has victimized them, a school system that has failed them, a community that has racially or economically labeled them, and a child protective system that has ignored them. Their actions, they learn, are the result of an environment that shapes them, and those who offer treatment employ the negative images of this environment to excuse the conduct. There is no accountability for one's own actions. Popular theory wants to avoid stigmatizing the violent offender by denoting external factors to justify his brutality.

It is in this context that the Abruzzi case disproves the basic maxims of the juvenile justice system. As a young white male of Italian heritage he could hardly lay the blame for his violence on a racist society. Nor could he attribute his violence to the rage of being poor in the ghetto. His neat single-family home in Baychester would not compare to an adolescence in the rough streets of New York. His *alma mater,* Baychester High School, is one of the finest secondary schools in the city of New York. Baychester High School routinely produces students who earn or have been nominated for National Merit Scholarship awards, thus rejecting the fashionable excuse of having the schools fail the child.

Michael is the product of two loving and caring parents. Initially, they may not have been willing to accept their son's guilt, but surely their show of support must be counted toward dedication and commitment from family. Furthermore, unlike most parents of the youths who come through the system, Michael's parents have a stable marriage. There was no evidence of domestic violence in the home, nor was there any concern that Michael had been abused or neglected at any time.

Mr. and Mrs. Abruzzi were apprehensive about the ability of the court to fashion an appropriate disposition for Michael.

After the judge found Michael guilty of arson, they realized that their son was no longer manageable at home, but they were very hesitant about the short-term harm and long-term effects of placement upon Michael. They understood from talking to the court's psychologist and to Michael's psychiatrist that the youth could not remain in the community. Although they perceived Michael to be "spoiled," they also recognized that more trouble for their son was just around the corner. Furthermore, the parents were aware that Michael's attraction to fire would undoubtedly turn deadly in the near future.

It is clear that the parents of Michael Abruzzi were able to realize something about their son that the rehabilitation experts within the juvenile justice system refused to see. They finally recognized that Michael, not the people and place surrounding him, was the true controller of his own fate. Michael had to be held accountable, and Michael would ultimately have to pay the price for his crimes.

In a show of love, respect and strength, the Abruzzi family consented to placing Michael with the Division for Youth. Because he was adjudicated an arsonist, there were no private facilities that would consider taking the boy. Arson is a crime that guarantees rejection from private facilities—they too have an interest in self-preservation.

Michael was sent away from home and remained in placement until his mandatory release at age eighteen. His parents, DFY and his psychiatrist all knew that his release was purely the result of statutory limitations, rather than a sign of rehabilitation. Michael is still an arsonist. He is still dangerous. He is still expected to continue to light fires. He is still expected to kill.

Michael Abruzzi is the product of a home, community

and family that are the antitheses of the popular social theories on the origins of juvenile violence. His case suggests that a youth's disposition toward the perpetration of violence may be innate, or "genetic" (for those interested in fact over politically correct fiction), rather than the product of some external societal policy or prejudice. After years of placement with DFY, Michael is also the product of a rehabilitation system that does not accept the notion of accountability and that places a deadline on the time by which rehabilitation must be accomplished.

Michael Abruzzi is living proof that the popular explanations for the exclusive origins of juvenile violence are steeped in myth.

Guess what? There was another fire in Baychester. . . .

41.

The four men and two women left the bar at closing time. It was 4 A.M., and these folks still wanted to party. One of the guys called a cab service, and within two minutes a van arrived in front of the bar. Everybody was drunk and feeling good. The van driver knew this crew. They were part of a wild crowd from West Harlem, and he was reluctant to take these people into his car. His caution was confirmed when Mike pulled out the revolver and started firing it into the air. He pointed the gun to the sky and started dancing about to the rhythm of the gunshots.

Before the driver could pull away to safety, Hassan pulled the front passenger door open. The driver didn't know this kid, but he could tell that he was trouble. Hassan said something to the driver about being afraid, but the last gunshot drowned out the youth's comment.

The side panel door slid open and the rest of the crew followed Hassan into the van. Bouncing from seat to seat the crew slammed the door shut and somebody yelled "DRIVE!" The van driver, looking to avoid a confrontation with six drunks and a gun, followed orders and stepped on the accelerator.

"Click-click" went the gun as someone squeezed the trigger. "Click-click" again, as the driver realized that the gun was either empty or at least partially loaded. "Click-click" a third time—and the driver felt a chill run down his spine. He wondered if the next squeeze of the trigger would be the last thing he would hear.

"Drive," yelled one of the young men again from the rear.

"Where to?" said the driver.

"Just drive," yelled another.

As the van raced across town on 125th Street, the young men were fumbling with the pistol. They unloaded the spent shells, and in their drunken revelry attempted to load other rounds. All the while, the livery driver nervously shifted his gaze from the street to the gun and back to the street.

Hassan, the young kid in the front passenger seat, reminded the driver to keep his eyes front. "Just keep driving 'til I tell you," said the punk. To enforce that point, the driver felt the muzzle of the gun jammed into his ribs. "We're goin' for a ride," said a voice from the rear. "Keep driving," he continued.

As the driver pleaded with the passengers for his life, he

was rewarded with another shove of the muzzle into his side. "Please" begged the driver, "you can take what you want—just leave me." But the celebrants just laughed at the frightened driver and ordered him to keep going. They could see the sweat on his face, his hands, and all over the back of his shirt. Hassan was so close to the frightened driver that he could actually smell the fear—and Hassan liked that smell.

"Uptown, motherfucker," screamed a voice from the rear.

"No, asshole, go downtown," came another voice.

Again the driver heard the click of the empty gun.

"Damn—can't you load shit?" said someone from the rear. Just then the driver heard the gun open again and someone fiddling with bullets. He focused his attention on the sounds of the bullets slipping into the chambers in the cylinder. Again he wondered whether the bullet being loaded at that very moment would be the one that killed him. He was sure that sooner or later these drunken idiots would load it correctly, and he would be dead.

Once more the driver felt the gun jammed into his ribs. "Now you're mine," said fifteen-year-old Hassan. "I tell you where to go and maybe I won't kill you."

The driver felt sweat on his body and heaviness in his chest as he contemplated his fate. His life depended upon the whims of a drunken crowd led by a teenager. He thought about his family and he wondered whether they would have to identify his body. Would his killers blow his head off? Would he be recognizable? Could his family afford a funeral? Why did he work so hard at such a dangerous job? Was it all worth this? To be killed by drunken punks with no respect for life or law? Did all murder victims feel this way right before they died? He was sick with fear when Hassan yelled "Turn here!"

As the driver turned the corner, the lights from a police car lit up his rear view mirror. The siren offered a welcome relief to a man who was sure death was only a few blocks away. For the predators riding in the van, the party-time atmosphere changed to panic as the blare of the siren grew louder. The gun was shuffled about the car until it landed with a dull thud somewhere in the back. Hassan opened his window and tossed the bullets and spent shells toward the sidewalk. In a matter of seconds the party was over. All the passengers were suddenly sober.

Family Court practice holds the prosecution to a very high standard for the filing of a case. Unlike New York's adult criminal system, where a complaint may be filed by a police officer on behalf of a victim, all juvenile proceedings must be arraigned upon a complaint that contains the statements of actual witnesses. Thus, the inability of a victim to come to court because of injuries sustained in a mugging will not excuse the prosecutor from filing a complete set of charges. Instead, the New York statutes allow the court to hold a pre-petition hearing to continue detention up to four days so that a petition may be filed. At this hearing the court may hold the youth when it finds that the court has jurisdiction.

The terrified driver of the van could not appear in court the day that Hassan McVie was brought before Judge Ned Merchant for a pre-petition hearing. The youth had been arrested for kidnapping the driver of the van and for possession of a loaded firearm. Because the gun needed to be tested for operability and because the driver's statement had yet to be finalized by the prosecution, no formal charges were to be lodged that day. The prosecution was asking Judge Merchant to put the matter over for one day so that the interview with the complainant could be completed.

Judge Ned Merchant is known as "Crazy Neddie" among lawyers practicing regularly in New York's Family Court, because his decisions are insane. As witnesses testify he appears to sit upon the bench listening carefully to each word. His head is bowed in a pensive gesture, and his hand holds his chin like the well-known sculpture, Rodin's "Thinker." But those who know Crazy Neddie can separate his appearance of thought from his ability to process information. Ponderous questions related to some unknown world spring forth from the judge's lips, to the amazement of counsel and witnesses. Bench conferences are called to resolve issues put in play by the court. Most depressing, of course, are the decisions. Win or lose, you lose.

Crazy Neddie's brand of insanity is prominently displayed when he sits in the arraignment part of the Family Court.[49] Proceedings that should take a matter of minutes may last an hour or more to satisfy a point that would be easily decided with the application of a little common sense. But Crazy Neddie likes to takes his time, and everyone else's time as well.

The matter of Hassan McVie was no exception. Before any other judge in the court, there was no question that the level of violence alleged by the police would guarantee a swift and sure order for the secure detention of Hassan McVie. But Crazy Neddie, with uncanny ability to evade the obvious, took the high road and launched into another extra-jurisdictional judicial inquiry.

The cop who arrested Hassan was the first to testify at the pre-petition hearing. He told Crazy Neddie that he was on routine patrol when a call came over the radio about shots being fired from a maroon van. The officer proceeded to the given location and began a pursuit of the speeding van. When he pulled the vehicle over, he told the occupants to exit the vehicle. At that point the officer's partner entered the van and found a .38 caliber revolver in the rear of the vehicle.

The officer then testified that he arrested the youth and his companions for kidnapping and possession of a loaded firearm. The cop continued, telling Judge Merchant that the driver of the van was dispatched to pick up several people in front of a well-known dance club in northern Manhattan. The driver told the officer that upon arriving at the club, one of the youths pulled out the gun and started wildly shooting into the air. The group of young men and women jumped into the livery van and started playing with the gun. They loaded and unloaded the revolver, and they dry-fired the empty pistol. One of the youths then ordered the driver to drive them to an undisclosed location.

The killing of cab and livery drivers in the city of New York is an ever-present event. Drivers literally risk their lives to provide a service that is indispensable to a city as large as New York, yet they continually fall prey to those hungry for a quick cash score. So it was at the time that this matter was being heard, that a number of livery driver killings had made the news. Robberies of cash receipts had left six or seven drivers with bullets in their heads—and the police had no clue as to the identity of the perpetrators. Everyone in the courtroom, attorneys, clerks and court officers, tried to imagine the driver's fear as he contemplated the last few moments of his life. Everyone recognized the probable outcome of those early morning events had the cops not stopped the van. Everyone except Crazy Neddie.

Ignoring the violence, Judge Merchant asked to hear from the mother. Instead of focusing on the gunshots that rang out that evening, Crazy Neddie asked the mother about her employment. Instead of considering the muzzle of a gun shoved into the ribs of a hostage, Crazy Neddie asked the mother about her boyfriend and his relationship with Hassan. Rather than contemplating the purpose for Hassan to toss the bullets and spent shells out of the car, Crazy Neddie asked the youth's mother what time her son finished school every afternoon. Instead of considering the public safety concerns of the citizens of the city of New York, Crazy Neddie released Hassan McVie to the custody of his mother.

Two weeks after Hassan was released by Crazy Neddie, he met Kenny Carter, an acquaintance from the neighborhood, on the street. The two youths had recently quarreled about a coat, and Hassan was determined to resolve the dispute. Hassan reached into his jacket pocket and pulled out a small pistol. He fired a shot from point-blank range into Kenny Carter's head. As the young man lay dying on the street, Hassan discharged another round into the doomed man's body.

Kids and guns are the deadliest combination in urban America. So say the newspapers, the television media, the politicians, the myriad of miscellaneous advocates, the clergy and the community leaders. Yet the people sworn to protect us, like Crazy Neddie Merchant, have not been listening.

42.

The woman asked if she was speaking with the supervisor.

"Yes, I'm the supervisor," was the reply.

"I want to complain about Ms. Smith," said the agitated woman. "My son Elijah was in court yesterday and Ms. Smith was rude—and she lied."

The supervising attorney was used to these complaints. Victims and their families often were unhappy about the results of the case. Perhaps they didn't like the plea, or they may not have approved of a prosecutor's statements in court. But the prosecutor was not expecting this kind of complaint.

"My son was in court yesterday. Your attorney kept telling the judge about my son's other case."

"Wait a second," said the prosecutor. "Was your son arrested? Is he the perpetrator?"

"Yes," came the reply, "and I don't like it when your lawyer lies about my son. She was settin' him up. Them two robberies was both cases of mistaken identity. Wrong place and wrong time."

"Wait a moment, ma'am. I don't think you should be discussing this case with me. I am a prosecutor. You should be discussing complaints with your son's attorney," said the supervisor.

"I can't reach my son's lawyer. He spent all day with your attorney. They make deals. They're probably lovers."

Shit, thought the supervising attorney, why did I take this call? Obviously this woman was more than confused. "Look, ma'am. This is a criminal case. This is not some government agency that runs a program. You just don't talk to the supervisor when you don't like the result. This is a criminal matter. There is a felony charged here. You are hardly the first parent to protest the guilt of your son."

The lawyer continued to tell the woman that it was not wise for her to discuss this matter with him. She would not yield.

"Your lawyer kept talking about my son's other case. Why would she tell this judge about the other case if she was supposed to be prosecuting this new case?"

"Ma'am, your son's legal history is always relevant. Please ask your lawyer."

"I can't talk to my son's lawyer. He won't talk to me any more. You're all in this together. Your attorney keeps talking about the other case, and my son's lawyer won't stop her. Besides, all your lawyer keeps saying is bad stuff about my son."

"We are the prosecution, ma'am. We are not here to praise your son. We are trying to put him in jail."

"Oh. Well that's no help." Click.

43.

They say that education is *the* savior. It is the process by which the offender will turn himself around. It is the key that will unlock all the potential that violent criminals harbor deep within their souls. So goes the theory.

After all, argue the advocates, so many of the young criminals are truant. Surely, this common thread must be a key to a reversal of fortunes for most delinquents. It should be the obligation of the school system to get these young offenders back into the classroom and back into a lifestyle within the law.

Much data supports the belief that youths who attend school will fare better than those who drop out. A recent study completed by the Commonwealth Fund[50] found that urban black youths who dropped out of school were more likely to be arrested. When these young men remained in school, the survey found that they were "systematically more likely to have good support from parents and teachers and positive experiences growing up."[51]

These findings are not, however, logically equivalent with keeping dropouts in school to guarantee—or even significantly increase—the likelihood of their success. Those people who remained in school and did not succumb to the pressures of the street may have had better support networks, stable home lives, and perhaps even more internal fortitude. In any event, remaining in school voluntarily is significantly different from being pushed back into the classroom. Just as rehabilitation requires the criminal offender to desire a change, so too does education need a willingness to learn.

It is sheer folly to assume that all will succeed via the same regimen—whether that regimen is schooling, counseling, intensive therapy or shock incarceration. Many offenders will never be saved by education because they cannot be educated. Schools provide these young criminals with nothing more than opportunities for crimes and further victimization.

Rather than keeping violent offenders *in* school, it makes better sense to keep them *out*. No matter how you calculate the statistics, keeping violent offenders with the general school population endangers the student body by increasing the probability of violent crime. If learning is best in a safe environment, then safety can be better assured by keeping predators out of school. Of course, some will say that expelling students from school will only put them back into the streets and a life of crime. But do these advocates prefer that the offenders remain in school to commit their crimes in hallways and classrooms? Why keep the gun-wielding offender in the locker room or cafeteria as opposed to having him roam throughout the rest of the city? Chances are he will be predatory wherever he happens to be. Are the safety and education of an entire student body worth the small probability that education will lead to some small reform?

Those who advocate for teaching the unteachable fail to look at the obvious factors of life. These young offenders and their families (to whatever extent a family exists) see no value in education. If they are told that education is the route out of poverty, then the road for them is too long. They want fast cash, fast women and the fast life. Unfortunately for them, such a lifestyle means either a fast death or a fast trip to a life in prison.

The advocates refuse to recognize that the young offenders may not have the cognitive ability to compete with their more successful peers. More common than truancy among delinquents is low IQ. Most offenders facing disposition in New York City's Family Courts test well below average in their intellectual functioning.[52] Predation does not take intellect; predatory behavior takes guts and pride. There is plenty of this available in the streets: The Commonwealth study confirms that self-esteem is not a problem among young men in the ghetto.[53]

Naturally, child advocates scorn the mandatory expulsion of any youth from school—even where that youth is a convicted violent felon. When a prior chancellor of the New York City Public Schools wanted to expel violent felony offenders from the high schools, his plan was rejected by the state chancellor of education. New York State does not permit students to be expelled from school—they may only be suspended for short periods (usually five days) after a hearing.[54] All students have a right to be educated, and apparently this is a right—

even in the wake of violent crime—that cannot be waived. It is ironic that in New York violent offenders may waive their right to remain silent, their right to an attorney and their right to a speedy trial (among other constitutional and statutory rights). They just cannot waive their right to a public education.

Education policy wonks suggest that it is necessary to preserve the absolute right to public education. If schools are the path to a rehabilitated offender, then the student must be allowed access to learning. The schools may move him to an alternative program filled with other predators, but they will still try to educate him. More likely, the education mavens will classify him as emotionally disturbed and place him in a special education program. There he can enjoy high teacher to student ratios and special programs and curricula developed on behalf of muggers, robbers, rapists, drug dealers and other nefarious types. Special education costs the city of New York about one billion dollars per year. It is a growing tax burden that is mandated by city, state and federal regulations. Where the regs are not written, the courts—through the perseverance of tireless child advocates—have stepped in to fill in the blanks.

Some educators, however, now support limiting the role of special education. New educational and social theories have moved violent and disruptive children out of their over-priced quarantines and into the regular classroom. The criminals have been educationally *mainstreamed*. Some educators say that in regular classes offenders will avoid the *stigma* and *label* of special education and will have the chance to work with and emulate mainstream children. No one has offered apologies to the regular education students who have to be terrorized by these offenders now in their classes. Nor have the education mainstreamers grappled with the fact that a class can only move as quickly as its slowest students. By bringing in those with the lowest IQ, those behind in reading and math, education's reformers stifle classroom environments for those who want and need to learn. Once again, the rights of an individual have trampled the needs of an entire student body. In the process, public education has been trampled as well.

It is no wonder that the policies of public educators have resulted in the breakdown of public education in urban America. Revisionists have decided to demonize Columbus, just as multiculturalists have chosen superintendents, principals and assistant principals without regard to qualification. Students are taught about civil rights and its leaders—but can they explain the roles of Madison and Jefferson in this genre? In an area unrelated to curriculum, the Manhattan Institute published an article in its *City Journal*,[55] which reported numerous scandals by local school board officials who use their positions for money, political power and higher public office.[56]

The students who want to lean will never be taught so long as the qualifications for teaching and administrative positions exclude scholastic competence. Principals who cannot spell do not belong in primary and secondary educational institutions. People who have been passed through the educational institutions of New York and other big cities as a means to accommodate their attendance—rather than to acknowledge their academic performance—should not be teachers and principals. People who are intellectually disadvantaged should not be teaching—even in special education.

Unfortunately, too much of what ought not to be is already established. When Darnell Papp[57] was arrested for a robbery he committed in his junior high school, the principal came to his defense.[58] The principal wrote the prosecutors a letter on office stationery alleging that a school investigation found Darnell to be a minor participant in the crime. It further minimized the crime by suggesting that only a small sum of money was stolen and that a charge of robbery tended to blow the incident out of proportion. The letter recommended that the case be dismissed.

It was not the fact that the principal wrote the letter that angered and amused the entire prosecutor's office. Letters on behalf of students come from educators regularly, although usually in support of the student's character. It was wrong for the principal to request dismissal of the case, and it was inappropriate to suggest his own version of the facts as the absolute truth. But the issue for the prosecutor's office was the quality of the letter itself. The letter, written without an appropriate salutation, was a conglomeration of spelling errors, bad grammar and general illiteracy.

The body of the letter—exactly as it was written—is contained below. Apologies are offered to the reader because it will take time to decipher the content.

As the principal of JHS—I am writing you on behalf of Darnell Papp, a student in my school. Darnell is being put through the court system do to the involvement of a theft for $1.00. Darnell was present during the time of this robery, however he was not the main culpritnore shuld he be charged based on the schools investigation. Darnell was traveling home with a friend, Mario when the robery took place. Mario doesn't go to JHS—, however, Darnell is being charged for the theft and I feel this is being blown out of porportion and for the courts to have to address such a minute situation.

Mrs. Papp, Darnell's mother does not have the time on her job to report to court. She already has come to court on two occassions and the complaintant was not present.

It is my recommendation that this case be dismissed thd thrown out of court based on the school's investigation.

If you have any questions or concerns please feel free to contact me at the above address and phone number.

The letter was signed by the principal and FAXed to the prosecutor's office. An original mailed copy was received by the prosecutor several days later.

The fact that the principal minimized the crime (there was no concern for the victim in the letter), and then requested dismissal based upon his own investigation, warranted a response. Yet the poor spelling and the lack of sentence structure demanded more than a prosecutor's rebuke. The following is the body of a letter sent to the chancellor as a response from the prosecutor:

My office is responsible for the prosecution of juvenile crime in the City of New York. One of the cases being investigated by my office is an alleged robbery committed by Darnell Papp, a student at Jr. High School. The assistant assigned to handle the matter received the annexed letter this past Friday.

I am aware that the schools are often asked to provide services that extend beyond their primary educational role. Schools have often taken advocacy positions in court cases where teachers and principals believe that they can help implement a particular disposition or sentence. The annexed letter, however, extends the role of the school official beyond appropriate advocacy. The letter recommends that the prosecution discontinue this case because the principal cannot comprehend the meaning of accomplice liability or the procedures within the criminal justice system.

Just as I would not, in my official capacity, challenge the development of curriculum, I also suggest that your principal is out of line in his assessments and recommendations. In his barely literate communication, [the principal] has minimized an event that may have been very frightening to the victim. It is also clear from his letter that he has a very limited knowledge of the facts.

I suggest that Principal—remove himself from the role of advocate, and perhaps use this energy to sharpen his own writing skills.

A short note from an aide to the chancellor was sent to the prosecution indicating that the matter would be investigated.

While the letter from the principal lacks the clarity that one would expect from an average sixth grader, the letter makes many things about the quality of public education in New York City all too clear. Students will not learn to read and write from illiterates. They will, however, learn that illiterates can be given prestigious and well-paying positions in the public schools based on every criterion but the quality of their academic capabilities. This is obviously a lesson that New York's public schools teach quite well, and perhaps it is why they deem it appropriate to keep violent offenders in the classroom. This is the one lesson that can give them hope without any need to change their behavior.

Part 2

The Law

44.

Everybody has an agenda. The prosecutors have their agenda, the defense attorneys have their agenda, and even the judges have an agenda. A trial is the time when agendas clash in a courtroom. The central issue at a criminal trial may well be the crime or crimes for which a defendant stands charged, but much of the time is consumed by the presentation of partisan agendas. "Public safety" routinely squares off against "individual rights." "Congested calendars" are pitted against "due process." Sidebars (the conversations held at the *bench* among prosecutor, defense attorney and judge), often have accusatory undercurrents. Everyone at sidebar places blame on the other side, thus prolonging the hearing well beyond its appropriate conclusion. The conferences at sidebar often stretch the limits of common courtesy beyond the breaking point. The muted whispers at sidebar belie the passion employed by trial lawyers in support of their agendas.

The American Bar Association has promulgated standards of conduct for lawyers within the criminal justice system. Although these rules are merely guidelines, they are cited with binding authority. Within these standards are the rules for the defense bar and for the prosecution.

"The duty of the prosecutor is to seek justice, not merely to convict." It is with these words that the defense bar (through their control of the Bar Association) has defined the role of the prosecutor. Virtually all aspiring prosecutors fresh out of law school know these words and cite them as gospel. Most veteran prosecutors cite them with a smile.

The system, designed to promote and encourage fictions about the perpetrators, also develops fantasy roles for its protagonists. How many bureau chiefs in the prosecutor's office would be content to hear that a staff attorney had dismissed seventeen felony cases in one week but was convinced justice was done? How many participants would be satisfied knowing that a case so carefully and tirelessly prepared was dismissed in the "interests of justice"? Trial lawyers, of whom prosecutors are a subset, are fierce competitors. They do not accept defeat gracefully, even if the ABA thinks it is ethical.

Although the "duty" of the prosecutor may not be to convict, it is surely his or her *job*. From the moment a case enters a complaint room, a prosecutor is looking for a conviction. The equities of a case, especially mitigating circumstances, are not readily apparent as the prosecutor drafts the complaint, interviews the victim and develops a trial strategy. Trial work is battle, and nobody goes into battle with a notion that fairness must come before victory. Because the prosecutor seeks to punish the transgressor for his or her violence, experience and common sense say that punishment and retribution are inextricably linked. The prosecutor who denies a component of vengeance in his work either lies or refuses to admit the truth about himself. The ABA and the public expect honesty of every prosecutor, and it should also be expected that he or she be candid about the job description. There is nothing unethical about believing that the good guy should get the bad guy every time.

The prosecutor is the only voice for the victim in the criminal justice system. Purists will argue that the people of the state are really the aggrieved party and that the complainant is just another witness in a case. Such an analysis tends to obscure the purpose of criminal proceedings as much as it misrepresents the role of the prosecutor. It is the prosecutor who puts the victim on the stand to tell the story. It is generally the victim's evidence that gets considered when it comes time to weigh culpability, and it is during questioning by the prosecutor that the victim gets to point at his or her attacker in the courtroom to say, "That's the one."

In truth, the identification at trial is the victim's moment of revenge. It is the victim's only opportunity to point to the attacker and tell the world that the defendant is a criminal. There is retribution in this act, and the actual process of identification is prepared again and again (along with other testimony) in the prosecutor's office. Thus, it is the prosecutor who sets the table for the victim's courthouse vengeance. While this role is understood by the practicing bar, it remains unrecognized in the ABA's standards for professional conduct.

The standards of conduct promulgated for the defense bar are unambiguous. Defense counsel is not bound to do justice. Rather there is a duty to the administration of justice—to represent the accused with courage and devotion. Effective, quality representation must be rendered and guided by the standards of professional conduct. In other words, doing whatever is legal to secure an acquittal is the agenda of the defense attorney.

According to the ABA's rules, the defense attorney provides a check on the court and the prosecutor. In seeking acquittal, the prosecutor is challenged, and often the court is challenged as well, at virtually every turn. The defense is bound to "stimulate efforts at remedial action" when "inadequacies or injustices in the . . . law" appears. Roughly translated, the ABA's guidelines designate defense counsel as the guarantor of due process and a fair trial.

In practice, however, a "fair" trial has come to mean that

the defendant must be afforded a sporting chance at winning acquittal. Rules of evidence are twisted, turned and manipulated until the court is satisfied that the facts are *fair*—but not necessarily *true*. For instance, recalling the grisly facts at a criminal trial via photographs of the victim may provide an accurate picture of the crime, but courts are reluctant to admit such evidence. Although true, the evidence is excluded because its prejudicial effect may outweigh its probative value. It is irrelevant that the details accurately describe the agony and torture experienced by the victim. A trial is not, contrary to popular myth, a "search for the truth." It is a sanitized version of the events that have passed all the evidentiary smell tests for admissibility.

The logical question becomes: *At what point is a trial absolutely fair?* Since new law is made every day by adherence to, and building upon precedent, the quest for a "fair trial" continues from one case to the next. When the defense bar earns a major procedural victory from an appellate court, it seeks to apply the case to future proceedings with the hope of broadening its application. Thus the quest for the "fair trial" is a process of evolution where the challenger's limit will never be reached. Expansion of the defendant's substantive and procedural rights is proffered until a court finally accepts an argument. There is no incentive for defense counsel not to proceed with this agenda, since the rejection of any argument, without respect to its frivolous nature, has no consequences. The proponent is free to try again in the next case before another court and may continue to do so until a sympathetic judicial ear is found. Thus, it is clear that the only trial that can be deemed fair, where defense counsel no longer seeks to challenge the proceedings, is the trial that guarantees acquittal. So much for a "search for the truth."

So long as we resolve cases by trial, competing agendas will continue to clash in the courtroom. At times, the underlying proceeding takes a back seat to the sparring agendas of the court, the prosecutor and the defense attorney. "Prosecutorial misconduct" is the indictment regularly advanced by defense counsel, in keeping with the theory that the best defense is a good offense. There is irony in accusing the DA and the police of wrongdoing when the person making that charge stands at the table next to his client, the felon. The trial may concern the brutal rape of a child or the savage murder of a young mother. But the court's focus is routinely deflected away from the central issue toward an allegation of a violation of legal protocol. The defense may demand dismissal because the officer was too rough during the arrest or because the prosecutor withheld a piece of paper that seems inconsistent with innocence to everyone but the defendant's legal advocate. In every criminal case, the state is on trial along with the defendant. The police, the prosecutor and even the courts are perpetually accused of miscreancy by the one who stands indicted for the violent crime. Usually, the judges and jurors see through the smoke and the case proceeds over the defense attorney's objection. Of course, the matter is hardly settled. Upon an unfavorable ruling from the court, the defendant may choose to appeal. Sometimes, however, the court joins the procedural free-for-all and punishes the prosecutor. Whether it is by suppression of evidence, exclusion of testimony or by total dismissal of all charges, in some way the state's case will suffer because of an official's gaffe.

The charges by defense counsel of illegal behavior on the part of prosecutors and police are standard practice of the criminal defense bar. Motions alleging violations of constitutional rights are routinely filed by defense attorneys. They seek to "punish" the prosecutor for the police officer's bad search, the coerced confession, or the undercover cop's inaccurate application for a search warrant. The integrity of the justice system is always placed in issue, well before the accused is ever placed in jeopardy, by the one we have curiously dubbed "defense" counsel. Through it all, the system's ironies are again too clear as the deeds of the defendant are ignored in the preliminary litmus test of prosecution and police behavior. Failing that test, the prosecutor's case is stunted because the community must be punished. We are told that this procedure is part of our civilized notion of "justice."

As the defendant leaves the courthouse as a result of our "error," we are asked to celebrate this "justice." We have been taught that this is the price we pay for freedom. We have signaled the offenders that their violence is less culpable than the mistakes of their accusers. Our courts will sooner excuse the murderer for his or her crime than the officer who searches him with less than probable cause. For the defense attorney, it is the triumph of his agenda. For the criminal, it is an invitation to repeat the crime. For the community, it is the perpetration of a lie.

Competing agendas reach beyond the four walls of the courtroom. They prominently clash in the lawyer's safe haven, the bar associations. Dubbed as public service organizations that serve the community as well as the profession, bar associations are really unregistered lobbyists on behalf of the lawyer's agendas. For all practical purposes, the bar association is the lawyers' union. Bar associations form committees that investigate the agendas by giving them the opportunity to clash at their meetings. Rarely ideologically balanced, these committees generally have recommendations and opinions ready well before the facts have been gathered. The winning agenda is always assured by the ideological majority on that committee. After all the facts are gathered, the members of the committee bend, distort, delete and ignore the relevant facts—much the same as government commissions—so that they can reach a conclusion and then write a report that supports an agenda. These reports are often sent to legislators, governors and even presidents.

Prosecutors often join bar associations, but rarely are they able to exercise sufficient control of the issues. Except for those associations that cater to prosecutors (e.g., National District Attorneys Association), the criminal justice sections of the bar associations are predominantly comprised of defense attorneys. The defense bar is generally better paid, and the bar associations respond well to those who pay dues and make bigger contributions. Thus, prosecutors asked to speak at association meetings are often met with contempt, skepticism and distrust. Contrary to popular myths, career prosecutors and defense attorneys do not trust one another. Although they may, in some instances, like one another, they don't routinely walk out of the courthouse together to consume a liquid lunch or to share "war stories." This is not "L.A. Law." This is real life. Prosecutors and defense attorneys each sit with their agendas on their own side of the fence. This holds true whether they are in the courtroom or at the committee meetings of the bar associations.

When a local New York bar group invited a Family Court prosecutor to talk about the problems facing juvenile justice for the 1990s, the presentation was marked by a clash of agendas. The prosecutor was asked to present to the group the inherent problems of the absolute speedy trial rule in Family Court delinquency proceedings and to offer a solution. As a way of introducing the topic, the prosecutor chose to give an overview of the changing face of juvenile crime. Graphs were distributed that showed the near threefold jump in robberies, the sixfold increase in loaded gun cases and the rise in felony assault cases covering the prior six years. When this change in the caseload was presented in the context of an absolute speedy trial rule, the results were the loss of serious felony matters. It seemed, said the prosecutor, that these violent offenses should not be dismissed for speedy trial violations as a result of the offender's own failure to appear in court. Yet this was exactly what was happening following the Court of Appeals' decisions relating to speedy trial for young offenders.

What seems like common sense to some prosecutors may be a declaration of war to the defense bar. Defense lawyers may want their streets safe and their homes secure, but taking appropriate steps to impose these conditions seems inconsistent with their agenda. These attorneys expect their own community's schools to be centers of learning rather than zones of conflict. Therefore, much of the defense bar has taken the logical step of ensuring this desire. They have moved to the suburbs or placed their children in private schools. The calls for police restraint, for understanding instead of punishment and for community-based programs instead of incarceration are being trumpeted by many who have abandoned the community long ago. The bar association's forum gives the suburban attorney a chance to be the liberal social engineer— just one that doesn't have to live with the consequences of one's idealism.

In bar association tradition, one prosecutor presented his agenda to a large audience of defense attorneys. Disregarding this unbalanced breakdown of ideology and that the outcome of the evening was therefore predetermined, the prosecutor presented legislation that would toll the speedy trial time while a youth remained "out" on a warrant.

The defense response was expected. They began the presentation of their agenda with a familiar attack on the prosecution by alleging the unfair use of "scare tactics" (distributing the graphs that showed the actual increase in violent juvenile crime). They continued by calling for investment in prevention initiatives rather than incarceration. One attorney suggested that the graphs clearly showed that crime had increased as the economic climate of the late 1980s and the early 1990s stagnated; another attorney suggested that the numbers were the result of a failure to address social problems that culminated in minority over-representation in the criminal justice system. Not one defense attorney found fault with the offender. They were willing to condemn the crime but not the criminal. Fault and accountability are not part of that agenda.

At what point does a professional agenda take control of an individual's thought processes? When does a lawyer put aside civic concerns in favor of the promotion of their agenda? When did the primary purpose of the criminal courts cease to be the security of the society? When did we accept an agenda that promotes the deflection of individual accountability? That night at the bar association, bias, racism, class struggles and Reaganomics were the defense counsel's agenda. Individual responsibility was lost in the familiar attempt to find another place to put the blame. It never occurred to anyone in the audience that a youth with a gun can also kill lawyers. A lawyer's family is as easily cut down by a stray bullet as anyone else. Nor did anyone consider the possibility that the increase in felony assaults by kids could touch their lives, at least those few whose lives took them home on the subway rather than in a Lexus.

The defense bar pushed its agenda by supporting more community-based alternatives to incarceration. Suddenly those who ushered in a wave of social spending in the 1960s and 1970s had become fiscal conservatives. Prison costs, they warned, were way too high, and New York could no longer afford to keep putting offenders behind bars. Probation alternatives had to be instituted. Yet no one has been able to explain how keeping convicted felons in the community could better protect our society. Even when the rhetoric confirms that all community-based programs should not place additional risks on public safety, there can be no assurance that such a goal can be achieved in the absence of a locked cell.

Is there an alternative to incarceration? There are many when you are not planning for your own community.

It is not clear how long the city of New York can withstand the competing agendas of the lawyers and the community service of the bar associations. Big government, absolution from personal accountability and more offenders on the street are good business for the private defense bar. It means that they can all make enough money to live in Scarsdale.

45.

For ten years New York's highest court conferred special protection on the habitual felony offender. Without regard for public safety, and with contempt for common sense, the New

York Court of Appeals, behind the shield of the state constitution, gave recidivist felons an arsenal in the continuing war
of suppression. If the court's actions had been codified by a
legislature, the bill would have been known as the *Habitual
Felony Offender Protection Act.*

The old saying goes that hard cases make very bad law.
New York's law on the right to counsel for criminal defendants got very bad upon the extension of that right in *People
v. Rogers.*[59] Actually, the decision in *Rogers* was predictable. The
cops were interrogating Mr. Rogers about a robbery when his
lawyer phoned the precinct and demanded that the questioning cease. The questioning did cease—at least with respect to
that robbery—but the police continued to interrogate the
defendant about *unrelated* crimes. The Court of Appeals suppressed these statements and found that the police had violated the defendant's right to counsel, although the lawyer (at the
time of his phone call) did not represent the defendant on the
unrelated cases. Clearly, as a matter of fairness the cops had
crossed the line. The attorney knew nothing of the subsequent
interrogation and presumably would have instructed his client
not to speak with the police. Once a lawyer enters the case, or
even upon an assertion of the right to counsel, the defendant
may not waive counsel except in the presence of the attorney.
In the *Rogers* case, the result seemed evident.

The Court of Appeals, however, was not satisfied letting
Rogers serve as the outer limits of a defendant's right to counsel. Two years later, they decided *People v. Bartolomeo*[60] and set
a new standard for protecting the violent criminal. Peter
Bartolomeo was arrested in late May of 1978 for a bur-
glary/arson. He was arraigned in court and represented by
counsel at that proceeding. Nine days later, he was picked up
by police (a different officer from the same county police

department) and questioned about a murder from that previous April. Without any reference to his attorney on the arson case, Peter Bartolomeo waived his right to a lawyer and confessed to detectives his fatal shooting of the victim earlier that year. He was convicted at trial of murder, and that conviction was affirmed by the Appellate Division. The Court of Appeals threw out the confession, and with it, the murder conviction.

Peculiarly, there was no evidence to suggest that the cops who questioned Bartolomeo knew anything about his representation by counsel on the earlier case. Despite the lack of knowledge on the part of the police about counsel's role in the unrelated case, the court suppressed the murder confession by expanding the scope of the *Rogers* rule. The Court of Appeals imposed a duty upon the police to make an additional inquiry—that is, they should have asked Bartolomeo about the status of his case and whether or not he had retained counsel on the unrelated matter. Lawyers had become an umbrella to cover all the crimes of their clients, and the police were duty bound to explore the coverage. Knowledge was imputed to the police, so they *had* to ask. In effect, the court added another requirement within the *Miranda* warnings by holding that police had to ask perps about their prior cases.[61]

> . . . Hence, the interrogating detectives here, with actual knowledge of the outstanding arson charge against defendant, were under an obligation to inquire whether defendant was represented by an attorney on that charge. Having failed to make such inquiry, the officers were chargeable with what such an inquiry would have disclosed—namely, that the defendant did have an attorney acting on his behalf. With such knowledge they were foreclosed either

from questioning defendant or from accepting his waiver of counsel's assistance unless his attorney was then present. It was therefore error to deny suppression of testimony as to the statements made by defendant at the Suffolk County police station on June 5, 1978. For this reason, defendant's conviction must be vacated. [62]

Thus repeat offenders—who committed crimes while out on bail or released in their own recognizance—reaped the benefit of a blanket protection of counsel. The recidivist had become free from the possibility of police interrogation. Since the defendant's right to counsel could be waived only in the presence of the lawyer, the predicate felon was granted immunity from interrogation by the *Bartolomeo* decision.

The impact of the decision was not lost on all the members of the court. A stinging dissent noted that the benefits of the protections were vastly outweighed by the burden on law enforcement.

> . . . It is already the law that a suspect must be clearly told that he may refuse to say anything in the absence of his attorney. To say that the police must do more than this carries the right to counsel to unheard of extremes.

> It is the common criminal, not the one-time offender, who nearly always will manage to have at least one serious charge pending, so that the attorney in the picture can provide him with virtual immunity from questioning in subsequent investigations. I had thought it clear that although our courts are

sometimes required to let the guilty go free, this is not because the Constitution serves only the miscreant, but rather because our constitutional protections must apply evenly to us all. By its analysis I believe the majority has turned this basic principle completely around by providing what is in effect a dispensation for the persistent offender.[63]

The *Bartolomeo* decade ushered in a period of trivial distinctions by which the court slowly backed away from the impact of the decision. Of course there were casualties. A young offender, with a few juvenile cases in Family Court, confessed to twenty-six burglaries and an arson that destroyed a row of stores in Harlem. The magnitude of the damage that he had wrought was only overshadowed by the senseless suppression of these confessions. They were made within weeks of the *Bartolomeo* decision, and every offense was lost. The convictions on these cases were as illusory as the logic that excused them. Yet time began to prove to the trial courts, and to the Appellate Divisions, that *Bartolomeo* was unworkable. The dissenters were right.

Courts began to look for any loophole that would exempt them from the reach of *Bartolomeo*. A convicted defendant could not claim representation by counsel while the matter was on appeal. "Counsel," they opined, referred only to *trial* counsel.[64] In a set of facts similar to *Bartolomeo,* the court refused to suppress the statements of a defendant interrogated by the same police department that arrested him two months earlier. The court would not *infer* knowledge of that prior representation.[65] Later, the Court decided that the police must have *actual* knowledge of representation by counsel on the prior case in order to trigger suppression.[66] The burden of proving police knowledge of counsel's appearance was placed upon the defendant.[67]

In *People v. Bertolo*,[68] the Court of Appeals embarked on a giant retreat from the original principles of *Bartolomeo*. The court held that where the prior case was only a minor offense, the police could reasonably assume that the case was resolved in a short time. Again, actual knowledge of representation was required. Although a victory for prosecutors, the *Bertolo* matter is the most puzzling decision in this line of cases. While it limits *Bartolomeo's* overbroad application of the right to counsel, it holds that where prior offenses are minor (and somewhat remote in time), the police need not check the disposition of the case. Since minor offenses are disposed of quickly, the cops are free to assume that an old arrest for a minor offense has probably been adjudicated. Therefore, the counsel issue was nonexistent, since the court created a presumption that the offender is no longer represented. Yet looking at *Bertolo* from another angle, one can suggest that it took *Bartolomeo* to its most illogical and insidious conclusion. Since *Bertolo* only related to prior *minor* offenses, previous felonies were not covered by the exception. Thus, the New York Court of Appeals, in *Bertolo,* gave recidivist felons special privileged status. *Bartolomeo* was no longer just the product of a court that was soft on crime, it had become the product of a court that encouraged criminals to commit the most serious offenses.

A senior trial judge in Manhattan summed up the prevailing views on *Bartolomeo.* With total disregard for the binding force of appellate rulings—and with apparent contempt for the Court of Appeals—he referred in open court to the *Bartolomeo* case as a "damn fool decision."[69] Wiser words were never uttered.

In July of 1990, a divided Court of Appeals overruled

Bartolomeo in *People v. Bing.*[70] After a decade of suppressing the statements of New York's worst, the Court of Appeals—in an unusual display of common sense—rejected *Bartolomeo* as unsound policy.

> The appeals [presently before the court] demonstrate graphically the recurring problems we have had with the *Bartolomeo* rule. When it is applied to the circumstances in each case, the result is not only unworkable but it imposes an unacceptable burden on law enforcement. Nor can the results be avoided by modifying or creating exceptions to the rule without undermining its rationale. We conclude, therefore, that a fundamental change is required and, notwithstanding compelling concerns of stare decisis, we hold that *People v. Bartolomeo* should be overruled.[71]

In support of the reversal, the court's majority relied upon the words of the dissenters in *Bartolomeo.* Only now, the court could use history to prove that the concerns of the dissenters had in fact become an all too real nightmare. ". . . [T]he court, without apparent reason, had provided a 'dispensation' for persistent offenders. . . ."[72]

> This failure to elaborate the basis for the rule, and the questionable policy behind it, were to cause considerable difficulty in subsequent cases as the court tried to integrate the decision into existing law. Its application became uneven, introducing uncertainty into the rule itself and destabilizing the law on the

right to counsel in general.[73]

Bing was not an easy victory for the prosecution. Like *Bartolomeo,* it was a four to three decision. The Court's minority issued a strong dissent, urging the majority not to dispense so easily with settled precedent.

> Not often in our history have we explicitly overruled a recent precedent, and rarely *if ever* have we done so by a closely divided court.[74] Perhaps even more disturbing than the extraordinary step of overturning *Bartolomeo*—wrong and unnecessary as it is to do so—is that it cannot help but unsettle the belief "that bedrock principles are founded in the law rather than in the proclivities of individuals." [cite omitted][75]

Not surprisingly, the minority opinion in *Bing* was authored by Judge Judith Kaye and joined by Judge Fritz Alexander and the antiprosecution judge, Vito Titone. Also not surprising, Sol Wachtler (author of the *Bartolomeo* dissent), joined in the decision to overrule *Bartolomeo.* Despite the call to honor *stare decisis* and the immortality of the law, sometimes common sense must rule. Unfortunately, *Bing* was more of an exception to that rule than everyday practice.

Ten years of *Bartolomeo* took a tremendous toll upon the State of New York. Peter Bartolomeo was not the only convicted murderer to have his conviction vacated,[76] and there is no way to measure how many convictions and charges were lost because the police had their hands tied. We can never know how many felons enjoyed the protection of *Bartolomeo* by relying upon the immunity created by their recidivism.

Sometimes it takes a decade to get a court to apply common sense. Most of the time, it takes longer.

46.

Stigma. Everything in the juvenile system centers on that word. The purpose of confidentiality is to avoid *stigmatization* of the youthful offender. We keep the records of these young offenders separate from adult records to prevent a *stigma* from attaching to that child. We want to protect our young offenders from the scrutiny of the general public. We hope that a youthful error will not prevent a person from going to college, getting a good job and raising a family. If we *stigmatize* our youths, the theory suggests that hope for reform is lost. This philosophy is everywhere.

The theory flourishes in the legislature of the State of New York. Rather than pass a bill in 1986 that would have expanded the rights of the police to fingerprint juvenile felons, the chair of the State Assembly's Committee on Children and Families declared his opposition to the fingerprinting of young offenders. He said that the process would tend to *"stigmatize"* youths. According to him, the cops and the courts would just have to find another way to keep track of violent kids. Fingerprints mean permanent records, and our lawmakers apparently don't want police and prosecutors to keep an effective watch on those who are violent.

A logical question for this legislator, and all others who subscribe to this theory, is *who* is being stigmatized (assuming fingerprinting has that effect)? In New York, the state legislature doesn't allow police and prosecutors to fingerprint kids with loaded guns. The youth with an Uzi or Tech-9 in class may be arrested, but he will have no state record. After all, the legislators don't want to stigmatize people who carry guns in school. In fact, a kid arrested for gun possession in Brooklyn on Thursday, can get arrested for a second gun in Queens the following week. If he gives the cops two different names, chances are he won't be found out. But at least the chairman of the Assembly's Children and Families Committee can remain confident that this offender will not suffer *stigma*.

Who else must be saved from this terrible *stigma?* The youths who rampage around the streets and through the trains inflicting serious physical injury for fun can't be printed either. Or the kid who shoots his classmate/friend/mother/enemy, causing physical injury, this offender also can't be fingerprinted. Assault of a police officer by a juvenile is not a fingerprintable offense in the State of New York. The cops can't print the young felony sex abuser or the kid who commits "strong-arm" robberies in our streets and schools. These offenders have been spared the *stigma* of a record of their offenses. As far as the criminal justice archives are concerned, these people have never been offenders. Should they later commit a fingerprintable offense, or should they be arrested as an adult, they won't be *stigmatized* as a recidivist. They will enjoy the protections afforded first offenders, courtesy of the New York State Assembly. As first-timers these offenders will likely be placed on probation and then released back into the streets. Their records may even be sealed—so that we don't *stigmatize* the (recidivist) "first-time" criminal. Perhaps the

New York State Assembly does not care that by precluding *stigma* they have encouraged a criminal justice system that keeps its judges and prosecutors ignorant of an offender's past.

All new government employees are fingerprinted. Are they *stigmatized* by this process? The prospective college student taking the SAT is printed, as is the future lawyer before the LSAT exam. Armed forces personnel are also fingerprinted. Only the young felons of the State of New York have been spared this heinous process. Only the people who will go on to rob, rape and murder in our streets remain unknown to the government. The people sworn to protect and represent the public have turned their backs on their obligation. The State of New York does not know how many gun-wielding youths are in our streets because the legislature doesn't want to know. When the opportunity was there, it was thrown away.

Stigma. Is it wrong to label someone a criminal who carries a gun in to a school? Should we condemn as wrong the violent gangs that see assault as sport? Should offenders know that their acts will not be tolerated by the citizens of the state? Should we not single out those who have committed violence because they must learn that violence has consequences—for the offender?

Stigma. The New York State Assembly has accomplished its goal. We do not *stigmatize* offenders in the juvenile system. We do not cast blame in the juvenile system. The Family Court does not punish, and it does not require accountability. We don't even allow the police and the courts to keep records of the people we must fear.

Stigma. It's time we brought it back.

47.

Appellate practitioners[77] and judges are the Monday morning quarterbacks of the legal system. Everything related to an appeal depends upon the record below (i.e., trial transcript and other evidence), and the review of this record. Lawyers study the transcripts, review the evidence, research the law, and make arguments in their appellate briefs. After the case is argued before a panel of appellate judges, the court reviews the record and hands down a decision. Sometimes the panel's decision is split, and a judge or a group of judges will file a separate opinion. This additional opinion may concur with the majority's position, but cite alternative reasons for the decision. The separate opinion may also dissent from the majority's view when one or more judges think that the prevailing view was incorrect. The appeals process takes considerable time to complete. A split-second decision made by a lawyer in the midst of trial can be argued, discussed, second-guessed and decided in an appellate forum over several years.

The same lengthy review process applies to decisions that are made by police officers in their day-to-day work. Appellate judges are the final arbiters of the legality of a search, the suggestiveness of a lineup, and the voluntariness of a statement. A cop may well believe in his heart that he has probable cause to arrest a particular perpetrator, but the appeals court decides whether that belief was legal. Encounters on the mean streets of New York between police and offenders are generally reviewed in the wood-paneled civility of an appellate forum. No dirt, no grime and no defendant is present throughout this process—just a collection of lawyers and jurists supporting, condemning and explaining the propriety of a young cop's decision to stop a felon. With brief and law book in hand, judges discuss at length questions that cops have to answer in the time it takes to pull a trigger. For the judges it is intellectual gamesmanship; for the cops it is life or death.[78]

It is against this backdrop that the New York Court of Appeals decided a line of cases dealing with street encounters between police and civilians. Juvenile criminals, like most offenders, are usually apprehended within a short time period following the crime. Thus, the extent to which an officer may approach, question, search and arrest an offender is consistently an issue for practitioners in the criminal/juvenile justice system. While the Court of Appeals has made an effort to develop a set of objective criteria for all police–civilian encounters, the application of these rules has caused confusion among the lower courts.

In *People v. DeBour*,[79] the Court of Appeals identified four tiers of police intrusion during street encounters with civilians. In *DeBour,* two officers were patrolling a deserted drug-users' street around midnight when they saw Louis DeBour walking in their direction. When DeBour saw the police approaching, he crossed the street-leaving the officers suspicious about the man's sudden change of direction. The policemen followed him to the other side of the street and asked him for identification. When he told the officers he had no identification with him, one of the policemen noticed a bulge in the waist area beneath defendant's jacket. Concerned about his safety, the officer ordered DeBour to open his coat. When the coat was unzipped, the policemen saw a gun and arrested Louis DeBour.

The question before the court concerned the authority of the officers to stop and question the defendant and whether or not the circumstances in this case warranted that specific level of intrusion.[80] To decide these questions, the New York Court of Appeals in *DeBour, supra,* listed four tiers of police intrusion relating to street encounters and the requisite amount of suspicion to warrant each tier.

> The minimal intrusion of approaching to *request information* is permissible when there is some objective credible reason for that interference not necessarily indicative of criminality ... [cites]... The next degree, the *common-law right to inquire,* is activated by a founded suspicion that criminal activity is afoot and permits a somewhat greater intrusion in that a policeman is entitled to interfere with a citizen to the extent necessary to gain explanatory information, but short of a forcible seizure . . . [cites] . . . Where a police officer entertains a reasonable suspicion that a particular person has committed, or is about to commit a felony or misdemeanor, the CPL authorizes a *forcible stop and detention* of that person . . . [cite] . . . A corollary of the statutory right to temporarily detain for questioning is the authority to frisk if the officer reasonably suspects that he is in danger of physical injury by virtue of the detainee being armed ... [cite] ... Finally a police officer may *arrest* and take into custody a person when he has probable cause to believe that person has committed a crime, or offense in his presence ... [cite]. [emphasis added] 40 NY2d at 223.

With these words the Court of Appeals defined the permissible scope of all police-civilian encounters for the State of

New York. Unfortunately, police, prosecutors, defense attorneys and judges cannot agree on the meaning of this language. Rather than limiting the litigation surrounding the "stops" of individuals, the Court of Appeals has invited challenge to every encounter on the street. No one is sure which category applies to his or her specific case, nor is the language within each level of intrusion clear enough to allow objective analysis. Instead, one man's *request for information,* is the next woman's *common law right of inquiry.* Nor has the Court of Appeals clearly distinguished the limits of a policeman's authority while "requesting information" as compared to those limits while exercising a "common-law right to inquire."

The fact that there is conflict among all the leading cases relating to street encounters is a clear indication that the test defined by the court in *DeBour* is unworkable. Yet, as we shall see, rather than applying a common sense analysis to these cases as a means to resolve the conflict, the Court of Appeals has stubbornly and inconsistently applied the rules of *DeBour.* Such an approach may be appropriate for the mind games of appellate practice or the law school classroom, but the cop on the beat needs to know the limits of his or her authority. In this area, the Court of Appeals, and *DeBour,* have failed to provide definitive answers. Instead, they have exacerbated the conflict.

In upholding the "stop" (and the subsequent seizure of the gun) in *DeBour,* the majority opinion from the Court of Appeals said that the officers' *request for information* from the defendant was appropriate in these circumstances. Crossing the street to avoid walking past the cops was a proper ground for requesting identity in this high-crime area. ". . . . [T]he attendant circumstances were sufficient to arouse the officers' interest." 40 NY2d at 220. The bulge in the defendant's waist-band, taking into account the late hour and his avoidance of the police, authorized these officers to minimally intrude upon the defendant by opening his coat. Such a result seems consistent with common sense. Unfortunately, it is inconsistent with other cases that rely upon the same standards for police-civilian encounters.

DeBour was decided in conjunction with *People v. LaPene.*[81] In *LaPene,* police received an anonymous phone call that a black male in a red shirt was in Jean's Bar (a local Queens tavern) with a gun. The officers entered the bar and saw LaPene in a red shirt conversing with other patrons in the back of the pub. Without asking any questions, Police Officer Dennis Sheeran ordered the defendant to "freeze" and to raise his hands. The officer reached into LaPene's waistband and removed the gun.

The Court of Appeals applied the four-tiered analysis to these facts in their decision suppressing the gun. The court reasoned that ". . . Since the *right to request information* as delineated in *DeBour (supra)* and the *common-law right to inquire* do not extend to a frisk . . . "[82] 40 NY2d at 223, the cops were without reasonable suspicion to trigger a *forcible stop and detention* (sometimes called a *stop and frisk*). The judges looked to the nature of anonymous calls or tips and found them to be among the weakest types of information on which an officer may rely. Although the officers may have approached the defendant and asked for information consistent with the two lower levels of intrusion, they exceeded their authority, said the court, when they told LaPene to "freeze" immediately prior to the search. At first glance the *LaPene* scenario appears to fit neatly into the *DeBour* criteria. Upon closer examination, however, it conflicts with other cases that allow even greater levels of intrusion—including the policy concerns within *DeBour* itself.

People v. Howard,[83] better than any other case, illustrates the conflict between common sense and the application of the *DeBour* criteria. Archie Howard was strolling down the street in a rundown section of the Bronx that was noted for a high incidence of burglaries. It was about one P.M. when Howard was seen by two police officers on anticrime patrol. The officers became suspicious when they noticed him carrying a ladies' vanity case. As the cops drove past Howard, he looked over his shoulder at the cops in a "furtive manner." The officers made a quick U-turn and started to pull the car to the side of the street where Howard was walking. Just as in *DeBour*, he changed direction when he saw the officers turn in his direction. As the car got closer, Howard began to quicken his pace. When one of the cops displayed his shield and said, "Police Officer, I would like to speak with you," Howard looked directly at the officers and kept on walking. The police continued to follow, and again the officer repeated his request. This time, however, Howard pulled the vanity case to his chest like a football and began to run away from the officers. The cops gave chase, along with a college student who had apparently seen all or part of this exchange. The college student caught Howard just after he tossed the vanity case into a pile of junk. One officer arrived and asked him why he tried to run away. A few seconds later the other cop arrived and asked about the ladies' vanity case. The college student pointed to the case in the rubbish and the police officer opened it to find a loaded .38 caliber revolver and several envelopes of heroin. Archie Howard was arrested.

In a four to three decision (four judges in the majority and three dissenting), the court of Appeals applied twisted

THE LAW · 263

logic to suppress the vanity case and it contents. The majority opined that mere flight from police officers is not enough to warrant an arrest and subsequent search. While the Court was correct in this assertion, their application of this rule failed to consider the totality of the circumstances confronting the officers. Minimizing defendant's activities as well as their reasoning in *DeBour, supra,* the majority cut Archie Howard loose with a reckless thrust of the sword of social liberalism.

> While we hold that there was a sufficient basis to permit inquiry, we agree that the defendant had the right not to answer, that his running did not, absent any indication that any crime had been or was about to be committed, permit detention; that there was no probable cause for defendant's arrest. . . .
>
> As we have recently had reason to reiterate in *People v. Belton*[84] (50 NY2d 447, 429 NYS2d 574, 407 NE2d 420), "[t]he privacy interest of our citizens is far too cherished a right to be entrusted to the discretion of the officer in the field." 50 NY2d at 588.

The basis for the Court's decision in *Howard* is the failure on the part of the police to have "probable cause" for an "arrest." With a swift stroke of the pen, the majority in *Howard* rejected *DeBour's* three lower tiers of police intrusion, and assumed that "probable cause" was necessary for the detention of the defendant. Careful analysis of the facts, and common-sense application of the *DeBour* standards, should have demonstrated otherwise.

In considering the prosecutor's case, the Court of Appeals

found that the officers were well within their rights to *request information* (the lowest level of intrusion) from the defendant. "We have no difficulty in concluding that the officers' request for information from defendant was justified under those criteria." 50 NY2d at 589. Quizzically, the court next said that the criteria in this case did not meet the "probable cause" standard, so the officers did not have enough information to authorize an arrest of the defendant. Lost in this simple and hasty analysis are the two middle levels of police intrusion under *DeBour, supra.* No mention is made of a *common-law right to inquire,* and more importantly, the court ignored the ability of the police to make a *forcible stop* of the defendant based upon "reasonable suspicion." With one-half of the *DeBour* litmus test left out of the equation, it is easy to see why Archie Howard's gun and heroin were excluded from evidence.

It is suggested here that the police had more than just a right to request information from Archie Howard. They observed the defendant in an area categorized as a "high burglary" location. Upon seeing the police the defendant looked over his shoulder—in what the police called a "furtive" manner. When police approached the defendant, he suddenly turned and walked quickly in the opposite direction. All the while, the defendant was carrying a ladies' vanity case (the officer indicated that burglars often carry away their bounty in their victim's luggage). When the officer asked to speak with the defendant, Howard looked right at the cops and walked away. At the officer's second request to speak with the defendant, he—without any provocation from police—pulled the vanity case close to his chest and ran from the officers. Common sense told these officers—as well as the college student that also gave chase—that criminal activity "was afoot."[85] While each of these factors by itself was not enough to detain Archie Howard, taken together, any reasonable person would assume that the defendant was involved in criminal activity. That was evidenced by the uncontroverted testimony of the officer who asked the defendant as soon as he was grabbed, "Why did you run?" Archie Howard was not under arrest—Archie Howard was not going to be detained—Archie Howard was properly the subject of a *common-law right of inquiry* until he decided to run. As soon as the defendant made his unilateral decision of flight, however, the officers had "reasonable suspicion" to effect a *forcible stop and frisk* Flight alone, as the court suggested, did not warrant detention. But the flight, coupled with Howard's other actions, should have made the most benevolent jurist suspicious about his criminality.

The absurdity of the *Howard* decision was outlined in a stinging dissent by Judge Matthew Jasen. Allowing that common sense should rule these encounters, the dissenters pointed out that the totality of the circumstances was enough for a forcible stop—if not an arrest. Commenting on the majority's decision, the dissent said:

> Such a conclusion borders on the absurd. The officers had every right, if not the obligation to pursue defendant in order to investigate this highly suspicious conduct. 50 NY2d at 595.

As a matter of common sense, it is important to ask, what should the police officers have done? When the defendant—who had aroused suspicion by virtue of his furtive glances, change in direction and possession of a ladies' vanity case—ran from the police, should the officers have ignored this activity? The majority acknowledges that following the defendant was appropriate.[86] If so, how does one keep surveillance on a rapidly fleeing suspect without giving chase? Should the cops not inquire of the defendant his reason for running? Even if we do not permit the search of the vanity case—shouldn't a police officer as a matter of public policy investigate activities that a reasonable person finds suspicious? Isn't that the purpose of a police presence?

The answers to these questions posed by the *Howard* case should be found in *DeBour, supra.* Unfortunately, the analysis in *DeBour* did not find its way into the *Howard* holding. Perhaps it was ignored—or perhaps the *Howard* court missed the connection. More likely, it is the difficulty of trying to neatly fit complex descriptions of street encounters into one of the four tiers of intrusion. In any event, the policy concerns of reasonableness in *DeBour* never found its way into *Howard*. In *DeBour,* the court opined:

> . . . [W]e cannot say that the defendant's right to be free from an official interference by way of inquiry is absolute. . . . The crucial factor is whether or not the police behavior can be characterized as reasonable which, in terms of accepted standards, requires a balancing of the interests involved in the police inquiry. *People v. DeBour,* 40 NY2d 210 at 217.

Unfortunately, *Howard* and other street encounters were not judged by this reasoning behind *DeBour.* Instead, the four-tiered analysis has taken "reason" hostage. All analysis under *DeBour* has become a puzzle that is solved independently at each interpretation. Rather than ensure consistency, the four-tiers of *DeBour* promote adversity. It is hard to understand and is impossible to apply.

The conflict has never been more apparent than in a direct comparison of *Howard, supra* with a subsequent Court of Appeals case, *People v. Leung.*[87] In *Leung,* police officers saw the defendant pass a manila envelope to another man. Since the cops thought that it was the type of envelope that often was used in drug transactions, two police officers decided to approach defendant to investigate. Upon identifying themselves as policemen, the defendant fled. As he ran he discarded a hat and a black object under a bench. A search recovered a 9 mm pistol as the object discarded by the defendant. Relying on *People v. Howard, supra,*—and asserting that the facts were indistinguishable—the defendant argued that the pursuit by police was unreasonable and that the gun should have been suppressed.

Quite unexpectedly, the Court of Appeals in *Leung, supra,* cited *DeBour* to sustain the scizure of the weapon. With facts almost identical to the *Howard* situation, the Court of Appeals balanced the equities. For reasons unknown, the balance that had weighed in favor of Archie Howard, shifted against Leung.

> In *People v. DeBour,* we held that judicial review of the legality of police conduct must weigh the interference such conduct entails against the precipitating and attendant conditions known to the police as the encounter unfolds. . . . The present case presents a situation wherein the level of police intrusion was an appropriate response to the observations and beliefs of the officers involved. *People v. Leung,* 69 NY2d 734 at 736.

Naturally, the officer on patrol needs to determine the extent of his power to stop, question and detain a civilian. He must be able to apply an objective test to the facts at hand to avoid exceeding the permissible limits—or risk suppression of all evidence he has gathered. Applying the analysis of *People v. Howard,*[88] to the *Leung* case, it is clear that the defendant in *Leung* could have refused to answer questions. The *Leung* court, consistent with the decisions in *Howard* and *DeBour,* acknowledged the right of the officer to request information by suggesting that there existed an objective credible reason ". . . to support the intrusion attendant to a police approach of a citizen." The comparison ends, however, where the confusion begins:

> When coupled with defendant's immediate flight upon the officer's approach, the passing of the manila envelope in this narcotics-prone neighborhood establishes the necessary *reasonable suspicion* that defendant had committed or was about to commit a crime, such that pursuit by the officers was justified. [*emphasis added*]   *People v. Leung,* 69 NY2d 734 at 736.

Most puzzling about this portion of the *Leung decision* is the fact that the Court of Appeals cites *People v. Howard, supra,* in support of the officers' justification for pursuit. It is therefore instructive to ask, since *Howard* required "probable cause" for an "arrest" of a fleeing defendant, why did *Leung* authorize "detention" of a defendant who ran from the police upon "reasonable suspicion"?

This question can only be answered by accepting the fact

that relying on *DeBour, supra,* the same court—given two versions of the same facts—articulated different standards in allowing a police officer to pursue a fleeing suspect. The majority in *Howard* in vacating the defendant's conviction held that "[T]here was no *probable cause* for defendant's arrest." 50 NY2d at 588. A unanimous court in *Leung* defined the same scenario as a lower level of police intrusion, therefore requiring "reasonable suspicion" to detain, rather than "probable cause" to arrest. If these distinctions seem confusing, one can only imagine the split-second dilemma facing the officer on patrol.

The rules regarding street encounters are more complex when focusing on the two lower levels of intrusion as described in *People v. DeBour.*[89] These encounters, the *request for information* and the *common-law right of inquiry* are indistinguishable in language and in practice. Attempts by the Court of Appeals to separate these two levels have only been met with confusion. Since the Court of Appeals has failed to clearly separate the two levels by limiting both to interrogation, the officer's authority to investigate remains essentially the same, despite the heightened indicia of criminality.

This inability to distinguish between the request for information and the common-law right to inquire was highlighted in *People v. Hollman.*[90] In that case, the Court of Appeals took a tutorial approach to reaffirm their commitment to the *DeBour* standard and to instruct the lower courts on the fine differences between the lower levels of intrusion.

> . . . [W]e revisit *DeBour* in order to clarify the difference between a request for information and the common-law right of inquiry. Because the two terms on their face are so close in meaning, the legal

significance we intended each to have has become obscured. The result has been inconsistency in the evaluation of markedly similar police encounters. . . .

. . . We conclude, as a general matter, that a request for information involves basic, nonthreatening questions regarding, for instance, identity, address or information. As we stated in *DeBour,* these questions need only be supported by an objective credible reason not necessarily indicative of criminality. Once the officer asks more pointed questions that would lead the person approached reasonably to believe that he or she is suspected of some wrongdoing and is the focus of the officer's investigation, the officer is no longer merely seeking information. This has become a common-law inquiry that must be supported by a founded suspicion that criminal activity is afoot. *People v. Hollman,* 79 NY2d 181 at 185.

Careful analysis, however, along with comparisons with other Court of Appeals cases can only lead to the conclusion that the distinction proffered in *Hollman* is illusory. Clearly, the court has attempted to define different levels of interrogation. While the police may not be permitted to ask incriminating information during a request for information, the suspect— pursuant to *People v. Howard, supra,*—has the right to walk away. Yet even where the interrogation escalates into the common-law inquiry—where the police believe that criminal activity is afoot—the suspect still may not be forcibly detained. Implicitly, the suspect at this point is still free— under the *Howard* doctrine—to walk away. Since a response to

police questioning is not required under either of the two
lower levels of intrusion, and since the suspect may leave without fear of arrest, detention or frisk, any attempt to differenti-
ate between a request for information and a common-law
right to inquire is a mere academic exercise.[91]

Rather than developing fine-line tests like the four tiers
of *DeBour, supra,* the Court of Appeals ought to promulgate
rules that meet the privacy interests of the citizens as well as
giving the police an easy-to-apply rule for street encounters.
The court need look no further than the rules proffered by
the Supreme Court of the United States regarding the ability
of police to detain, arrest, frisk and search citizens on the
street. While concerns about state constitutional law in *Howard*
are noted,[92] the privacy interests of citizens cannot be protected if police cannot be provided with objective criteria for
investigatory work.[93]

In *California v. Hodari D.*[94] the United States Supreme
Court took a common sense approach to the situation posed
in *People v. Howard, supra.* In *Hodari D.,* the defendant was seen
by officers huddled around a car with several other youths in
a high crime section of Oakland. When the youths saw the
officers approaching, they fled. During his flight, Hodari D.
tossed away a rock later found to be crack cocaine. The officers gave chase and the defendant was apprehended a short
distance away. The court considered whether the youth after
fleeing from police had been seized within the meaning of the
Fourth Amendment.[95] In holding that no seizure took place
the court said:

> We have long understood that the Fourth Amend-
> ment's protection against "unreasonable . . . seizures"
> includes seizure of the person . . . [cite] . . . From the

time of the founding to the present, the word "seizure" has meant a "taking possession"... [citing several dictionaries] ... For most purposes at common law, the word connoted not merely grasping, or applying force to, the animate or inanimate object in question, but actually bringing it within physical control ... 111 SCt. at 1549–1550.

The Supreme Court went on to say:

An arrest requires *either* physical force ... *or,* where that is absent, *submission* to the assertion of authority. (*emphasis* in original) 111 SCt. at 1551.

If we apply the rules of reason from *Hodari D.* to the facts in *People v. Howard*,[96] the analysis and result are more in keeping with common sense. We need not wonder whether the police were "requesting information" or whether they were justified in making a "common-law inquiry." We need not reach the question of whether there was criminal activity afoot, since after flight both Howard and Hodari D. tossed their contraband away. Under the practical federal analysis, there is no question about the legality of police intrusion since neither individual would be considered "seized." Additionally, the Court of Appeals by adopting the common sense approach like that of *California v. Hodari D.* would have avoided the paradox of authorizing the surveillance of Archie Howard but disallowing police pursuit.

Simplicity is the key to an effective policy regarding police-civilian encounters. The simple reasonableness standard laid out in *Terry v. Ohio*,[97] ". . . [W]hether a reasonably prudent man in the circumstances would be warranted in the belief that his safety or that of others was in danger," 392 US at 27, ought to replace the complex four-tiered analysis that even the Court of Appeals admits is confusing.

The four tiers of *DeBour*, and the renewed commitment to this standard in *Hollman*, underscore the problem with the New York Court of Appeals' failure to remove academia from the day-to-day dangers of police work. Arguments on the propriety of a stop may be appropriately evaluated in the classroom on four or more tiers—but complex analysis guarantees failure in the street. How can the Court of Appeals honestly expect the "cop on the beat" to consider the limits imposed at every tier when the court acknowledges the past difficulty in separating the layers? Leaving the issue to common sense by requiring that the level of intrusion remain consistent with the totality of the circumstances is an easier rule to apply. In *US v. Cortez*[98] the US Supreme Court recognized the impossibility in defining a bright-line rule to cover all encounters between police and civilians. The Court said the "totality of the circumstances—the whole picture—must be taken into account . . . " *Cortez* at 417, when evaluating the propriety of detention for criminal investigatory purposes. Recognizing that each case was different, and that suspicion could never be universally quantified, the court opined:

> The process does not deal with hard certainties, but with probabilities. Long before the law of probabilities was articulated as such, practical people formulated certain common-sense conclusions about human behavior, jurors as factfinders are permitted to do the same—and so are law enforcement officers.

Finally, the evidence thus collected must be seen and weighed not in terms of library analysis by scholars, but as understood by those versed in the field of law enforcement. (emphasis added) 449 US at 418.

The ease and workability of the Federal common-sense rule was recently demonstrated in *Florida v. Bostick*.[99] In upholding a search against drug traffickers aboard a bus in a Florida terminal the Supreme Court again focused upon the "reasonable man" standard. While reasonable people can disagree so that results may vary (there was a heated dissent in *Bostick* that disagreed with the conclusions after application of the reasonableness standards), no one can dispute the appeal of a simple common sense standard.

We adhere to the rule that, in order to determine whether a particular encounter constitutes a seizure, a court must consider all the circumstances surrounding the encounter to determine whether the police conduct would have communicated to a reasonable person that the person was not free to decline the officers' requests or otherwise terminate the encounter. 111 SCt. at 2389.

The final analysis of a working rule is not whether it protects the citizens from crime or police intrusion, but whether police may apply the rule to meet those concerns. The four tiers of *DeBour, supra* are fine for application in any academic forum, but they fail to provide quick answers for the officer on patrol. Rather than worrying about "objective credible reasons" to approach a potential suspect, the officer's investigation should be governed (and eventually judged) by the reasonableness of his activity in light of the totality of the circumstances.

In developing analysis to determine the propriety of police encounters, the New York Court of Appeals should first consider a policy of simplicity. The use of a common-sense standard to govern street encounters would preserve our constitutional right to be free of *unreasonable* seizures and would also provide a practical boost to crime prevention and investigation. The four tiers of *DeBour* have fared well over the past fifteen years; the society they are supposed to protect has not been so lucky.

48.

Rosario material is every prosecutor's nightmare. It is the proverbial "technicality" that inures to the benefit of the criminal at the expense of the law-abiding people of the state. It has become a crusade for the Court of Appeals, with prosecutors and victims feeling the brunt of the court's wrath. As a dissenter, Judge Bellacosa described it: "It is a law enforcer's nightmare and a perpetrator's delight." It also makes a living for many defense lawyers.

Simply put, *Rosario* material is statements of a prosecution witness about the crime that is charged—statements, made to law enforcement officials. The legislature has said that all such statements must be turned over to the defense *prior* to the commencement of a trial. That statute was based upon the New York Court of Appeals' decision in *People vs. Rosario.*

It is not the underlying premise of *Rosario* material that prosecutors find unfair. It has been the zealous enforcement of the rule, taking *Rosario* material beyond common sense and the fairness that the rule was meant to promote. In bending over backward in support of murderers, rapists and the most socially deviant individuals of the Big Apple (and beyond), the New York Court of Appeals has decided that failure to turn over *Rosario* material is *per se* error. That is, no good faith, harmless error or good intentions will save a case from reversal when there is a *Rosario* failure. If the prosecutor fails to provide the material, the conviction is lost.

So strict is the *Rosario* requirement, that many defense lawyers build their cross-examination around the search for missing *Rosario* material. The hope of defense counsel is that some obscure police form or statement will surface, thereby mandating the exclusion of testimony, or the outright reversal or dismissal of a case. Instead of focusing cross-examination upon the acts of their client or the ability of the witness to make an observation, the *Rosario*-keen advocate questions the witness about statements that may have been written down by the police. It is not uncommon to hear defense counsel ask each witness: "When you spoke to the officer, was he writing?" In short, some lawyers have chosen to ignore the facts and are using *Rosario* violations to force the courts to ignore the truth. The fear of a *Rosario* violation holds every prosecutor hostage. Any defense attorney worth his salt knows this— and uses it well.

In a small town where crime is at a minimum and police paperwork is limited to a single form, the Court of Appeals'

Rosario rule might work. The NYPD, however, has thousands of forms and about 36,000 police officers. This does not include the hundreds of officers in the Port Authority Police Department, the Sanitation Police Department, the Long Island Railroad Police Department, the Amtrak Police Department, the Health and Hospitals Police Department the Metro-North Railroad Police Department, and the State Police. These police forces have their own forms as well. In addition, detectives and patrol officers use different forms when investigating a case.

Besides the Police Department's forms, almost every cop carries a "memo book." This is a notepad that officers use to keep personal accounts of the case, with contents varying from accurate descriptions of crimes to the phone numbers of good-looking complainants. Of course, if the cop testifies, his memo book must be turned over to the defense attorney; or if a statement of the victim or other testifying witness was recorded, then the book must also be provided.

The *Rosario* rule has become the impetus for the mad search for statements. Prosecutors must thwart the bureaucratic paper shufflers at Police Plaza to avoid the strict liability of the rule. Cops who may never be called to testify must be tracked down at their precincts for their memo books, complaint forms, follow-up forms, etc. Yet despite the scorched-earth search for *Rosario* material, no prosecutor is ever 100 percent comfortable that he has found every piece. With a *per se* error rule, the possibility of reversal hangs over every conviction in the State of New York. All this thanks to a Court of Appeals that places form over common sense.

The radical view of New York's highest court stands alone in American jurisprudence. The court has steadfastly refused to inject a "harmless error" analysis into the *Rosario* fray. This would allow the appeals court to review the evidence and make a determination as to whether the failure to provide the statement was benign. In a harmless error analysis, the court would look at the testimony and exhibits to determine whether the outcome would have been affected by the missing material. Where there is question as to the outcome, the court would reverse and remand the matter back to the trial court for a new trial. Where the evidence of guilt is overwhelming, and it is clear that the unserved material is of little or no value, the court would affirm the conviction. This type of analysis is done by appellate courts daily. On issues of the competency of counsel, the review of exculpatory evidence, and the existence of prejudicial information put before the jury, the appeals courts review the matters with harmless error in mind. It is only with the *Rosario* issue that the Court of Appeals has refused to apply these traditional methods of case review.

In support of their unforgiving position on *Rosario* material the court has suggested that they cannot review the importance of the missing statement and, in effect, substitute their judgment for that of the defense attorney. Thus, the Court of Appeals is willing to review a record to see if counsel served effectively, but they are not willing to second-guess that same lawyer as to whether an insignificant statement could be put to good use.

The problem with the New York Court of Appeals is its judges refuse to accept the world as it is. Police officers write things down. They make notes of descriptions, notes from witnesses, notes about their observations. The careless loss of a note may result in a loss of the case. The failure of the cop to turn over the scratch piece of paper on which he or she hurriedly took a description mandates reversal. It doesn't even matter if the perpetrator suffers no prejudice. The rule is clear and dumb. "When the prosecution fails completely in its obligation to deliver *Rosario* material to defense counsel, the courts will not attempt to determine whether prejudice accrued to the defense," states one opinion. Thus, despite a lack of any demonstrable prejudice, the murderer, rapist or armed robber may be back on the streets of New York—courtesy of the state's highest court.

After the *Rosario* rule was strengthened in the late 1980s, it was unbelievable that the courts would expand its scope even further. But in 1992, Judge Vito Titone, the ranking anti-law enforcement member of the Court of Appeals, wrote the unanimous decision in *People vs. Young.*[100] In *Young* the Court of Appeals leaped to new heights in judicial activism: They held that *common sense* analyses are not appropriate for *Rosario* violations.

"It is thus apparent that while we have from time to time referred to the general notion of 'common sense limits' on the *Rosario* rule . . . [cites omitted], the specific exception to the per se reversal rule that is proposed here is simply not consistent with the principles underlying our case law."[101] Does this mean that after the *Young* case (where a "common sense" exception to *Rosario* was sought), the courts should reverse the conviction of a killer where the failure to provide a statement would have no effect on the outcome of a case, even under a common sense analysis? Can the Court of Appeals refuse to exercise common sense or their best judgment in favor of reversing the conviction of a felon?

Judge Titone in his opinion in *Young,* says, "The common sense exception posited by the appellate division is nothing more than a substitute for the harmless error rule."[102] Clearly, he is right in such a suggestion, but should the highest court of the state be rejecting "harmless error" in *Rosario* violations when such a position is equivalent to common sense? Does this suggest that the Court of Appeals' decision to reject 'harmless error' is inconsistent with common sense?

The *Young* opinion continues by proving the direct relationship between common sense and harmless error. Yet despite that direct proof, the unanimous court concludes that *Rosario* violations are *per se* error where the prosecution has failed to turn over the statement. ". . . [T]he degree to which the undisclosed material bears on the accused's (note that the defendant herein had already been convicted) factual guilt or innocence—[is] a consideration *unrelated* to the values of procedural fairness that inform the *Rosario* rule."[103] [parenthesis added] Thus, where the material bears no relation to the innocence of a felon, the Court of Appeals has decided that this statement is still important enough to require the reversal of a conviction. That is, harmless error is out. Common sense be damned. The killer is free. In the case itself, Jeffrey Young was convicted in the murder of a man named Booker. Booker and Young had committed a prior crime together, and Young believed that Booker was going to "rat him out." So Young murdered Booker, placed his body in a plastic bag and disposed of it in a nearby dump.

At the murder trial of Young, the main witness against him was Marie Somie, Young's former girlfriend. Young had confessed the entire crime to Somie, and her information was corroborated by the location of the bag containing Booker's body. It would be interesting to ask Marie Somie, in light of Young's previous method of silencing witnesses, whether she takes comfort in the court's abandonment of "common sense" in order to reverse the conviction of a killer. And if Young is released to practice his craft upon Somie, would such a killing qualify as the Court's "harmless error"?

When the highest court in the State of New York rejects common sense in favor of procedural formality, the message of our criminal justice system is all too clear. Can we really continue to survive these judges? Or is that just a question of *common sense?*

49.

The right to a speedy trial guarantees the accused that a case will commence in a timely fashion. When the People fail to begin a trial within statutory time limits, the court must dismiss the case. Statutory law and fundamental fairness require a prompt resolution of criminal proceedings.

In the criminal justice system, the laws relating to speedy trial have grown in complexity with each year's judicial interpretations and legislative modifications. Prosecutors and defense lawyers are continually "counting the days" to make sure that the proceeding is commenced within the Criminal Procedure Law's specified time periods. These calculations have been made more complicated by the rules allowing the exclusion of certain time periods from the speedy trial timetable. For instance, time does not run against the prosecutor during the periods when defense counsel has caused the delay and when the defendant has absented himself or herself from the court proceedings. More importantly, in the criminal courts, the speedy trial time clock stops running as soon as the prosecutor states that he or she is "ready" for trial.[104]

The juvenile justice system in New York does not operate under the same statutory framework for speedy trial as the adult criminal justice system. Under the Family Court Act, there are no specific periods of excludable time. The delay occasioned by the defense attorney will not toll the time for speedy trial purposes, nor does the statement of readiness by a prosecutor stop the speedy trial clock from running toward the dismissal date. Unlike the criminal statute, the juvenile procedural rules are ". . . a true 'speedy trial' provision, in that both its language and its underlying purpose are directed towards bringing the juvenile to trial within a specified [time limit]. . ."[105] After a juvenile case is arraigned, the speedy trial time begins to run. Until dismissal or disposition—absent waiver from the juvenile—time is never tolled.[106]

The right to a speedy trial is defined in §310.2 of New York's Family Court Act.[107] The specific time limitations, defined in another section of the law,[108] say that a *fact-finding hearing* must be commenced no later than sixty days following the conclusion of the *initial appearance*. Upon a showing of "good cause," the period may be extended another thirty days. Special circumstances—which may not include court congestion—may take the proceeding beyond the ninetieth day.

Under New York's juvenile delinquency code, the source of the delay does not control the speedy trial time clock. Even if the perpetrator himself causes the delay to extend beyond the statutory time period, New York's highest court has decided that the offender must go free.[109] Without addressing the impact upon community protection, the Court of Appeals has consistently insisted upon the literal application of rules that challenge common sense. Following the lead of the Court of Appeals, trial and appellate judges have repeatedly released the violent criminal because of delay that is unrelated to the prosecution or the courts.

It is instructive to step back and look at the cases that have led to the wholesale dismissal of serious crimes because of extraneous delays. In June of 1984, a youth named Frank walked into the Manhattan Family Courthouse with cocaine. As part of a routine security check, court officers required Frank and everyone else who entered the courthouse to pass through a metal detector and to empty their pockets. When the drugs were discovered, Frank was arrested by the court officers and another juvenile delinquency petition was filed against the youth. At the *initial appearance,* the case was set down for a *fact-finding* hearing, and the youth was released to a parent pending the trial.

The matter was set down for trial thirty-seven days following the initial appearance. Although the prosecutor answered "ready for trial" that day, the case was adjourned for one month to give the court time to decide the discovery and suppression motions made by the defense attorney. On the next court date, the trial calendar was clogged and the judge marked the case "ready and passed."[110] Two months later, defense counsel made a motion to dismiss the case for failure to provide the youth with a speedy trial under the time limitations of the Family Court Act. *Although no delay was occasioned by the prosecutor,* the defense argued that the respondent had been denied a hearing within the mandatory sixty-day limit prescribed in New York's Family Court Act. Furthermore, argued the defense, no specific finding of good cause was made by the court to push the matter well beyond this statutory time limit.

The trial judge, finding no fault with the prosecution, dismissed the case for failure to commence the fact-finding hearing within sixty days. That decision was affirmed without an opinion by the *Appellate Division,* First Department, and was then argued before the *Court of Appeals.*

A unanimous Court of Appeals affirmed the dismissal of the proceeding. "It is clear both that the delays were not permissible under the statute and that the *presentment agency* was not at fault."[111] The court opined that the legislative goal of a prompt disposition in juvenile cases mandated dismissal of the charges for failure to strictly comply with the time limits of the statute. Although the statute does not refer to dismissal for failure to commence a fact-finding hearing within sixty days, the Court of Appeals chose to read such a requirement into the law.

> While no specific provision for dismissal is made in the statute . . . [cite] . . . , the statute's specific and mandatory language, as well as its precise deadlines and clear legislative history, lead to the conclusion that the legislature did not intend to leave the sanction for noncompliance to the Family Court. Rather, a holding mandating dismissal of the charges seems necessary to effectuate the legislative goal of prompt adjudication and to ensure consistency in the statute's application. 70 NY2d at 414.

This reasoning, however, is replete with contradictions. It was illogical for the court to *infer* the sanction of dismissal as a matter of legislative intent, when the court similarly found the statute's language to be "specific and mandatory." When the court found no ambiguity present in the statute, inferring a remedy not in the legislation conflicted with their premise of a "clear legislative history."

In dismissing the charges against Frank C., the Court of Appeals was fully aware of the problems that the Family Courts would face by attempting to abide by the legislated time constraints. "Moreover, the fact that the Legislature enacted the statute despite the concerns expressed by some regarding the undue burden its strict time limitations would impose on the Family Court system . . . [cite omitted] . . . strongly suggests that the Legislature weighed all of the competing considerations and found the goal of speedy resolution of charges against juveniles to be paramount."[112] The court was referring to memoranda from the Association of Family Court judges and from the state's own *Office of Court Administration* (OCA) that argued that the time limits proposed in the statute were impossible to cope with the tremendous volume of cases that were before the Family Court. These opinions were offered in 1982, prior to the "crack" epidemic in New York. Thus these concerns were expressed prior to the 400 percent rise in child protective caseloads and the doubling of the juvenile delinquency cases throughout New York City in the late 1980s. If these time limits were inappropriate by 1982 standards, they defy the reality of the 1990s caseload crises.

The Court of Appeals ignored the warnings of those trained in Family Court practice, and decided that all cases must proceed to trial within the specified time limits or the petition would be dismissed. ". . . [W]e hold that the source of delay is not controlling and that dismissal is required whenever the statutory requirements for commencing a fact-finding hearing are not satisfied."[113] Thus, when the defense seeks to adjourn a case, speedy trial time still runs against the prosecutor. Similarly, when the court's calendar is too congested for the case to proceed to trial, then the speedy trial period still runs against the prosecution—even when the prosecutor is ready to commence the fact-finding hearing. Should the calendar be congested beyond the sixtiethth day following the initial appearance, then the matter against the juvenile must be dismissed. Apparently the Court of Appeals believed that dismissal of a felony case against a young offender was more in keeping with the statutory purpose of prompt adjudication than delaying the hearing. In a system originally designed around the rehabilitation of the offender, on-time performance has usurped the paramount goal. Strict compliance—not its consequences—is the high court's key to achieving a perceived legislative mandate.

The effects of *Frank C., supra,* were felt immediately throughout the juvenile justice community. Cases that had historically taken far longer than sixty days to commence faced certain dismissal. The good faith of the prosecution was irrelevant. In one case the court dismissed a robbery matter because the young victim was away in summer camp in Maine.[114] The court found that because the parents of the young mugging victim had refused to produce their child within the specified time period, the case had to be dismissed. Relying on *Frank C.,* the Family Court found that the victim had an obligation to surrender part of his vacation to satisfy the speedy trial rights of the people who mugged him.

If the rationale for *Frank C., supra,* defies logic, then the cases that followed extended that defiance. Nothing epitomizes the sacrifice of common sense better than *In the Matter of Randy K.*[115] There the Court of Appeals, in a four to three decision, found that where the youth causes the delay by failing to appear for trial, speedy trial time still runs against the prosecution. Under the *Randy K.* holding, when the prosecution fails to regularly seek adjournments for "good cause" or "special circumstances"—even though the offender remains at large—the case must be dismissed. There is no indication in the opinion relating to the purpose of adjourning a case where the perpetrator is "out" on a warrant. The failure of the trial court, however, to routinely find "good cause" or "special circumstances" while the warrant was extant resulted in dismissal of the petition against Randy K.

Randy K. committed an armed robbery in the Bronx. He and a buddy, each armed with a knife, approached a young man and demanded money. The two robbers shoved their victim to the ground, kicking and beating him. Then, in a gratuitous display of barbarism, Randy cut the victim's arm with his knife.

When Randy was arrested for the robbery, the police issued the youth and his parent a *Family Court Appearance Ticket* (FCAT). When the youth failed to appear in the Family Court on the ticket's return date, a case was filed and a warrant was issued for Randy's arrest. Shortly thereafter, he was involuntarily returned to court by the police warrant squad. The judge, however, chose to release Randy to his parent when the parent and the youth promised to return to court. The judge warned the young offender that his failure to return would result in certain incarceration.

Randy ignored the court's warning and again failed to appear in court. The armed robber was again returned by the police to the Family Court seven months after the issuance of a second warrant. Upon his return, and despite the fact that the youth's only court appearances were due to involuntary returns on the warrants, the defense attorney moved to dismiss the case because his client had not received a speedy trial. The attorney for Randy alleged that the prosecution had not commenced a trial within sixty days of arraignment and that his client's failure to appear did not constitute the "good cause" necessary to allow for an adjournment.

It is a running joke among lawyers that *chutzpa* is defined by the person who murders his parents and then asks the court for mercy because he is an orphan. That joke, however, became a reality when the Court of Appeals allowed a youth to delay the proceedings as a result of his own failure to appear in court and then profited by the dismissal of the charges because of that delay.

Once again, the high court looked to the prompt resolution of delinquency proceedings as a reason to dismiss the armed robbery case against Randy K. The four judges in the majority said that the prosecution was duty bound to request an adjournment of the case during the pendency of the warrant, even though the youth had caused the delay by absenting himself from the proceedings. This, the court said, would have been proper procedure and would have avoided the required dismissal of the armed robbery petition. Permitting the case to be prosecuted ". . . based solely on a failure of a juvenile to appear for a hearing and the issuance of a bench warrant would in no way advance the aims of ensuring a swift and certain determination of the proceeding and supervision of the juvenile."[116] Of course, the opinion offered no explanation as to how the dismissal of the petition against a youth who has failed to appear as directed will ". . . advance the aims of ensuring a swift and certain determination of the proceeding and supervision of the juvenile."[117] Nor is there any guidance in the majority opinion as to how successive adjournments for "good cause" will ensure the swift resolution of delinquency proceedings.[118]

Within one week of the *Randy K.* decision, the court also

decided *In the Matter of Vincent M.,* 70 NY2d 793, 522 NYS2d 527 (1987). In that case, the court relied upon the *Frank C.* reasoning to dismiss a case that contained delay occasioned primarily by the prosecution. The case was dismissed 161 days following arraignment for speedy trial violations. It would be absurd to suggest that any other result was appropriate in light of the continuing adjournments secured by the District Attorney. The failure of the D.A. to secure "good cause" adjournments appropriately placed the blame on the party causing the delay. Yet *Randy K., supra,* in light of *Vincent M.* must mean that the blame for delay may be placed upon every party and nonparty—except for the person with the legal responsibility for being present. When the offender fails at his responsibility, he is rewarded for his noncompliance and the system is blamed for failing to adjudicate the case quickly. How can we expect to hold young offenders accountable for the escalating violence in our society when the highest court of the state excuses their obligation to come to court?

Some might suggest that the majority in the *Randy K.* case may be excused for their decision on the grounds that there was little consideration for the impact of the holding. Juvenile delinquency is often portrayed as less serious than adult criminal proceedings (although the victims do not minimize their injuries because of the youth of their attackers). In *Randy K.,* however, the first premise of law school, that one cannot profit from his own wrongdoing has been turned on its head, in a criminal case! Surely the lack of foresight is illustrated in the conflicting language that constitutes the majority opinion:

> It is certainly possible, even probable, that some adjournments would have been permitted because

of respondent's failure to appear [in court]. . . [119]

and

Holding that a juvenile's failure to appear and the issuance of a bench warrant affect an "automatic" adjournment for "special circumstances" would be contrary to the clear mandate of the statute . . . [120]

That these two quotations appear in the same opinion indicates a lack of consideration regarding the policy impact of the holding. That they appear on the same page reflects a lack of consideration for the practical impacts of the decision.

The dissent in *Randy K.* questions the majority's commitment to the juvenile justice process and to community protection. The dissenters distinguished the *Randy K.* facts from those in *Frank C.* by looking to the source of the delay. Although the delay in *Frank C., supra,* was not the fault of the prosecution, it was delay occasioned by the system itself (i.e., calendar congestion and motion practice). Therefore, reasoned the dissenters, the dismissal of the case in *Frank C.* was appropriate. The delay caused by Randy K., however, was due solely to his own failure to appear. This was not delay caused by the system, but rather delay promoted by the design of the perpetrator. By choosing non-appearance, Randy K. deceived the court when he promised the arraigning judge that he would appear for trial. Yet based upon his deception, the offender was exculpated. Did the high court think that this was an important lesson for the juvenile consistent with the goal of swift adjudication?

The dissenters suggested that the decision in *Randy K.* actually thwarts the purposes of prompt adjudications in juvenile proceedings. Asserting that punishment is not a benchmark of juvenile dispositions, the dissenters attacked the majority view that failure to commence the process in a timely fashion failed to meet the legislative purpose. Dismissal is a drastic remedy when compared to the other dispositional alternatives available to the Family Court and ". . . We have no basis whatever to assume that these [dispositional] alternatives do not do exactly that, and that releasing a respondent because of his failure to appear is a superior alternative."[121]

Interestingly, Judge Judith Kaye, the author of the dissent in *Randy K.,* reviewed the legislative history and cited opposition to the proposed time limitations from the state's *Office of Court Administration* (OCA) and the Family Court Judges' Association. These concerns, she alleged, were evidence of the hardship that the speedy trial rules would bring to the system. This same argument was previously offered by the unanimous court (including the three dissenters in *Randy K.*) in *Frank C., supra,* to support the view that the legislature had rejected these concerns and demanded adherence to the strict time constraints within the Family Court Act. This time, however, the opinions of those familiar with day-to-day Family Court practice were not summarily rejected by a unanimous Court of Appeals. Perhaps the dissenters in *Randy K.* were no longer sure about the wisdom of *Frank C.*

The dissent further emphasized the majority's failure to consider the effects on community safety resulting from the *Randy K.* decision. Noting that the Family Court Act requires the court to consider the needs of the youth as well as the need to protect the community,[122] the dissent said:

> While the majority opinion makes no mention of it, the Family Court Act also mandates that the community's need for protection be considered in any delinquency proceeding (Family Ct. Act §301.1). That need is ill served by a rule which permits respondents to evade the law by their own acts or omissions—a rule which, since announced less than a year ago by the Appellate Division, will apparently require dismissal of more than 100 cases [cite omitted].[123]

Both the number of cases jeopardized by *Randy K.* and the effect on community protection were seriously underestimated in the dissenting opinion. Hundreds of cases in New York City alone were dismissed as a result of *Randy K.* In the year following the decision, over 300 cases, most of them felonies, were lost for the simple reason that the youth failed to return to court as ordered. All these crimes went unpunished because the highest court of the state inferred from the statute a mandatory dismissal rule occasioned by the person most likely to benefit from delay. Perhaps someone should have asked the Court of Appeals: Why would any offender come to court?

Randy K. had changed the historical view of speedy trial from an important right embedded in American criminal procedure to an offensive weapon. The intent of the legislature to achieve a prompt resolution of juvenile cases had been placed solely in the hands of the person whom the state alleged needed treatment, supervision and confinement. Suddenly the offending (and perhaps violent) juvenile had virtually complete control over the course and outcome of the proceedings. The court and the prosecutor were no longer in control of the case—they could only seek to adjourn the matter for good cause while the speedy trial limits and the at-large offender both remained uncontained. Even if "good cause" or "special circumstances" to adjourn the matter were found time and again, it is clear that the court's goal of prompt adjudication was lost. A matter could proceed indefinitely under the *Randy K.* rationale. All that had changed was that the prosecutor and court had to perform a monthly charade to satisfy the havoc wrought by the criminal.[124]

The result of the *Randy K.* decision was a change in speedy trial law from a rule designed to provide fairness and order to a process tumbling toward chaos. Logic has been sacrificed in favor of an odd view of technical purity. In the *Matter of Roshon P.,*[125] the Appellate Division, Second Department extended the mandatory dismissal rule to the *dispositional* phase of delinquency proceedings. Roshon P. pled guilty to attempted robbery at the fact-finding hearing. On the scheduled disposition date, the defense attorney failed to appear in court. The judge adjourned the case for twenty-five days to allow counsel for the youth to appear. On the date set for disposition, the defense attorney asked that the case be dismissed because the court adjourned the matter fifteen days longer than the ten-day dispositional adjournment limit. Quoting the relevant statute, the defense attorney argued that the court may adjourn the dispositional hearing:

"(a) on its own motion or on the motion of the presentment agency for good cause shown for not more than ten days; or

"(b) on motion of the respondent for good cause shown for not more than thirty days."[126]

Although the disposition was completed within the prescribed fifty-day period,[127] the Appellate Division said that an adjournment for more than ten days mandated the dismissal of the petition.[128] The original concerns for prompt adjudication of juvenile proceedings had devolved into requests for timely adjournments.

Roshon P. raises serious questions about the conduct of defense counsel during the course of juvenile delinquency proceedings. Since the failure of the defense lawyer to appear at disposition causes speedy trial time to run against the prosecution, should defense counsel—in her role as advocate—appear at all? Even where the court would adjourn the case at ten day intervals, if the lawyer's non-appearance continues to keep the speedy trial time running against the prosecutor, then the attorney would best serve his client by not appearing within the fifty-day mandated period. Clearly, under *Roshon P.* it is only the lawyer who appears in court that risks the conviction of his client. Non-appearance, on the other hand, leads to the dismissal of the charges. In any event, non-appearance of counsel at least once seems consistent with proper defense advocacy—especially if the non-appearance takes the proceeding beyond the allowable time limits of disposition.

Other interesting questions are raised by the decision in *Roshon P.* Since the prosecution invariably bears the burden of demonstrating "good cause" for an adjournment when defense counsel has failed to appear, what must the prosecution demonstrate to satisfy this standard? Is it the responsibility of the prosecution to produce the offender's attorney? If efforts to locate and produce the defense attorney are met with resistance, should the prosecution seek a warrant for the lawyer? Upon failure to seek these remedies, has the prosecution failed in its burden to meet the "good cause" standard?

Shortly after the decision in *Roshon P., supra,* the Appellate Division, Second Department again extended the rationale of *Randy K.* into the dispositional scheme. In the *Matter of Faruq F.*[129] the court held that the failure to commence the dispositional hearing within fifty days mandated dismissal of the petition—even when the youth caused the delay by failing to appear. In *Faruq F.* the youth was released after pleading guilty to a lesser count in a car theft petition. The court set the matter down for disposition, but on that date the youth failed to appear. He was involuntarily returned on the warrant by the police about one hundred days after he pled guilty. Relying on the rationale of *Randy K., supra,* the Family Court judge dismissed the case because the prosecution did not routinely seek ten-day adjournments of the proceeding during the time that the youth remained at large on the warrant. The Appellate Division affirmed and said:

> As with Family Court Act §340.1, the Legislature, in Family Court Act §350.1, has seen fit to require as a condition for adjourning a hearing that the court make findings on the record of good cause for the adjournment and of special circumstances for subsequent adjournments. [citing *Randy K.* and *Roshon P.*].[130]

The majority in *Faruq F.* chose to ignore contrary decisions from the Appellate Divisions in the First and Third Departments.[131] Those cases, along with other Family Court decisions,[132] recognized a fundamental difference between fact-finding and disposition. Where there has already been an adjudication of guilt, said the Family Courts, the delay precipitated by the offender should not be deemed a *per se* violation mandating dismissal. A strong dissent in *Faruq F.* echoed these sentiments:

> . . . [W]hen the offender's miscreance is at the root of it all, it strikes me as inappropriate to reward that miscreance with a release, while punishing the agency to the same degree as in the case of a fact-finding hearing, at which factual guilt was as yet undetermined. While the source of delay . . . is not controlling. . . , it is at least relevant in weighing the remedy to be imposed, and in my view, tips the balance. [133]

Although the dissent is correct in its conclusions, its reasoning further demonstrates the contradictions and inequities within the *Randy K.* holding. The dissenting justice in *Faruq F.* noted the unfairness in "punishing" the presentment agency by dismissing the petition. Nowhere, however, does the dissent—or even the majority—discuss the other mandate of the Family Court Act's delinquency code: community protection. The punishment referred to by the dissent is not really directed against the prosecution. Rather, it is an assault on the society that must continue to live with offenders because courts have freed them as a consequence of their own failure to appear.

Further, the dissent in *Faruq F.* opines that, in keeping with the holding of *Frank C.,* the source of the delay is not controlling for speedy trial purposes. Yet the dissent's assertion that the source of the delay is ". . . relevant in weighing the remedy to be imposed . . . and *tips the balance,*" suggests that the source of delay actually *does* control. Clearly, the dissent herein was handcuffed by the holding of *Randy K.* and sought to escape from its grasp.

The lower courts followed the *Randy K.* rationale even when such a course was unwarranted. Perhaps the extreme position taken by the Court of Appeals in support of prompt adjudication of delinquency cases has forced this response. The application of a mandatory dismissal rule as a by-product of a speedy trial right at disposition, as in *Faruq F., supra,* is such an example. FCA §310.2 specifically says that the youth is entitled to a "speedy fact-finding hearing." No similar right is designated for disposition, except that there are time restrictions imposed upon the dispositional hearing. But the right to a speedy *fact-finding hearing* creates the mandatory dismissal rule. The specific language of FCA §310.2 has apparently been rewritten by some of the judiciary to include dispositional hearings.[134]

Although the Court of Appeals denied leave to appeal in the *Matter of Faruq F.*[135] they agreed to review the question a few months later in the *Matter of Jose R.*[136] To the surprise of all Appellate Divisions, and to the surprise of counsel, the Court of Appeals refused to recognize the denial of a speedy disposition right when the offender caused the delay by failing to appear.[137] The court relied on the plain language of FCA §310.2 which only provides for a speedy fact-finding hearing. While such a result seems obvious in light of the statute, the failures of the Appellate Division to follow this line of thought (after *Randy K.*) says much about the message on speedy trial from New York's highest court.

In fact, it is still unclear as to the extent to which the right to a "speedy disposition" will continue to exist. While the failure of a youth to appear will no longer trigger the dismissal of the petition, the court did say that ". . . where the juvenile is not solely responsible for the delay, the Family Court retains the authority to dismiss." Does this mean that a defense lawyer's failure to appear will still implicate the time clock as previously held in *Roshon P., supra?* Does the Family Court still have to "adjourn" warrant cases set for disposition? If so, what does the prosecutor have to demonstrate if no dismissal is warranted at this point in the proceeding?

Wholesale changes in the statute or in their interpretations by the Court of Appeals are necessary before common sense can return to this corner of the criminal justice system.[138] Various courts have recognized the folly of this entire line of cases and have called for legislative modifications.[139] These changes will have to provide a lucid program for speedy trial reform. While it is important to ensure prompt adjudication in all juvenile delinquency proceedings, it is equally important that community protection and common sense are not sacrificed in the process. At the same time, any attempts to modify the existing scheme will likely benefit the chances for the ultimate rehabilitation of the youth. Surely a later disposition of a juvenile case is more likely to ensure the delivery of appropriate social services than the high court's fuzzy rule of dismissal.

Unfortunately, in attempting to apply the high court's speedy trial rationale, some Family Courts have felt compelled to reject community safety requirements and common sense. For example, in *The Matter of Lawrence C.*[140] the prosecutor answered ready for trial on the ninetieth day following arraignment. (There was a "good cause" adjournment that had taken the case beyond the sixtiethth day.) The Court's calendar was congested that day and the matter was not called until 5:10 P.M. Since the case was past the official close of business for the ninetieth day, the Family Court judge—eager to dismiss a petition from his calendar's backlog and cognizant of the strict statutory construction demanded by the Court of Appeals—ruled that the proceeding had actually exceeded the ninety-day limit. Relying on this ten-minute overrun of the speedy trial rule, the defense lawyer moved for dismissal. In overturning the Family Court's dismissal, the Appellate Division, Second Department, said:

> We conclude that under these circumstances, the dismissal of the petition was an improvident exercise of discretion, particularly in view of the minimal delay presented. [141]

The determination previously exhibited by the Second Department in support of a rule of reason for speedy trial issues has been limited since the *Lawrence C.* case. Prior to *Randy K.,* the Second Department decided speedy trial issues for the Family Court via a common sense approach. For instance, it was the Second Department that refused to allow a juvenile to profit via dismissal because of his or her own failure to appear at trial. In the *Matter of Jerome S.* [142] the judges attacked the "logic" of the lower court for failing to recognize that a youth who declines to appear in court cannot claim that the resulting delay mandates dismissal of the petition.

> It is unreasonable to assume . . . that the Legislature intended to reward a respondent who fails to appear with outright dismissal of the petition under the circumstances presented.
>
> To require summary dismissal of the petition

merely because the presentment agency has failed to redundantly seek successive adjournments of the fact-finding hearing in the respondent's absence neither accords with the logic of the statutory scheme nor promotes the desired end of "swift and certain" delinquency proceedings. . . . The adjournment provisions of the statute were intended to function as a means of forestalling unwarranted delay, *not as a sword to be employed by a respondent who delays the proceeding and then subsequently argues that it must be summarily dismissed as a consequence.*[143] *[emphasis added]*

Since the reversal of the *Matter of Jerome S.* (via *Randy K.*), the Second Department has obediently—although somewhat reluctantly—gone along with the high court's rules of strict construction.[144] Although the Second Department found that it was "unreasonable to assume" that the Senate and Assembly supported mandatory dismissal for youths who defy their obligation to appear in court, the Court of Appeals evidently found such an assumption quite reasonable. Their position is supported by the fact that in the two years following the decision in *Randy K.*, the Legislature—although presented with proposals to ameliorate the *Randy K.* problem—refused to change the law. It may well be that New York's legislature is comfortable with a rule that allows violent felony offenders to defy the court by not appearing—with the result that they can then use this defiance to earn a dismissal.

By promulgating statutes that allow for dismissal when an accused or his lawyer fails to appear in court, the state legislature has taken fairness beyond the bounds of traditional criminal procedure. In developing the line of cases that began with *Frank C.*, New York's highest court has carried the procedural rights of an accused into uncharted waters. Together, the appellate courts and the lawmakers in Albany have made sure that the prosecution and the trial courts can no longer fulfill their obligations without the complete cooperation of the perpetrator.

NOTES (PART 1)

1. Names have been changed.

2. The names of the victims have been changed to protect their privacy.

3. Quote from the *I & R* prepared for the dispositional hearing.

4. Names have been changed for the purposes of reporting.

5. George lost his job with Legal Aid. He has never been able to obtain permanent employment since.

6. Under Judge Zuckerman's order of placement, the youth could have been released by *DFY* at any time. Without the specific order for a statutory minimum, any other language in the order is deemed wishful thinking.

   Prior to her reading the *I & R,* Judge Zuckerman had already determined not to require a six-month minimum term in residential placement for Che. In the minutes at the dispositional proceeding, she angrily admits not having read the report, but assumes —without the necessary factual background—that the youth was not a "special" case. Such an assumption placed faith ahead of community protection.

7. All surnames have been altered.

8. This story adapted from an Op-Ed piece I wrote for the *New York Daily News*.

9. In reality, the crowding of juvenile facilities has reduced the average time in placement to eight to nine months. Tarion W. was one of the many serious offenders that enjoyed an early release—serving approximately one-third of the initial placement period.

10. There is little doubt that no hope exists for the most vicious offenders with no coherent family history. Programs that offer violent criminals "parenting skills" (or similarly titled therapies) to counter generations of antisocial behavior ignore overwhelming rates of failure. The application of common sense in the criminal and juvenile justice systems would undoubtedly save wasted budget dollars, as well as legitimize an evident truth: Violent people with no sense of civilized life must be isolated from civilization.

11. Names have been changed.

12. Although prison populations have increased significantly throughout the 1980s,the number of offenders placed on probation or in other community-based sentences has increased at a greater pace. By their own logic, the advocates' use of alternative sentencing programs and the growth of the crime rate indicate the failure of the present community-based systems. Throughout the 1980s, the *real* alternative sentencing

practice has been incarceration.

13. To a non-student of the social work/psychology regimen, the presumption of malleability of teenagers appears more to be an act of hope rather than fact. Surely nobody is as surly or obstinate as a teenager, and no age group listens less to the experience of elders. Parents and positive role models are often mistrusted or ignored by most teens as a matter of instinct; their own sense of immortality and invincibility makes change (without aging) appear impossible. As these youths age into their twenties, a corresponding reduction in violent activity is often noted. Perhaps the juvenile justice system ought to redefine its basic presumptions and precepts about allowing proverbial "second bites" by ensuring that the most violent of these offenders remain isolated until they "age-out" of their predatory behavior. Certainly the reluctance of DFY and other service providers to do exhaustive recidivism studies only intensifies the belief that little can be done to reform the violent teen.

14. Whether this is actually true is open to question. Since Family Ties is a new program, there are no long term recidivism studies. We have no idea whether or not it has actually *prevented* a placement, or simply *deferred* incarceration. Surely a Family Ties youth who is arrested either as a juvenile or as an adult within three years of the program can hardly be called a success story. Thus, the claim for millions of dollars in savings is misleading.

15. The probation end of the Family Ties system is not an

issue for prosecutors. The program, termed JISP (Juvenile Intensive Supervision Program) is not under DJJ control and thus immediately fares better. JISP may incur the wrath of the prosecution, but that is usually in connection with a specific programmatic component. Unlike the DJJ end of the program, the JISP people can be trusted to report fairly to the court.

16. The Giuliani Administration is trying a newer and more conservative approach to Family Ties via their new DJJ Commissioner, Jose Maldonado. Maldonado, a former prosecutor, has promised to run a program that is geared toward nonviolent offenders. This more responsible approach will likely run afoul of those who seek to return offenders to our communities.

17. A popular and well-respected Austrian-made 9mm handgun.

18. The Grand Jurors never met Luis. He did not testify before the Grand Jury. According to Luis' recorded statements, it was self-defense or it was otherwise justified. The statement to the detective during fingerprinting was heard, but the written admission and the videotape were directly from the kid. They had more of an impact than the words of Detective Chung.

19. The kids admitted to DAP were originally detained in Spofford or in one of the several *NSD* facilities.

20. Family Court Act as amended in 1976 and 1982. The original statute of 1962 had no references to a need for community protection. Incarceration is still not possible unless all other alternatives have been explored. See

FCA §§352.2, 353.3.

21. Two parents appearing is a rarity. Most juveniles appear with their mother. Paternal involvement is uncommon in the lives of most offenders.

22. This version of the events was reviewed by the prosecution as a possible attempted murder charge against Roshad, but the matter was dropped. The prosecution believed that Karim was trying to curry favor with law enforcement officials by fabricating a serious charge against Roshad. Karim seemed to think that he would deflect his own culpability by pretending to be a necessary and cooperative witness against his friend. Unfortunately for the manipulative young man, there was no evidence from the victim or Roshad to support his lies.

23. Had Karim committed this offense as an adult, he would have faced a maximum prison term of five to fifteen years in a state penitentiary. His youth served him well. How well the community was served will be known in due time.

24. *NY Daily News,* July 26–27, 1992. *Juvenile Injustice,* a series by Heidi Evans.

25. Names have been altered for the purposes of reporting.

26. See *Schall v. Martin,* 467 U.S. 253, 104 S.Ct. 2403 (1984). In that case, the Supreme Court recognized that in some cases the probable cause hearing and the *fact-finding* hearing are merged into one hearing.

27. In the summer of 1992 the issue was almost put to rest

in the Appellate Division's opinion in the *Matter of Jeffrey V.* A youth is not entitled to a probable cause hearing unless he is charged with the highest felony offenses. No misdemeanor cases would warrant a probable cause hearing after the *Jeffrey V.* decision. This opinion, however, was subsequently reversed by New York's Court of Appeals. The divergence of legal opinion clearly demonstrates the ambiguity of the statute.

28. This is not to suggest that a prosecutor can never be held in contempt. Where the conduct of the lawyer is unrelated to the prosecution of the case—but is designed solely to defy judicial authority—then holding in contempt may be appropriate. It is, however, a remedy of last resort. Where, as here, the differences related to interpretations of the law, the disagreement with the court was not personal—it was legal—and the court was left with other options. Judge Carmen, however, sought compliance with his legal opinion through force.

29. Brief of the Legal Aid Society *F.A.O. Schwarz, Jr., Corporation Counsel of the City of New York, et al. v. Carmen Cognetta* N.Y. Sup. Ct. Index Number 15747/86 at page 12.

30. id., at page 19.

31. Technically, the judge was without any power to make that order. The court may order a remand to the Department of Corrections, but he is without power to tell the executive agency where or how to lodge the prisoner. After the two lawyers were placed into the cells, the corrections officer checked with his commanding officer about keeping the lawyers in the cells.

The captain told the officer that the attorneys may be kept in the vestibule and that the judge had exceeded his authority.

32. The Legal Aid Society had no interest in the jailing of the attorneys. It bore no relationship to the guilt or innocence of their client, nor could it serve as means toward a procedural dismissal. Their position has engendered a deep distrust for Legal Aid among management at the Office of the Corporation Counsel, which is unlikely to change until either agency changes leadership. The personal animosity, however, will remain for life.

33. Names have been changed.

34. FCA §352.2 mandates that at disposition the court must impose the least restrictive alternative consistent with the needs of the youth and the protection of the community.

35. As written in the federal court petition.

36. It is a common misconception that the failure to read a suspect *Miranda* warnings will universally violate the rights of an accused. *Miranda* rights are only required when the suspect is in custody and when the police begin interrogation.

37. Names have been changed.

38. FCA §353.3 establishes the time periods for placement of juveniles on felony and misdemeanor offenses. There is a longer and more restrictive type of placement available when the court finds that the youth has com-

mitted a *designated felony* act. Under FCA §353.5 a youth found to have committed a designated felony act could serve up to five years with an initial placement in a secure setting. Randy Nicholas, however, could not be charged as a designated felon because he was under thirteen years of age at the time he committed his crimes.

39. One notable exception has been the 1976 modification regarding "designated felony acts." These are a very narrow classification of offenses prosecuted in the Family Court. The restrictions on designated felony status are so strict that very few acts are actually charged within that category.

40. Juvenile delinquents—except those charged under *designated felony* petitions—may not be sent by the court into secure facilities. Youths are sent to "limited secure" facilities that may be inside or outside of their home community. Doors are unlocked, and youths can leave without much effort. Only those facilities located in remote areas can serve to hold offenders without fear of escape. In fact DFY staff often tell the young residents that carnivorous bears and other animals are the best reasons to stay put.

    Youths may be moved to secure facilities via an administrative process within *DFY.* A hearing must be held and the youth is entitled to representation by counsel. The agency must demonstrate that, because of the youth's poor adjustment in an open environment, he must be transferred to secure care.

41. Despite the request for placement in a secure facility,

courts may not place juvenile delinquents (except those convicted of "designated felony" offenses) into a secure environment. The court may recommend secure care, and may even authorize DFY to place a youth in a secure facility within the first sixty days of placement. The decision, however, remains solely within the discretion of the Division for Youth.

42. *New York Daily News,* Monday, July 27, 1992, page 7.

43. A suspect cannot be convicted of a crime based solely on the testimony of an accomplice. There must be independent evidence that corroborates the accomplice's testimony.

44. A fifteen-year-old charged with murder in New York is considered a *Juvenile Offender* (JO). This means he is tried in the adult court. The case may be tried in the Family Court after the case is *removed* from the adult system.

45. NY Family Court Act §301.1.

46. Sobie, Merril. Practice Commentary. McKinncy's Consolidated Laws of New York, Family Court Act §301.1 (1983).

47. Oddly, the failure of the state to redeem the offender within the required time results in the release of that offender. Surely time limitations and the rehabilitation of offenders are mutually inconsistent notions.

48. Michael later told the probation officer preparing the *I & R* that he regularly set fires around Baychester during the winter months in order to "keep warm."

Michael would not discuss the damage caused by these fires, and would not detail their times and locations.

49. This part is called the Intake Part in the Family Court's traditional euphemistic style. In effect, most of what happens is the arraigning of all types of cases.

50. *Pilot Survey of Young African American Males in Four Cities,* The Commonwealth Fund, 1994.

51. Ibid. at p. 2.

52. In *The Bell Curve* (The Free Press, 1994) Charles Murray and Richard Herrnstein offer a view of the literature about crime and intelligence. See infra at p. 242: ". . . incarcerated offenders average on IQ of about 92, 8 points below the mean. . . . More serious or more chronic offenders generally have lower scores than the more casual offenders."

53. Ibid. at p.11. "A striking majority of these young men (89 percent) had strong self-respect."

54. Suspension hearings are required as a matter of due process. A principal no longer has complete authority over the school. The right to suspend a youth—for even the five-day period—is subject to adversarial hearing. The youth may be represented by counsel, and is entitled to a script should he seek to challenge the matter further. The loss of teacher and principal author accompanied the forfeiture of quality public education.

55. Segal, Lydia. *Who Really Runs the Schools? City Journal,* Winter 1995, p. 46.

56. "Not surprisingly, the most politicized districts rank among the lowest in citywide test school this climate, instead of spending time developing creative lesson plans, teachers feel pressured to stick." Ibid. at p. 48.

57. Name has been changed.

58. Some might be puzzled as to why a principal would come to the aid of an offender. Yet this is more often the rule than the exception. Principals do not want their schools to have high levels of reported crime. It makes the school look dangerous (which may be the truth) and thus he places his position in jeopardy. So schools in New York often cover up crime to make it appear that the school is safer than it is. Crimes like robbery, gun possession and even *forcible rape* have been covered up—or at least an attempt was made to do so.

(PART2)

59. 48 NY2d 167 (1979).

60. 53 NY2d 225 (1981).

61. Besides the usual warnings relating to a right to remain silent and the right to counsel, the police in effect had to ask the defendant whether he was *presently* represented by counsel on a pending criminal matter. Where the answer was affirmative, the court required that all questioning cease.

62. *People v. Bartolomeo,* 53 NY2d 225, at 231-232.

63. *People v. Bartolomeo,* 53 NY2d 225, at 239. The *Bartolomeo* decision was a split decision with four judges for the majority against three for the dissent. Within several years, only Sol Wachtler—the dissenter—would remain on the court.

64. *People v. Colwell,* 65 NY2d 883 (1985).

65. *People v. Servidio,* 54 NY2d 951 (1981).

66. *People v. Fuschino,* 59 NY2d 92 (1983).

67. *People v. Rosa,* 65 NY2d 380 (1985).

68. *People v. Bertolo,* 65 NY2d 111 (1985).

69. *People v. Thornton,* 539 NYS2d 344 (App. Div. 1st Dept., 1989).

70. 76 NY2d 331 (1990).

71. 76 NY2d at 337.

72. 76 NY2d at 342.

73. 76 NY2d at 342.

74. Note that *Bartolomeo* was decided by a closely divided court—and that it in fact overruled precedent. While some of the overruled precedent was not *recent* in relation to the *Bartolomeo* case, the decision in *People v. Kazmarick,* 52 NY2d 322 (1981), was several months old when *Bartolomeo* effectively overruled it.

75. 76 NY2d at 361. The majority's assertion that *Bartolomeo* is a case resulting upon "bedrock principles" is puzzling. The majority asserted quite correctly that in all other jurisdictions where a *Bartolomeo* defense was asserted, it was rejected by the courts. Clearly, a case that is uniformly rejected in other jurisdictions, and that has been continually modified since it was decided, rests upon principles less solid than *bedrock.*

76. See *People v. Smith,* 54 NY2d 954 (1981). Murder conviction of the defendant was reversed because the court found that the police were aware of his eight-month-old sodomy arrest.

77. This section adapted from an article in the *New York Law Journal,* September 8, 1992.

78. The failure of some appellate judges to seriously consider the dangers of street encounters for the police officer is evident in Judge Vito Titone's concurring

opinion in *People v. Allen,* 73 NY2d 379, 540 NYS2d 971, 538 NE2d 323 (1989). In *Allen,* this associate judge of New York's highest court concurred with the detention of the defendant, but would not subscribe to the broad interpretation of case law proffered by the majority opinion. He wrote: "Use of phrases that evoke vivid images of police officers in danger may have some superficial appeal, but they ultimately serve to obscure, rather than enhance analysis." 73 NY2d at 381.

Such a position is inconsistent with common sense and knowledge about the everyday dangers of police work. Perhaps Judge Titone considers the constant threat of police work to be superficial or inconsequential. Yet there are hundreds of families across the nation whose loved ones have died in the line of police duty. To these people, the danger is not superficial.

Judge Titone's comments are also out of step with much of the federal case law. The Supreme Court of the United States, in the leading case on street encounters, has held that a pat-down frisk is justified by a police officer when there is reasonable suspicion to believe a suspect is armed. *Terry v. Ohio,* 392 US 1, 20 L Ed2d 889 (1968). The court, by Chief Justice Warren, wrote ". . . [T]here is the more immediate interest of the police officer in taking steps to assure himself that the person with whom he is dealing is not armed with a weapon that could unexpectedly and fatally be used against him. Certainly it would be unreasonable to require that police officers take unnecessary risks in the performance of their duties. American criminals have a long tradition of armed violence, and every year in this country many law enforcement officers are killed in the line of duty, and thousands more are wounded." 392 US at 23.

79. 40 NY2d 210 (1976).

80. Naturally, any evidence—like DeBour's gun herein—seized from a defendant as a result of an unconstitutional "stop", would have to be suppressed (i.e., not permitted into evidence at trial). Suppression of evidence occurs via the "exclusionary rule."

81. 40 NY2d 210 (1976).

82. Since neither the common-law right to inquire nor the request for information allows a "frisk," the distinction between these two levels of intrusion is—despite attempts by the Court of Appeals to suggest otherwise—one of semantics.

83. 50 NY2d 583, 430 NYS2d 578, 408 NE2d 908 (1980).

84. *Belton* was reversed by the United States Supreme Court in *New York v. Belton,* 453 US 454 (1981). The Supreme Court denied the motion to suppress, and the evidence against Belton was deemed properly admitted at trial. In 1982 the case returned to the Court of Appeals, which agreed with the Supreme Court's decision to admit the evidence at trial but specifically held that the right of privacy under the State Constitution exceeded the minimum limits proscribed by the Federal Courts. *People v. Belton,* 55 NY2d 49, 447 NYS2d 873, 432 NE2d 745 (1982)—also known as *Belton II.*

85. The term "criminal activity afoot" was used by Chief

Justice Warren in his holding in *Terry v. Ohio*, 392 US 1 at 30, 20 L Ed2d 889 at 911 (1967). The Supreme Court, in deciding *Terry*, chose to develop simple criteria to justify detention where the officer has information regarding criminal conduct falling short of probable cause. No four-tiered analysis like *DeBour*, 40 NY2d 210 (1976), is suggested. Instead, a simple equation for police, prosecutors and judges was devised:

> We merely hold today that where a police officer observes unusual conduct which leads him reasonably to conclude in light of his experience that criminal activity may be afoot and that the persons with whom he is dealing may be armed and presently dangerous, where in the course of investigating this behavior he identifies himself as a policeman and makes reasonable inquiries, and where nothing in the initial stages of the encounter serves to dispel his reasonable fear for his own or others' safety, he is entitled for the protection of himself and others in the area to conduct a carefully limited search of the outer clothing of such persons to discover weapons which might be used to assault him. 392 US at 30-31.

Such a simple standard is far easier than the four-tiered analysis of *DeBour, supra,* for the officer on patrol to apply. It also causes a likely change in the suppression of the gun in *People v. LaPene*, 40 NY2d 210 (1976). In that situation, it was reasonable for the officer to order defendant to freeze as a means to ensure not only his own safety, but the safety of all the patrons in the bar.

86. "The circumstances justified the inquiry made and would have justified the officers in keeping defendant under observation. . . ." *People v. Howard,* 50 NY2d 583 at 590 (1980).

87. 68 NY2d 734, 506 NYS2d 320, 497 NE2d 687 (1986).

88. 50 NY2d 583 (1980).

89. 40 NY2d 210 (1976).

90. 79 NY2d 181 (1992). *Hollman* was decided in conjunction with *People v. Saunders,* also at 79 NY2d 181. Two other companion case were decided with these two matters: *In the Matter of Antoine W.,* 79 NY2d 888 (1992), and *People v. Irizarry,* 79 NY2d 890 (1992). These cases all concern the inability of the lower courts to work within *People v. DeBour,* 40 NY2d 210 (1976) and its progeny.

91. Some might argue that the distinction is important where the product of the interrogation is an inculpatory statement. Since the suspect is never in custody during the request for information or during the common law inquiry, any statement obtained should be free of taint. See *People v. Yukl,* 25 NY2d 585, 307 NYS2d 857 (1969), *People v. Huffman,* 41 NY2d 29 (1976).

92. *People v. Howard,* 50 NY2d 583 at 588–589 (1980).

93. ". . . [A]ny time an intrusion on the security and privacy

of the individual is undertaken with intent to harass or is **based upon mere whim, caprice, or idle curiosity,** the spirit of the Constitution has been violated and the aggrieved party may invoke the exclusionary rule or appropriate forms of civil redress." *People v. DeBour,* 40 NY2d 210 at 217.

The concerns of the court regarding the actions of officers based upon whim are similar to the concerns of the police acting upon conjecture. Police officers, without an objective test to follow, may lose a case to the exclusionary rule since one judge's permissible level of intrusion is not the same as the next.

94. 111 SCt. 1547 (1991).

95. The Fourth Amendment to the U.S. Constitution guarantees the right to be free from unreasonable searches and seizures.

96. 50 NY2d 583, 430 NYS2d 578, 408 NE2d 908 (1980).

97. 392 US 1, 20 L Ed2d 889, 88 SCt 1868 (1968).

98. 449 US 411, 66 L Ed2d 621, 101 SCt 690 (1981).

99. 111 SCt 2382 (1991).

100. 582 N.Y.S.2d 977 (1992)

101. id.

102. id.

103. id.

104. See CPL §30.30.

105. *Matter of Frank C.,* 70 NY2d 408 at 413, 522 NYS2d 89 at 92 (1987).

106. During the initial appearance the matter may be returned to the Probation Department for reconsideration of the adjustment process. The Court of Appeals, *In the Matter of Aaron J.,* 80 NY2d 402, 590 NYS2d 843 (1992), held that "a referral for 'adjustment services' made pursuant to Family Court Act §320.6 tolls the time specified . . . for commencing the fact-finding hearing . . . "

Although the Court's refusal in *Aaron J.* to dismiss the petition for failure to comply with the speedy trial time limitations was the appropriate conclusion, the Court missed the proper argument to support its holding. Speedy trial time (pursuant to FCA §340.1) does not begin to run until the conclusion of the initial appearance. Where a referral back to the Probation Department for adjustment services has been made, the initial appearance has not concluded. The arraigning court would still be monitoring the case and, if appropriate, will dismiss the case when adjustment services are successful. Failure of those services, however, would result in the conclusion of the initial appearance, including settlement of all questions regarding detention and a date for the fact-finding hearing.

107. FCA §310.2 says: "After a petition has been filed . . . the respondent is entitled to a speedy fact-finding hearing."

108. FCA §340.1 says that where the youth is not detained, ". . . the fact-finding hearing shall commence not more than sixty days after the conclusion of the initial appearance . . . " except that upon a showing of good cause the case may be adjourned for another thirty days. Further adjournments must be made upon a showing of special circumstances. "[S]uch circumstances shall not include calendar congestion or the status of the court's docket or backlog."

109. *Matter of Randy K.,* 77 NY2d 398, 568 NYS2d 562 (1991).

110. The term "ready and passed" usually means that the case was ready to proceed, but the court is beginning the proceedings at a later time.

111. *Matter of Frank C. , supra,* at 411–412.

112. 70 NY2d at 414.

113. 70 NY2d at 410.

114. *Matter of David C.,* 592 NYS2d 25 (1st Dept., 1993).

115. 77 NY2d 398, 568 NYS2d 562 (1991).

116. 77 NY2d at 403.

117. Id.

118. The practice commentary accompanying the Family Court Act called the request for successive adjournments an "empty act." Further, the writer believed ". . . that respondents should not benefit from their own misdeeds." Besharov, Supplementary Practice Commentaries, McKinneys Consolidated Laws of New York, Family Court Act.

119. 568 NYS2d at 565.

120. 568 NYS2d at 565.

121. 77 NY2d at 409.

122. FCA §§301.1, 352.2.

123. 77 NY2d at 410.

124. The dissent in *Randy K.* refers to the adjournments for "good cause", etc. while the youth is at large as "empty acts". 77 NY2d at 410.

125. 588 NYS2d 614 (1992).

126. FCA §350.1

127. FCA §350.1

128. The Appellate Division does not discuss whether the failure of the defense attorney to appear should be considered a respondent's application for an adjournment. Such a view would have allowed a thirty-day adjournment. See FCA §350.1(3)(b).

129. 588 NYS2d 914 (2d Dept., 1992), lv. den.81 NY2d 706, 597 NYS2d 936 (1993).

130. 588 NYS2d at 915.

131. *Matter of David R.* 150 AD2d 161, 540 NYS2d 780 (First Dept., 1989); *Matter of Brion H.,* 161 AD2d 832 (Third Dept., 1990). But note that the 3rd Department changed its view in the *Matter of Christopher WW,* 596 NYS2d 199 (3rd Dept., 1993)

132. *Matter of Jose Z.,* 154 Misc.2d 450, 585 NYS2d 658 (Fam. Ct. NY, 1992); *Matter of Gregory C.,* 131 Misc.2d

685 (Westchester Fam. Ct., 1986).

133. 588 AD2d at 916.

134. This assertion is briefly raised by the dissent in *Faruq F.,*
supra. There Justice Rosenblatt opined: "There is no
parallel statutory authority for dismissal based upon a
violation of Family Court Act §350.1 (time of dispositional hearing), and I would not extend *Matter of Randy*
K. (supra) by writing one in." Although this argument
is not the main thrust of the dissent, it is the best argument in light of the strict statutory construction that
resulted in *Randy K.*

    See also *Matter of Jose Z., supra;* but see also *Matter*
of Daniel C., 151 Misc2d 730 (Fam. Ct. Kings County,
1991) for a contrary view.

135. See 81 NY2d 706, 597 NYS2d 936 (1993).

136. 82 NY2d 656, 602 NYS2d 805 (1993) granting lv. of
194 AD2d 310, 598 NYS2d 243 (1st Dept. 1993).

137. 83 N.Y.2d 388 (1994).

138. With little fanfare, the New York legislature in 1994
adopted a statute that is supposed to fix the *Randy K.*
problem. The new law stops the speedy trial time from
running while a youth is out on a warrant, but upon
the offender's return defense counsel may challenge
the sufficiency of the prosecution's efforts to execute
the warrant. Thus, when the youth is finally returned
to court, the prosecution must retroactively demonstrate "due diligence" or face dismissal. Once again, the
burden is shifted to the government, where the offender has perpetrated the wrongdoing. This is in keeping

with New York's agenda of crime without guilt.

139. See *Matter of Faruq F.*, 588 NYS2d 914(2d Dept.,1992), lv. den. 81 NY2d 706, 597 NYS2d 936 (1993); see also *Matter of Daniel C.* 151 Misc 2d 730 (Fam. Ct. Kings County, 1991), where the court in a series of footnotes called for the legislature to review the entire speedy trial sections of the juvenile delinquency code as well as asking the "Legislature . . . to revisit the wisdom of expecting miracles of redemption from an underfinanced, underserviced Family Court . . . " *id.* footnote #1 at 731.

140. 152 AD2d 693, 543 NYS2d 750 (Second Dept., 1989).

141. Id. at 693.

142. 157 AD2d 286, 556 NYS2d 115 (Second Department, 1990).

143. 556 NYS2d at 118.

144. See *Roshon P., supra* and *Faruq F., supra*. Note the call for legislative reform in *Faruq F.* In *Roshon P.* the Second Department opinion dismisses the petition ". . . in light of the interpretations by the Court of Appeals . . . " Such references speak for themselves.

EPILOGUE:

WHERE DO WE GO FROM HERE? Pursuing *CHANGE* Along the Road to Disaster

Change is the promise of every political candidate. Once that candidate is elected, however, the promise of change faces the obstacle of government inertia. This is especially so when changes are promised for the criminal justice system and for the juvenile justice subsystem. Political candidates offer formulae to combat crime, but once in power the programs they implement—as well as the judges they often appoint—serve the continuing urban decline. Even the few elected officials who try to bring about real reform are thwarted by bar associations, screening panels and various advocacy groups. Those who profit from the *status quo* are intent upon preserving it—even when the *status quo* is the road to anarchy.

"The system is not perfect, but it still is the best in the world." Proponents of the *status quo* have offered this adage as a reason to thwart significant change. Assuming that our system is the best—and after O.J., Lemerick Nelson, Rodney King's uniformed attackers and the Menendez brothers' first trial that surely cannot be true—it should not preclude trying to make the criminal justice system even better. We virtually never ask the victims and the families of victims who have been dragged through the system whether they are satisfied with the process or with the outcome. When the daughter of a woman shot to death in Harlem asked why the police can't get guns off the streets, it was not hard to look at the decisions of the appellate courts to see that the rules of police work have been defined by those who choose to remain ideologically divorced from the dangers of walking a beat—and probably never stop in most of the neighborhoods where the crimes took place.

We are informed in law journals, judicial decisions and through various bar groups that these judge-made rules enhance our individual liberty. But is this "liberty" enough to satisfy the daughter of a murdered victim? Is there a victim of violent crime or a family member of a murdered victim who would not trade these judicially designed "protections" for the crime never having happened? Wouldn't they be happy to trade the "freedom" which afforded their victimization for a small dose of "tyranny" which could have provided them with protection? Would the father of a murdered teenage girl have preferred that police approach a rowdy group of teens at the 59th Street subway station, search the youths and remove the weapon which eventually killed his daughter? Are the extensive search and seizure protections invented by New York's highest court worth the life of his child?

Why does the price of being free from limited police intrusion have to be paid with the blood of those citizens? When the laws cannot protect us from the predators because these laws mandate individual rights before society's security, we are on the express route to community suicide. In their pursuit of expanded individual rights, some courts have forgotten that the crime victim is also an individual.

Judges, the elected and appointed officials with the power to make immediate and sweeping changes, are supposed to be free from political and public pressure. An independent judiciary is supposed to be the hallmark of a democracy, but no one has adequately explained how absolute judicial independence differs from a total lack of accountability. When judges release dangerous offenders—even though common sense and legal history suggest otherwise—and when those offenders kill, criticism of the judge by public officials brings sharp rebukes from senior judges and the organized bar. But such action should be debated in the forum of public opinion—or any prospect for intelligent change is doomed. Judges who "take chances" by releasing violent offenders on whim or hunch are really gambling with the safety of the general public. The public, therefore, should have the right to comment and to criticize. The public has the right to make changes to support their own safety—even when that change concerns the judiciary. Those who disagree need not look far to find examples of governments whose officials are insulated from criticism.

Not all judges have failed to recognize that the primary obligation of the criminal justice system—public safety—has been lost in the rapid build-up of constitutional case law. These judges, however, have been labeled controversial, cynical or just plain jaded. Sitting judges who speak their minds about the insanity of *Miranda* or the overuse of the exclusionary rule—and who offer reform—become pariahs in the legal community. Their recipe for change involves a retreat from a system of law that traditionally moves in the direction of expanding individual rights. Yet other jurists, who change existing law by swelling the scope of the exclusionary rule and the due process rights of criminal defendants are often hailed as civil libertarians. Of course, their style of change vacates convictions of guilty defendants, defines *Rosario* material to become a "prosecutor's nightmare" and takes the speedy trial rights of violent felons beyond the realm of common sense.

Change is the last item on the agenda of the New York legislature and for the policy die-hards in the criminal justice system who seek to preserve their failing principles as a matter of faith. Perhaps the desire to safeguard their leadership roles and their committee positions has held juvenile justice reform hostage in New York's legislature. As prosecutors' caseloads doubled in the late 1980s and as crime became more violent, New York's legislature ignored the blood of the victims of juvenile predation. Of course, the obligatory hearings were held and the speeches were made, but the wave of crime provoked no action from our elected representatives. As prison space tripled for adults throughout the 1980s, New York's DFY missed every opportunity to add more beds.★ The legislature actually cut DFY's budget during this rise in juvenile violence. It was as if violent juvenile crime had left its mark on every corner of the state except in the halls occupied by Albany's law and policy makers.

By the end of Mario Cuomo's tenure as governor, his "Decade of the Child" saw juvenile justice in total disrepair. Violent crime was up, and incarceration time for violent young offenders was down. Gun-toting offenders could not be fingerprinted and photographed, and prosecutors in the juvenile system could still not obtain arrest and search warrants. In the midst of the rising violence the New York Court

---

★ Lobbying the legislature for more money to build or expand facilities was not undertaken by the agency.

of Appeals continued to carry the banner for anti-law enforcement sentiment. Among their decisions, they ensured that speedy trial time would run against the prosecution even when the youth remained outstanding on a warrant. In that same spirit the court extended the requirement for prosecutors to serve every piece of paper containing any prior statement of a witness made to law enforcement, or risk automatic dismissal of the case. "Good faith" exceptions to the exclusionary rule were rejected by the high court, and gun smuggling teenagers were given the right to travel through the Port Authority Bus Terminal without fear of interdiction by police. The "Decade of the Child" had become a decade of child violence with the help and sanction of New York's highest court.

The decline of law and order in urban America appears inevitable, but some politicians have attempted to slow the pace. The administration of Mayor Rudolph Giuliani, through his former Police Commissioner William Bratton, developed a Youth Strategy aimed at the apprehension of violent young offenders. Detectives were assigned to arrest unapprehended youths in group robberies and other violent felonies. Truants are being picked up by police and truant officers and returned to schools. Any of these truants with weapons are arrested. All juvenile arrestees are being "debriefed" at precincts and upon referral to court to learn about their own crimes and—even more important—about other crimes that have not been solved. New York's new Governor, George Pataki, had sought to make more beds available in DFY and thus ensure longer stays. This will also increase the likelihood of placement for many youths otherwise kept in the community—a fact too late to matter for Craig Peters or his grieving mother, who had sought her own son's incarceration to protect him from himself and the violence of the streets.

But the positive steps of Mayor Giuliani, Commissioner Bratton and Governor Pataki are meeting stiff resistance from those who want to preserve the *status quo*. As violent crime among teens escalates, advocates for young offenders continue to oppose incarceration in favor of alternative programs. The new buzzword among the policy wonks (replacing the old and lost *rehabilitation*) is *prevention*. Silly slogans like "Build schools, not jails" suggest that education is a viable alternative to prison. Yet this simplistic approach—high in appeal and empty in content—cannot deal with the already violent teen who rapes, robs or kills. Even if such a person were educable, the end result of the process is probably just a criminal with a diploma. Realistically, the opportunity for education does not translate into a success story. Without genuine commitment from the student, money for educating violent offenders would be better funneled into more prison space. Those advocates who disagree ought to consider calling 911 and asking for a teacher the next time *they* encounter juvenile violence.

Preventing crime ought to be a government priority. Arrest and prosecution of violent offenders is a reactive approach and will never make people feel as safe as the outright prevention of violence. Unfortunately, the present criminal justice system does its utmost to block the best prevention efforts government has to offer. Experienced police officers in New York (and in other jurisdictions) have been handcuffed by the courts in their best crime detection efforts. New York's appellate courts have severely restricted the authority of officers to stop, frisk, and search suspects during street encounters. The courts view these restrictions on law enforcement as an extension of individual rights for all New Yorkers—by leaving them free of police interference. But every extension of indi-

vidual rights defined by these judges results in a broader application of the exclusionary rule. Thus, when cops cannot stop
and frisk suspects because of judge-made rules, crime prevention takes a giant leap backward. The gun or the knife that
would be confiscated via good police work remains in the
hands of the robber, rapist or murderer. The rights of a
would-be defendant remain fully protected—only an innocent victim is violated.

Unfortunately, in trying to prevent crime among the
young, the city and the state cannot substitute for the role of
a parent—although that is exactly what they are consistently
told to do.

The morally corrupt approach of some reformers who
rename fragmented households as "nontraditional families"
cannot displace the continuing dysfunction of the people they
are allegedly attempting to serve. Values that are learned from
a solid nuclear family have little chance of being instilled by
counselors, therapists or teachers—and become impossible to
convey as the child reaches adolescence. The schools should
no longer be singularly blamed when kids don't learn, and
society should not be indicted when a youth gets violent.
Stigma, the societal pressure to avoid self-destructive conduct,
has been eradicated in some segments of society. It has been
replaced with payments from the government to do that
which was previously likely to be stigmatized—and often prevented.

Explaining behavior cannot serve as an excuse for violent
conduct. Accountability needs to be highlighted in any
reform of the criminal justice system. Individual rights are
meaningless without a concomitant level of individual
responsibility. In one generation we have gone from "Ask not
what your country can do for you . . ." to asking the country,

the state and the cities for everything.

The criminal justice system, originally designed to protect the public, has now become a game that places the government on trial in every case. The actions of the perpetrator—no matter how heinous—are secondary until we assure ourselves that the police and the prosecution follow rules designed by defense counsel, their bar associations and other guardians of due process. Murderers are allowed to walk out the courthouse doors because police officers used the "N" word, and defense attorneys rejoice with jurors when they acquit their obviously guilty client. These celebrated cases, however, are never condemned the way "experts" decry the fictional violence of television and the movies. For some odd reason those who displace individual blame suggest that the televised trials of real life killers and other felons—and their ultimate acquittals—are less likely to poison the minds of impressionable youth than Wiley Coyote or Bugs Bunny.

There are no definite answers because there are no true solutions to crime. Every civilized society has had its criminals, and ours cannot rewrite history by *solving* the crime problem. Those who suggest "solutions" to crime problems are selling modern-day snake oil to buyers who are tired of living under the gun. Crime can, however, be limited and it can be displaced. People can turn their lives around, but it is not the obligation of the government to do this for them. Similarly, their failure to reform is not the government's failure to reform them.

As people flee the cities for greener pastures, urban America needs to undertake programs designed to keep its shrinking tax base. Businesses will not remain in the cities—despite tax incentives—when employees are afraid to stay late and finish work. Social services cannot become the primary function of the urban government since those who are likely to pay for the services are less likely to require them. *Change, despite the politicians, needs to be quick and it needs to extensive.* Without change that affords public safety, the thoughts of Dwayne Jones—as he lay sprawled on a Bronx street following the robbery of his bicycle at gunpoint and contemplating the violence of New York's youngest predators—become too clear for every city resident: *It is time to move out of the city.*